目录

中国戏曲

目 录

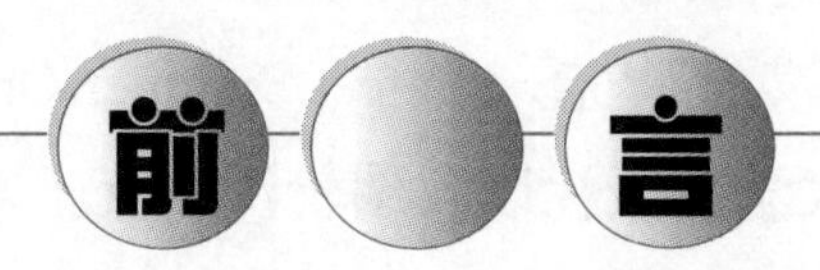

前言

这是一本介绍中国戏曲的教材。它主要是为母语为英语的大学生而写的。这些学生想学习关于中国戏曲的一些基本知识,从而可以更好地欣赏这门独特的中国艺术。想进一步了解中国戏曲以及中国文化的读者也可以使用本书。

笔者的教学理念是教材应该集知识性与学术性于一体。因此本书不仅对中国戏曲进行了全面系统的介绍:从发展史、戏曲种类、地理分布、表演特点,一直到社会功能与剧场的演变,而且还试图介绍一些当今对中国戏曲的学术研究,在每一章之后还提供了一些思考题,以激发学生的兴趣,便于课堂讨论,同时引起读者对一些问题的思考。

本书为汉英对照,笔者在两种语言的处理上侧重点略有不同。英语是为母语为英语的大学生所写,笔者从他们的角度、水平出发,行文尽量浅显流畅。在一些戏曲选段的翻译上,也尽量使用日常规范语言,能让其理解。另外,还加了不少注解,使来自不同文化的学生能更好地理解一些段落、句子或某些文化现象。中文则主要是给教师以及中文程度较好的学生作学习上的参考。笔者已经尽量简化行文,以适应外国学生学习的需要。但因为话题本身涉及古代文化的阐述,对于古代文献的引用,所以如果学生有文言文的基础,则对阅读带有文言句法的引文会有帮助。

笔者在完成本书书稿时，得到了美国华李大学（Washington and Lee University）夏季蓝菲斯特基金（Lenfest Summer Grant）的资助，谨此致谢。笔者也向北京大学出版社以及编辑沈岚女士对我的信任以及在写作过程中的鼓励与支持表示感谢。书中存在的错误缺点，尚祈专家学者不吝指正。

作者

2011年12月

于美国弗吉尼亚州列克星敦镇

Table of Contents

FOREWORD

This is a textbook for learning and teaching Chinese drama. It is aimed at those college students who speak English and who want to learn some basic fact about Chinese drama so that they can better appreciate this unique Chinese artistic form. It can also be used for those who want to further their knowledge about Chinese drama and to learn more about Chinese culture.

It has been my teaching philosophy that a textbook should combine coverage of knowledge with an introduction of scholarship. As a result, this book not only provides a comprehensive discussion of Chinese drama from its history of development, its variety and geographical distribution, its performing characteristics, to analysis of its social functions and evolution of Chinese theater, but also tries to introduce some modern scholarship on Chinese drama, and to provide a few discussion questions at the end of each chapter, the purpose of which is to stimulate student interest, to facilitate class discussion as well as to further a reader' s thought on the subject.

Since this is an English-Chinese bilingual book, I have handled the two languages therein with slightly different emphases. The English version is mainly for English-speaking college students. I have tried to express ideas and concepts in a way that is clear and lucid so that the content is easy to understand from their perspective. In translating the excerpts from some Chinese dramas, on the other hand, I have also tried to render them in everyday and standard English accessible to most college students. There are also quite a few notes I have supplied just to make a passage, a phrase, or certain cultural phenomenon better understood by people of different cultures. The Chinese version, on the other hand, is mainly for teachers' reference or for readers with more advanced Chinese. I have tried to simplify as much as possible the language so that it is accessible by foreign students. But since the subject itself involves narration of ancient Chinese culture and citation of ancient literature, some knowledge of classical Chinese may be needed occasionally when it comes to some passages with a bit of classical Chinese syntax and classical Chinese phrases and idioms.

I would like to acknowledge my thanks to Washington and Lee University for its Lenfest Summer Grant, which has enabled me to complete my manuscript in time. My thanks are also due to Peking University Press and to its editor Ms. Shen Lan for their trust, encouragement and support over the course of writing this book. All the remaining errors are, without doubt, entirely my own.

Author
December, 2011
in Lexington, Virginia
U. S. A.

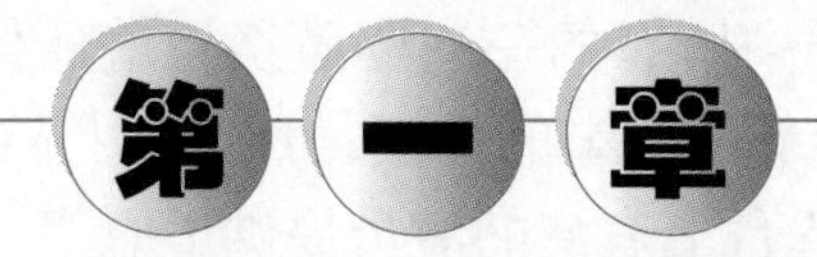

中国戏曲的起源

中国戏曲的起源到底在哪里？这是在中国近代历史上颇有争议的。有些人把它归因于古代巫觋，也有人把早期的歌舞表演看做是戏曲的先驱，还有人把古代宫廷里的优孟表演看做是戏曲活动的开端，更有人主张将在汉代（公元前206 —公元220）流行的所谓百戏看做是中国戏曲的来源……不过，无论哪种看法，都无法令人信服地说服彼此。[1]我们也许可以从以下的视角去看这个问题。

现代中国戏剧因为包含了“话剧”这样一种类似于西方戏剧的剧种，所以常称之为“戏剧”；与此不同，传统中国戏曲则一般被称为“戏曲”，因为它不但有西方意义上的戏剧——“戏”，而且还包含音乐和歌曲——“曲”。中文“戏”一字实际上可以表示两层意思：其一是指戏剧本身，另外它还可以表示“戏耍”、“娱乐”、“游戏”、甚至“杂技”等，如以上所说的“百戏”中所包含的内容。因此，要更好地了解中国戏曲的起源，就不仅得了解模仿、扮演、表演的传统，还应该考察在这种表演中所具有的音乐和曲调。

一、与戏曲有关的活动

与中国戏曲有关的最初的活动或许可以追溯到古代的宗教祭祀。

1 关于较详尽的对中国戏曲起源的讨论，参看黄天骥、康保成主编《中国古代戏剧形态研究》，郑州：河南人民出版社2009年版，第3–19页。

巫觋们在祭祀中扮演鬼神，吟唱、舞蹈。至今在安徽、湖北、江西一些农村流行的傩戏或傩舞中所有的一些驱魔祭祀就还保存着这种活动的踪迹。这种具有简单情节或故事的扮演，虽然很明显还没有任何艺术表演的意识，却给日后在舞台上表演的演员提供了原型。

以后，春秋时期(公元前722—481)的宫廷倡优，则也从一个方面给早期中国戏曲的发展提供了素材。根据司马迁(公元前145或135—?)《史记》所记，楚国优人优孟，看到楚相孙叔敖死后他儿子所受到的不公平的待遇以及他的窘迫境遇，便扮做孙叔敖，模仿孙的神态，去见楚王。楚王见了大惊，以为孙叔敖复活，便想重新请他做宰相。优孟于是进谏楚王，成功地说服了楚王聘用孙叔敖的儿子。为了一些政治上的目的而采取现实生活中的扮演，再加上一些纯粹的笑料，这些都是宫廷倡优以及一些乐人所常用的手法，来表达一些有掩饰的讽刺与嘲弄，或给予一些劝告，因为除此之外，很难让别人接受这种劝告。这种有对话、有情节的、基于现实生活的模仿也可能促进了以后中国戏曲的诞生。

另一个与中国戏曲起源有关的活动是前面所提到的"百戏"。"百戏"大约产生于秦代(公元前221—206)，而流行于汉代。"百戏"是一个统称，可以泛指各种娱乐活动，如各种杂技、武术、魔术、歌舞、杂耍以及角抵等。表现人与兽之间的角斗便是角抵戏中的典型表演。东晋葛洪(284—364)所著《西京杂记》中所记的一出叫《东海黄公》的小戏便是一出角抵戏。它表演了黄公的悲惨故事：黄公会法术，能以法术降服蛇、虎。秦朝末年，东海一带出现了一只白虎。黄公仍想以他的法术去制服这只白虎。可是，这次因为他年老体衰，再加上饮酒过度，结果他的法术非但制服不了虎，自己最后反而被虎所咬死。与以前的娱乐表演不同，这出角抵戏不再是由倡优乐人进行即兴表演，而是演出一段事先制定的情节，其人物、冲突以及结果也都是预先制定好的，就像是在演出一个剧本。也许是因为《东海黄公》在当时比较新颖，所以这出角抵戏以后被召入汉朝宫廷，为皇帝演出。

从以上对中国戏曲早期所产生的一些戏曲活动的一番简略探索，我们可以看到，就其本身来说，也许这些活动没有一个可以被认为是中国戏曲的起源：古代巫觋所主持的祭祀确实载歌载舞，可是它的内容太神圣、太充满宗教气息、情节也太过于简单而不能视之为戏曲情节。另一方面，那些宫廷小丑、倡优及乐人的表演可能会有较复杂的故事情节，这些情节也都来自于现实生活。但这些大多数属于即兴表演，而一般不作为可以重复演出的节目。角抵戏《东海黄公》在这方面则确实跨出了一大步，因为它的情节较为复杂，也很有意思，而且此情节亦可以不断地、一次次地演出，就像以后的戏剧剧本一样。但是，我们不清楚戏里是否有歌舞作为它的基本成分。

二、与戏曲有关的音乐

另一方面，戏曲表演中的曲（音乐和歌曲）也有一个很悠久的传统。中文里，“曲”常与“歌”和“诗”相联系，因为诗本来是要吟唱的。所以“曲”可以指歌曲，也可以指一种可以歌唱的韵文。虽然音乐与歌曲在早期中国历史中就已存在，与舞蹈相伴或用于祭祀中，但它们成为戏曲中一个必不可少的组成部分，却是较晚才出现的。直到北宋、金朝（公元1115年—1234年）时期，我们才看到一些谱有歌曲的最早的戏曲。这些歌曲是专为那些戏曲而谱写的。一开始时，这些戏曲曲调大多数采自当时流传的民歌或俗曲。因为当时的歌曲作者熟悉音乐曲调，所以他们在创作新的歌曲时只需要依着音乐旋律填词即可。因此，那些曲调一开始对曲文的韵律（平仄叶韵）并没有严格的要求。可是随着时间的推移，后来的人们开始对那些曲调原有的音乐旋律不太熟悉了（就像我们现在对那些戏曲中的音乐旋律已几乎一无所知）。于是这些歌曲作者便开始模仿前人所作的曲子的韵律来作新曲。而且为了方便以后曲家作曲和以韵律，人们开始将每一曲调中词曲的韵律固定下来。这样一来，以后的曲家就不再依据音乐填词，而是依据每一曲调的诗文韵律填词为戏曲作曲。只有当戏曲中的组曲是以固定下来的韵律填词而作，而不是按照它的音乐旋律而作时，中国的戏曲才真正进入了它的成熟阶段。

很显然，正如常言所说，罗马不是一日之内可以建成，中国戏曲也并非于某一特定时期出现。相反，它是长期逐渐形成的。因此，我们在这儿所说的古代的祭祀以及各种娱乐表演活动，都对中国戏曲的形成作出了贡献。它们中的每一种活动也都可视为中国戏曲尚未成熟的形式。随着这些尚未成熟的戏曲形式的日积月累，中国戏曲才最终走向成熟。

讨论题：

1. 关于中国戏曲的起源都有哪些不同的观点？你认为成熟的戏曲应该有些什么基本成分？
2. 在哪些方面中国戏曲与西方戏剧从一开始就有所不同？是什么因素有可能导致这些不同？

第二章 中国戏曲的发展

一、唐宋时期的戏剧活动

唐朝(618—907)是中国历史上一个繁荣富强的朝代。唐王朝不仅在政治上强盛,经济上发达,而且在文化上也非常繁荣。很多艺术与娱乐形式在当时都得到了长足的发展,包括一些处于萌芽状态的戏剧形式。这些娱乐活动的发展当然是同官府的首肯,甚至帝王的鼓励密不可分的。根据历史记载,唐代的一些皇帝都偏爱百戏与散乐。散乐是百戏的同义语,内容包括歌舞、游戏、小戏,甚至杂技等。[1]比如,唐玄宗李隆基(685—762)本人就精通音乐,在很小的时候,就能歌善舞。他修订制作的一些乐曲,至今尚存。公元712年李隆基登基之后不久,便对当时的官方掌管歌舞、戏剧的机构——教坊进行了大力改组和扩充。各个教坊中的乐人也常被召来为皇帝、大臣演出。此外,李隆基还创建了教习音乐、舞蹈以及表演的机构“梨园”。因为这个机构就在一个梨园旁边,所以便使用了“梨园”这个名称。李隆基还挑选了三百名学生进梨园学习,由他亲自教习歌舞。从那以后,“梨园”就成了戏班的代名词,而中国戏曲演员则被称为“梨园子弟”。

正是在这种唐朝宫廷的促进和支持下,各种早期的中国戏剧形式得到了快速的发展。参军戏即其中之一,是整个唐代最盛行的戏曲娱乐活动之一。据记载,参军戏本来是在东汉年间(25—220)以戏曲形式嘲讽

1 参看刘昫等撰《旧唐书》,中华书局1975年版,第8册第2799页;或王溥撰《唐会要》,中华书局1955年版,第1册第623页。

官僚(参军)腐败的一种表演,之后成了一种固定的戏剧形式,由两人表演,一人嘲讽另一个,类似现代的相声或脱口秀。[1]唐代很多其他娱乐也继承了这种传统,旨在讽喻官僚腐败。由于参军戏的盛演,其中的两个人物在舞台演出中便逐渐有了固定的角色名称:一个叫做参军,而另一个则一般叫做苍鹘。一些学者据此认为这标志着中国古典戏曲中各类角色的雏形。[2]参军戏原本是由两个人物表演喜剧式的对话,其目的只是为了逗人一笑,可是之后这样的表演日趋复杂,而且也不一定只是为了逗笑或讽喻,有时还会不止两人的表演,甚至还有女艺人参与其中。除此之外,因为唐代歌舞也非常盛行,所以参军戏也加进了歌舞的成分,使它更接近于产生于宋金年代的成熟戏剧形态。

宫廷倡优及其他乐人们的表演,比如以上所提到的盛极一时的参军戏表演,究其本质大都是对话。但另一方面,主要为歌舞的表演也在当时非常盛行。在这方面比较有名的一些小戏包括《兰陵王》、《钵头》、《苏中郎》以及《踏摇娘》等。其中《踏摇娘》特别值得关注。该戏表演的是隋代末年一个姓苏的人,丑陋无业,而且常醉酒,但他喜欢自吹有中郎官衔。他的妻子则美貌,而且善歌舞。每当苏酒醉,便殴打妻子。妻子则只好向她的邻居哭诉。因此这个戏便将这种好笑的过程戏剧化。首先有演员扮演苏的妻子,一边歌唱一边舞蹈,倾诉她的怨恨,然后有演员扮苏回家跟他的妻子发生争吵,引人捧腹大笑,由此产生喜剧性效果。在演出过程中,观众也与演员产生互动:妻子一边唱,申诉苦衷,观众则齐声和之,复述其不幸。值得注意的是该戏合歌舞于简单的情节之中。另外,它也开了戏剧中男扮女装的先河。

宋朝(960—1279)标志着中国的一个转折期,从一个繁荣富强的国家沦落为一个柔弱,最终被女真族、蒙古征服的民族。但是,宋代的戏剧活动仍然继续、发展着,并最终趋于成熟。北宋时期(960—1127),随着经济的发展与商业的繁荣,大都市如汴京(今河南省开封)或金朝都城中都

1 参看段安节著《乐府杂录》,载《中国古典戏曲论著集成》中国戏剧出版社1959年版,第1册第49页。

2 参看陶宗仪著《南村辍耕录》,载《景印文渊阁四库全书》台湾商务印书馆1986年版,第1040册第685页下;或廖奔、刘彦君著《中国戏曲发展史》,山西教育出版社2000年版,第1册第225页。

(今北京)的人口迅猛增加。而人口的迅速增加则产生了对各种娱乐的需求。因此,在汴京和中都,便产生了大量称之为“瓦舍”和“勾栏”的娱乐场所。前者一般指的是商业娱乐活动场所,而后者则具体指的是在“瓦舍”之中,表演所使用的场地。之前,一些喜剧性的表演如参军戏都是以对话为主,而另一些娱乐表演则侧重歌舞。两者各自独立地发展着。现在众多的瓦舍、勾栏建立起来,这些娱乐活动便都在一起进行表演,互相交流,互相学习,于是,不久一种叫做“杂剧”的新型戏曲形式便于宋金之际诞生了。这种杂剧开始将戏剧表演和歌曲结合起来,形成一种固定的表演模式,除此之外,还创立了更多的戏曲角色。这种宋金杂剧还常分两部分进行表演,类似以后戏曲中的两场。所有这些都表明中国戏曲的成熟形态即将到来。但是,遗憾的是,由于之后北宋与北部女真人之间连年不断的战争,不但经济和民生遭受了重创,而且文化体制和戏曲发展也受到了很大程度的破坏。

根据一些学者的意见,中国戏曲最早的成熟形态是南戏,它大约是在北宋末年产生于中国南方。因为来源于浙江温州(以前叫永嘉),所以也被称为温州杂剧或永嘉杂剧。[1]宋朝年间产生的这些南戏为纯粹的戏曲表演,没有杂耍之类的技艺娱乐穿插其中。每出南戏都着重在舞台上表现一个完整人生,而不是人生片段的故事。由于南戏在表演上的灵活性,所以它并不像之后的元杂剧那样一定要遵守一个固定的结构,有的一出戏就可多达五十多场。另外,南戏还发展出了七种角色行当,如“生”、“旦”、“净”、“末”、“丑”、“外”及“贴”。这些角色与宋杂剧中的角色是有一定联系的,但并不完全一样,而且全都是由男艺人充任,包括女角色的充任。至于其音乐,鉴于当时有很多音乐形式盛行,如鼓子词、唱赚以及诸宫调,而这些音乐形式都以成套的曲子来表达较复杂的内容,所以南戏也开始借用这种成套的歌曲,作为它最重要的戏曲表演手段,来叙述剧情、表达人物情感以及烘托气氛。元代以前最有名的南戏有《张协状元》以及《赵贞女蔡二郎》。

---

1 参看徐渭著《南词叙录》,载《中国古代戏曲论著集成》,第3册第239页。

二、元代戏曲

(1) 北曲元杂剧

元代是中国戏曲发展的黄金时代。在13世纪后半叶至14世纪初这段时间里，特别是在元贞与大德年间(1295—1307)，突然涌现出了大批的戏曲，这些戏曲一般被称之为“元杂剧”。当时，在不到一百年的时间里，出现了约一百多位戏曲作者，而他们创作出的戏曲剧作则远远超过了五百部。[1]假如我们考虑到当时的历史现实正是中国在外族统治之下，“这种美学上的突然爆发……实在是料想不到的”[2]，那么产生于中国土壤而又令人惊叹的这一杂剧高峰便更会让人觉得不可思议。当然，可以有不少理由来说明这种戏曲上的发展。首先，在元朝的大部分时间里，蒙古统治者在中国废除了长期以来盛行的科举考试制度。他们依赖蒙古人以及西域色目人作为他们最主要的盟友，并选拔他们作为官府行政人员来统治中国。这极大地伤害了中国文人的自尊心，降低了他们的社会地位。因为仕途被杜绝，无法施展其才华，于是这些人只好以写作戏曲剧作来糊口。而此前，戏剧创作是其不屑而为的。其二，蒙古人所建立起来的庞大的蒙元帝国客观上促进了帝国内各个不同民族之间在政治上、经济上以及文化上的交流。蒙古人以及西域色目人酷爱歌舞，他们带来了大量本民族的歌舞在宫廷中表演。这也间接地促进了戏曲活动的发展。另外，经济的快速发展，各民族之间的贸易往来则使城市规模发展，形成像大都(今北京)和临安(今杭州)这样的大都市，也产生了大量对娱乐的需求。最后，或许由于蒙古统治者在文化控制上无意亦无能，所以元代朝廷总的来说采取了一种较为宽松的文化政策。因此地

1 根据元钟嗣成的《录鬼簿》，元代有111位剧作者。傅惜华的《元代杂剧全目》中共有737个剧目，其中550个是元代剧作者所写，另外187个则为元明之际无名氏的作品。

2 J. I. Crump, *Chinese Theater in the Days of Kublai Khan* (Ann Arbor: Center for Chinese Studies, The University of Michigan, 1990), 第3页.

方上的戏曲作者常常可以想写什么就写什么,并无太多的官方审查。这就是为什么我们可以发现在元杂剧里有这么多令人惊讶的丰富多彩的内容,包括针对元代朝廷和元代社会尖锐的抨击。

作为一种成熟的戏曲形态,元杂剧在格律与音乐上都有较严格的戏曲格式。一出杂剧常常由四折戏组成。如果四折戏还不足以表现其内容,则剧作者会再加上几个曲子,组成所谓的“楔子”。“楔子”常被置于戏的一开始或置于两折之间。元杂剧每一折都主要由一组套曲组成。曲是元杂剧的灵魂,因为它们主要用来表达戏剧情节、情感波澜以及人物性格。每一支曲子有两部分内容:音乐与歌词。音乐一开始来自于一些民间小曲。一支曲调经常使用之后,便流行起来,于是便形成了固定的曲调。以后的曲作者便开始按照严格的平仄韵律为这一曲调填词,形成新的曲子。填进曲子里的词,一般称为元曲,不同于唐诗宋词。创作元曲时,作者为了取得表演上的灵活性可以在格律之外增加若干个字,这些字称之为“衬字”。因此,在元杂剧里,不同曲调的曲子被放在一起便组成一组套曲,不过,同一组套曲中的曲子都得用相同的宫调。因此四折里的四组套曲便用四个不同的宫调。此外,同一组套曲中的曲词都要押同一个韵脚,一韵到底。至于演出体例,在元杂剧中,一般只由一个主要男演员或女演员来演唱所有的曲子,当然此演员可以在戏中扮演不同的角色。从这儿我们也可以看出杂剧中歌唱的重要性。

因为文献的缺乏,我们现在对元剧作者知道的很少。如元代一百来个剧作家中,很多我们都是只知其名而已。比如,关汉卿来自于大都,是其中最杰出,也是最有名望的。但我们只知道他是医户出生,喜欢与下层社会的很多人交游,包括不少剧社的剧作者、男女演员、歌舞者,甚至一些伎艺人士。正因为同这些人的交往,所以他剧作中大部分写的是普通民众的爱情和痛苦。关汉卿剧作的特点是他表露出的激烈的情感,以及他对他所创作出的人物的强烈的爱与恨。这一点得到了历代批评家的赞同。作为一个多产作家,关汉卿一生共写了六十多部杂剧,其中今存仅约十余种。他的一些有名的杂剧包括《窦娥冤》、《救风尘》、《单刀会》以及《蝴蝶梦》等。

王实甫大约是与关汉卿同时期的人，也是元代最杰出的剧作家之一。他的戏剧着重表达男女之爱。其剧作充满文采，曲词优美。他最有名而且影响最深远的剧作是《西厢记》。该剧讲述出身高官家庭的崔莺莺与年轻学子张生的恋情，以同情、赞许的笔调描写两人之恋情及最后之团聚。其反封建婚姻的意识不仅在青年男女中激起巨大反响，而且也深受各阶层人民的欢迎。该剧有众多版本。剧中一些人物名字如“红娘”现在已经成为当今中国社会中家喻户晓的名字。王实甫一共创作了十四个杂剧，但只有三个剧本流传于世。

元代其他重要的剧作家包括马致远、白朴以及郑光祖。他们的生卒年现在也都无法确知，不过，同关汉卿一起，他们四个并称为“元曲四大家”。

据钟嗣成《录鬼簿》记载，马致远也是大都人，曾做过江浙行省的一个小官。[1]马致远以他的神仙道化剧知名。他创作的神仙道化剧表达了一种隐居、遁世的思想。马致远剧作的语言常为世人所称道：自然、朴素、不事雕琢、貌似平淡无奇，但却含意深远。马致远一共写作了十五个杂剧，现存七个，其最有名的剧作有《汉宫秋》、《岳阳楼》及《黄粱梦》。

白朴出生于一个具有良好教育背景的家庭，其祖父、父亲及叔父都是金朝知名的知识分子。[2]但因为他生活在蒙古灭金的时代，所以自幼便经历了国破家亡的痛苦。这一切都给他的戏剧创作带来了巨大的影响。也许是因为对蒙古人对他的国家及人民的所作所为而感到愤愤不平，所以他终身不仕元朝朝廷。他的剧作中所表达的情绪也大多是怨愤、怅惘、或带有怀旧的回忆。白朴一共写了十六个杂剧，只有《梧桐雨》、《东墙记》及《墙头马上》三个剧本流传了下来。

郑光祖来自北方的平阳襄陵，后来赴杭州谋一小官职。郑性耿介清高，在那儿不太与人交往。[3]他的剧作有两个主题：历史故事与男女爱情

1 参看钟嗣成撰《录鬼簿》，载《中国古代戏曲论著集成》第2册第108页。
2 参看章培恒主编《十大戏曲家》，上海古籍出版社1990年版，第2–3页。
3 参看《录鬼簿》，载《中国古典戏曲论著集成》第2册第119页。

故事。其剧作之语言常为批评家所称道,认为优美俊朗、意境高远。郑光祖共创作了十九部杂剧,今存八部,其代表作为《王粲登楼》与《倩女离魂》。

(2) 元代南戏

起源于北宋末的南戏,在元杂剧兴起时仍然在继续发展着。但因为南宋与蒙元的政治与军事对峙,这两种戏剧形式遂各自在南北方以自己的方式独立地进行发展,并无什么接触。而当蒙古人逐渐将其势力南推,并最后推翻南宋政权时,元杂剧也随之南下同南戏发生交流,从而在各个方面影响了后者。

南曲与北曲在很多地方不同:就音乐而言,前者用的是五声调式(比如现今流行的民歌《茉莉花》即使用这种调式),而后者则使用七声调式;前者最初来自于民间歌谣,因其"顺口可歌"而并未考虑其宫调如何,[1]而后者用于一组套曲中时则严格遵守同一宫调。再就用词而言,前者多口语,俚俗而无文采,因为作者多为普通的未受过良好教育的民间艺人,而后者则因为是由赋有才华的文人学士填写,因此具有良好的文学性,有文采,而且严格遵守词格韵律。

与北曲元杂剧接触后,南戏开始吸收一些北曲的元素:首先,南戏在套曲联套上也日趋规范,尝试像北曲一样由同一宫调的曲子来组成一组套曲。其二,南戏曲文的用韵也开始使用北曲所使用之韵部。之前,因为南戏基于南方一些方言,因此语音基础及韵律都与北曲大不相同。最后,在歌曲的用词上,南戏作者也试图改进其语言,使其较优雅,有文采。这在高明的《琵琶记》中明显可见。

因为文人学士最初鄙视南戏,所以元代南戏的总数很难确切统计。有些人认为,应当在六十或七十部左右。[2]但是除了极少数几部剧作的

1 徐渭著《南词叙录》,载《中国古代戏曲论著集成》,第三册第241页。

2 参看廖奔及刘彦君著《中国戏曲发展简史》,山西教育出版社2006年版,第88页。

作者我们知道以外，其他绝大多数的作者则均为无名氏。随着元杂剧在元末的式微，南戏却加速了其发展的步伐。这一方面是因为其改进的结果，另一方面则是因为其音乐结构与剧作长度方面的灵活性—它可以因剧情需要随意调整或增加曲子或套曲，而且它整个剧作的长度也有伸缩性，没有限制。正因为有了这些特点，南戏才能够在有元一代生生不息、发展壮大，最后超越元杂剧而繁衍为今天的一些现代戏曲。元代南戏的代表作为《琵琶记》、《荆钗记》、《刘知远白兔记》、《拜月亭》及《杀狗记》。最后四部通常被称之为"四大南戏"。

《荆钗记》

此剧相传是由宋元时期苏州柯丹邱所撰，用戏剧形式写出王十朋与钱玉莲起伏跌宕的人生。王十朋是温州一个穷书生，赴京城赶考高中状元。钱玉莲为一年轻女子，入嫁王家便决定无论发生什么都忠贞于自己的丈夫。为了对王表示她的忠贞，她不惜牺牲自己的生命。王十朋也珍惜他与钱的感情，勇敢地抵挡住了各种诱惑和压力，拒不再婚。在一连串的事情发生之后及各自经历了各种苦难以后，两人最后终于夫妻团圆。此剧深受民间欢迎，一部分是因为它歌颂了剧中两个主角在顺境、逆境中不变的爱情，一部分是因为剧本本身的结构紧凑、针线细密。

《刘知远白兔记》

剧本撰者不详。虽然剧本题目指的是后汉高祖刘知远，但是此剧着重写的则是其妻李三娘。刘知远的哥哥和嫂子因为想谋取父亲的财产继承权，所以对三娘竭尽折磨，乃至横加迫害。李三娘含辛茹苦，直到多年之后，当她的儿子打猎追赶一只白兔到他们村庄，巧遇李三娘，夫妇俩才最后得以团聚。李三娘受苦受难但仍然忠贞不屈的形象深受各界人士同情，也使此剧历来盛演不衰。

《拜月亭》

又名《幽闺记》。此剧相传为元代施惠所作，[1]而且有可能改编自关汉卿的同名杂剧。它讲述了年青人蒋世隆与朝廷高官小姐王瑞兰在蒙古入侵，逃难途中邂逅、相爱及私订终身的故事。当瑞兰的父亲发现他们私订终身之后，却硬将其拆散。日后，蒋世隆在科考中一举中榜，高中状元，他们俩才在最后夫妇重圆。此剧一般被认为是喜剧，它歌颂了女主人公勇敢坚持婚姻自主，坚决抵制父亲的封建包办婚姻。其喜剧情节的安排以及词曲之优美常为人称道。

《杀狗记》

此剧一般认为是明初徐畛所作，讲的是两兄弟的家庭纠纷。哥哥孙华被当地两个无赖所蒙骗，虐待他弟弟孙荣。弟媳妇杨月真为了使他明了真相而杀了一条狗，用人的衣服把整只狗裹住，然后把它丢弃在哥哥的门前。鉴于这两个无赖与孙荣不同的处理狗尸的态度，孙华最终明了血浓于水。该剧明显宣扬儒家的道德观。其语言非常接近口语，质朴自然，因此常为后代一些学者所诟。

《琵琶记》

元明时期高明所撰，本于前人所作南戏《赵贞女蔡二郎》。在《赵贞女》中，蔡伯喈在科举考试中状元之后，与宰相之女结婚，拒不与其糟糠之妻相认，相反用马将其妻踹死。蔡之后则遭雷击而死。高明的《琵琶记》则改变了剧情，使蔡伯喈因圣旨被迫再娶。而当赵五娘来京城找他之时，他亦迎接。这样就促就了蔡一夫二妻的美满结局。《琵琶记》也强调了赵五娘在蔡伯喈离家之后所遭受的苦难以及她对公婆的虔孝之心。该剧因其道德教化而大获赞誉，正如剧作者自己所说："不关风化体，纵好也枉然。"《琵琶记》关目安排完美，语言与曲词优雅，曲调格律整齐，因此一般被誉为"南戏之父"。高明的《琵琶记》问世之后，文人们开

1 但因钟嗣成的《录鬼簿》与朱权的《太和正音谱》都未于施惠名下载有此剧，所以有些学者并不认同此说。

始改变了他们长期鄙视南戏的态度。南戏进一步得到成长与发展，最后取代北杂剧而成为中国戏曲传统中的一个主流剧种。

三、明清传奇戏曲

“传奇”一词，其本来的意思就是“情节离奇的故事”，但在历代被用来表示不同的事物。唐宋之时，“传奇”指的是以文言文写作的短篇小说；宋元年间，则因为不少北杂剧和南戏文都以这些故事为素材，所以一般也称这些戏曲为“传奇”；而从明朝开始并且一直到清朝年间，“传奇”一词则都表示唱南曲的长篇戏曲，以区别于北杂剧。

(1) 明代传奇

在明朝前期约一百五十年的时间里，北杂剧同南戏一样仍在演出，虽然它们各自都被限制在自己的地盘——北杂剧在中国北方作场(大约现今安徽、山西、河北、河南及一些相邻省份)，而南戏则在南方表演(大约在现今浙江、江苏、福建、江西、广东以及一些相邻省份)。南戏在表演方式上具有很大的伸缩性，包括词曲格律，所以它可以吸收各种地方曲调，而且也能适应很多地方文化。因此南戏得以迅速向外流传，缩小北杂剧的影响范围，使其相形失色。大约到了万历年间(1573—1619)，北杂剧已经基本上无人问津了，而成化(1465—1487)之后，南戏则方兴未艾，其戏曲活动越来越繁荣，而且还陆续变化出不少南戏腔种来。据史载，共有十五种这样的南戏腔种，其中海盐腔、余姚腔、弋阳腔及昆山腔是最流行的南戏腔种。[1]这些南戏腔种在明代大多局限于中国的东南部。昆山腔则经过昆山一些艺人在艺术与声腔上的创新与逐渐改进，于清代演变为昆曲，演出至今。

---

1 参看廖奔、刘彦君著《中国戏曲发展史》，第3册第38页。

到了明代晚期,北杂剧虽然已经衰败,但一些艺术家仍然在继续创作杂剧。不过,因为此时受了南戏的巨大影响,这些杂剧从形式上到曲调上都已经发生了很大的变化。标准的元代杂剧有四出戏,而明清杂剧可以像王九思(1468—1551)的《中山狼》那样只有一出戏,也可以如许潮《泰和记》一样多达二十多出戏。不过最重要的变化还是在乐曲上:这些杂剧将北曲和南曲夹杂使用,而有些则干脆全部套用南曲。因此,这些杂剧也被叫做"南杂剧",因为它的改变有时确实模糊了传统杂剧与传奇之间的界限。

明代传奇作者人数众多。首先值得一提的是来自现今江苏省昆山的梁辰鱼(约1519—约1591)。他写的《浣纱记》是昆山腔经过改良之后所演出的第一出传奇戏曲。该剧的巨大成功和声誉,使得昆山腔日后成为一种"高雅"的艺术,成为"官腔",地位远胜于那些"低俗"的被贬为"杂调"的其他各种声腔。

另一位值得一提的剧作家是郑之珍(1518—1595)。他以一百多出的鸿篇巨制写作了影响深远的《目连救母劝善记》,可以连演三天。郑之珍是第一位总括以前所有民间传说中关于目连的故事,并将故事全本以传奇形式写成的剧作家。因为在民间演出中极受欢迎,所以该剧成为以后所有戏曲改编本的故事原型。

万历年间,传奇创作趋向繁荣。徐渭(1521—1593)则是这一时期戏曲创作的先驱。他在戏曲上的声誉主要建筑在他那被统称为《四声猿》的四部杂剧之上:《狂鼓史》、《玉蝉师》、《雌木兰》以及《女状元》。这四部杂剧以戏曲形式演绎了一些非凡,甚至奇幻的故事,表达了徐渭对现实的不满和义愤。剧中表达出的徐渭狂放不羁的精神以及他对杂剧形式所作的改变深深地影响了之后的南戏创作。

沈璟(1533—1610)是明代戏曲中的重要人物。他最为人知的是他在曲学上所作的贡献。他写作的《南九宫十三调曲谱》为当时传奇戏曲中词曲的创作确立了规范。沈璟也写了不少传奇剧本,但因为他过于执著于自己帮助制定的曲律,所以他的剧作大多都不成功。

与沈璟不同，汤显祖（1550—1616）作为明代最重要的剧作家及文人，创作了很多成功的传奇戏曲与诗歌。他的《玉茗堂四梦》包括《紫钗记》、《牡丹亭》、《邯郸记》以及《南柯记》，给他带来了巨大的声誉，其中《牡丹亭》为他的代表作。深受明末哲学中“情”、“理”之争的影响，该剧大力提倡“情”，让出生于高官家庭的美貌小姐杜丽娘自己去寻找意中人。这种大胆、具有叛逆性质的举动在明代的封建社会里当然是不可想象的。因此汤显祖便设法使它只能在杜丽娘的梦中及她从冥界死而复活中得以实现。不管是在艺术上还是在思想上，《牡丹亭》都被认为是明代传奇之翘楚。

在晚明历史和文学上，阮大铖（1587年—1645年）的名字也值得一提。作为一个官僚、政客，阮大铖为很多人所痛恨，因为他卖身投靠明代宫廷里有权有势而又声名狼藉的宦官魏忠贤（1568—1627）。但作为剧作家，阮大铖又写出了一些有很高艺术造诣的剧作。他最有名的剧作是《燕子笺》，讲的是一个错综复杂的爱情故事，最后以美满幸福结局。剧中他以娴熟的手法，新奇、巧合构建的情节，制造出了一些意想不到的戏剧效果。这些都一直为人称道。

(2) 清代传奇

传奇戏曲在清代相当长的一段时期里仍继续盛行。但是由于朝代变更而带来的又一次外族统治中国，所以清初的传奇戏曲里常常充满着一种失落的情绪，带有明显的悲伤和怀旧之情。这一时期有不少剧作家进行戏曲创作，比如吴伟业 (1609—1671)、李玉 (约生活于1630年左右)、杨潮观 (1712—1791) 以及蒋士铨 (1725—1785)，但最知名而且最有代表性的则是洪昇 (1645—1704) 与孔尚任 (1648—1718)。

洪昇是钱塘（今浙江杭州）人，年轻时在很短暂的一段时间里曾踌躇满志，想在官场上有所作为，也过了一段舒适的生活，但之后的整个人生却是充满了挫折、失意与惆怅。这些情绪间接地反映在他的杰作《长生殿》中。唐玄宗与其贵妃杨玉环之间的爱情，历史上多有记载，而且关于他们的故事也有着数不尽的小说和戏曲演绎。但是与以前版本所不同的是，洪昇在剧中选取并着重描写了唐明皇对其爱妾永恒的失落与无尽的伤感。这一部分占据了全剧整整一半的篇幅。洪昇的《长生殿》是第一部将帝王之恋还原为普通男女之爱的戏曲，因此显得格外真实、感人。

孔尚任跟洪昇是同时期人，当时两人并称为“南洪北孔”，享有盛名。孔尚任出生于山东曲阜，之后在北京住了很长时间，却最终得不到清廷的重用。生涯上屡屡受挫，官运上也不得意，于是孔尚任倾注精力于剧作，特别是写他的《桃花扇》。该剧以儒生侯方域与歌妓李香君之间的爱情故事来反映政治，特别是用以说明南明王朝覆亡的原因。因为政治上相去不远，再加上孔尚任成功地运用当时盛行的昆曲这一形式来表达其内容，所以《桃花扇》获得了巨大的成功，也使孔尚任一夜成名。不过这同一出剧本，不久之后也给孔尚任带来了政治上的麻烦与官场上的失意。《长生殿》与《桃花扇》都是清代传奇的代表作。

四、京剧的兴起

明代万历期间，昆曲以其婉转的声腔，优雅的曲词赢得了文人的喜爱与支持。因此从那时起昆曲便成了一种“官腔”，在剧坛上取得了统治地位。但各种地方戏却并没有因此而消亡，而是经历了各种变化与转型。因此在清初，地方戏便获得了快速的发展。以弋阳腔为主的各种南戏逐渐统一为“高腔”。另一方面，在现今河南、河北、山西以及山东一带日渐消亡的北杂剧中所遗留下来的一些变种则几经变化，形成了“弦索腔”，而在今日陕西、甘肃一带的地方戏则被称作“西秦腔”。这些地方戏及其曲调在清代蓬勃兴起、互相影响、互相竞争、相互结合。它们之间日益广泛的互动便逐渐产生了一些新的混合的唱腔。例如二黄腔与西皮腔便源自于襄阳腔，而襄阳腔则又由西秦腔演变而来。

清朝乾隆(1736—1795)、嘉庆(1795—1821)年间,全国各地的地方戏日益蓬勃发展,对当时剧坛占统治地位的昆曲构成了强有力的挑战。这些地方戏以前曾被称为"花部"戏曲,而昆曲则被认为是"雅部"戏曲。虽然清廷进行了干预,甚至禁止了一些花部戏曲的演出,但是这些地方戏仍然在很多地方继续演出并得到进一步的繁荣。相比之下,昆曲则在迅速衰退。最终,这场"花部"与"雅部"的戏曲之争便在前者的全面胜利中宣告结束。

乾隆五十五年(1790),一个叫做三庆班的在扬州的剧团应召至北京,为祝贺皇帝八十大寿演出戏剧。三庆班原本徽班,善演二黄腔。他们的演出在京取得了巨大的成功,赢得了广泛的赞誉,于是便在北京留了下来,继续表演。看到三庆班的成功,另外三个徽班剧团也来到北京演出。于是,这四个徽班剧团在北京一起演出,互比高低,使二黄腔成了京城里最盛行的声腔。

当时,流行于湖北汉水一带的地方戏被称为"汉调",也就是现在汉剧的前身。因为其地理位置靠近安徽、陕西与甘肃,所以汉调在其发展过程中吸收了安徽的二黄腔,也吸收了陕西、甘肃的西皮腔。汉调产生之后,深受欢迎,其剧团也迅速发展。因此,在徽班进京之后,一些汉调剧团也逐渐来到北京一显身手。根据一些记载,至道光(1821—1851)八年至十二年间,这些汉调剧团已经在京站住了脚,赢得了广泛的赞誉。[1]于是,善演二黄的徽班与以二黄、西皮合唱的汉调艺人一同在京演出,互相影响。有时他们甚至同台联袂上演。久而久之,这种互动便产生出了一种新的声腔——皮黄。皮黄便是现在京剧所用的主要唱腔。道光之后,京剧正式形成,产生了很多有名的京剧演员。这些舞台艺术家一起将京剧推向顶峰。著名的京剧艺术家梅兰芳(1894—1961)甚至还带中国京剧代表团三次访问日本,并于1930年率团访问美国,让京剧艺术闻名于世界舞台。京剧之美与其魅力直至今日仍在继续。

1 粟海庵居士著《燕台鸿爪集》,载张次溪撰《清代燕都梨园史料》,中国戏剧出版社1988年版,第1册第272页。

1. 中国戏曲自唐代以来是怎样发展的？中国最早的成熟戏曲形态是从什么时候开始出现的？
2. 虽然元代是蒙古统治中国的一个相对短暂的历史时期，但它却是中国戏曲史上的一段黄金时期。有哪些原因促成了这种戏曲上的繁荣？
3. 谈谈元杂剧的戏曲形式是怎样的？有哪些组成部分？
4. 谈谈京剧是怎样在十八世纪末、十九世纪初产生的？

中国戏曲

一、中国戏曲的种类及分布

中国一共有三十四个省、直辖市与自治区(包括港、澳、台湾)。在所有这些地区都有当地的剧种。以下便是这些地区所有的当地剧种。[1]

(1) 直辖市[2]

北京市　　京剧
重庆市　　川剧
上海市　　沪剧
天津市　　河北梆子

(2) 省

安徽　　黄梅戏、徽戏、安徽目连戏、安徽傩戏、庐剧、凤阳花鼓戏
福建　　莆仙戏、梨园戏、高甲戏、闽剧
甘肃　　秦腔、陇剧
广东　　粤剧、潮剧、白字戏
贵州　　黔剧、贵州花灯剧、安顺地戏

1 此表大部分参照了李汉飞编《中国戏曲剧种手册》附录,北京:中国戏剧出版社1987年版,第847–981页;以及廖奔、刘彦君著《中国戏剧发展简史》,太原:山西教育出版社2006年版,第274–289页。

2 以下表中的省、直辖市、自治区以及其他地区均以其拼音字母顺序排列。

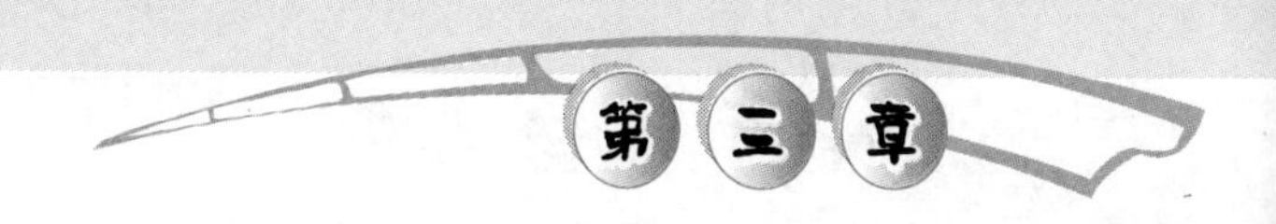

海南	琼剧
河北	河北梆子、评剧
黑龙江	龙江剧
河南	豫剧、河南越调、河南曲剧
湖北	汉剧、楚剧、花鼓戏、采茶戏
湖南	湘剧、祁剧、花鼓戏
吉林	吉剧、二人转
江苏	昆曲、淮剧、扬剧、通剧、锡剧、苏剧
江西	赣剧、弋阳腔、宜黄戏、采茶戏
辽宁	二人转
青海	青海藏戏
陕西	秦腔、陕西道情
山东	吕剧、山东梆子、山东柳子戏
山西	山西梆子(蒲剧/晋剧)、秧歌、道情戏
四川	川剧、四川灯戏
云南	滇剧、云南花灯、白剧、傣剧
浙江	越剧/绍兴戏、婺剧、绍剧、黄岩乱弹、瓯剧、杭剧、甬剧、湖剧、姚剧、睦剧

(3) 自治区

广西	桂剧、邕剧
内蒙古	二人台、大秧歌
宁夏	宁夏道情
西藏	藏戏
新疆	新疆曲子戏

(4) 其他地区

澳门	粤剧
台湾	歌仔戏
香港	粤剧

需要注意的是,不是所有的中国戏曲剧种都罗列于上。此表仅显示那些在各地区有代表性的或比较流行的剧种。根据1984年的一项调查,当时在中国有多达360个剧种。我们可以看到中国戏曲在分布上有如下的情况(虽然这是二十世纪八十年代的调查结果,但现在情况依然大致如此):[1]

一、在360个剧种中,京剧是唯一一个在全国各地都有影响力的全国性剧种。全国所有的省、直辖市以及自治区都有自己的专业京剧剧团,其影响显而易见。

二、有八个主要剧种是具有跨省影响力的,即这些剧种都在不止一个省份活动演出。这八个剧种是北方的评剧、二人转、豫剧、晋剧与秦腔,以及在南方的越剧、粤剧与川剧。这八个剧种中,每个都有70个以上的专业剧团分布在不同的省份。所以算上京剧,在中国一共有九大剧种。1984年在中国一共有2,302个专业剧团,其中1,299个是表演这九大剧种的剧团,占全国专业剧团总数的56.4%。

三、有些剧种只在本省内有影响,而且有25个以上的专业剧团。这些剧种包括山西梆子、河北梆子、山东吕剧、河南曲剧、安徽黄梅戏、江苏锡剧、福建闽剧、湖北楚剧以及湖南花鼓戏。1984年这九个剧种一共有341专业剧团。

四、有174个地方剧种,每种只维持少数的专业剧团组织演出。这些剧种共有专业剧团662个,平均每个剧种只有不到4个专业剧团。在这174个剧种里,92个剧种只有一个专业剧团。

---

1 以下材料根据胡兆量"中国戏曲地理特征"一文,载《经济地理》2000年第20卷第1期第84–87页。

五、没有专业剧团的剧种很多，总数达168个，差不多要占全国剧种总数的一半。这些剧种大多只有业余剧团在农村的农闲季节或节日期间演出。因为不常演出及一些其他原因，有10个剧种在上世纪八十年代末已经失传。

一般都认为，中国在地理上以淮河—秦岭为界划分成南方和北方。南北方的地理差异在很大程度上决定了南北方剧种的差异。

中国北方的气候一般要比南方冷得多，河流湖泊也比南方少。就土地而言，北方的可耕地比南方少得多，土地比南方开阔、空旷。因此，中国北方人口密度要比南方低，特别是中国的西北部分。因为人口密度不高，北方的语言便较统一，没有南方那么多的方言。因为有这些因素，所以北方的剧种倾向于高亢、铿锵、有力。这些特点也可能是受到了中国西北地区少数民族以及在那儿的中国邻国所表演的歌舞的影响。比如，蒙古的歌舞便以粗犷、豪放著称。[1]另外，有些学者也指出，中国东北的秧歌剧种多短节奏，快速度。这是由于秧歌演员在寒冷的气候条件下演出需要不停地活动、跳跃。[2]

形成对比的是，中国南方气候温和，河流湖泊众多，雨量丰富。从土地上来看，南方的可耕地比北方多得多，人口也稠密得多。因此，在南方，即使是在较小的地区比如长江三角洲地区，也分布着很多方言。在这种地理环境中，人们交流不用大声喧嚷，而温暖湿润的气候也使南方的口音，特别是东南沿海一带的口音，听上去比较低吟、柔和、流丽宛转。这也是南方剧种的特色。

实际上，很多文人学者很早就都注意到了南北方戏曲的不同特点。比如，明代著名学者徐渭（1521—1593）在其《南词叙录》中便指出“今之北曲，盖辽、金北鄙杀伐之音，壮伟很戾”，而且，“听北曲使人神气鹰扬，毛发洒淅……南曲则纡徐绵眇，流丽婉转，使人飘飘然丧其所守而不自觉。”[3]现代学者林语堂（1895—1976）则更具体地描写了它们之间的区别

1 乌兰杰著《蒙古族古代音乐舞蹈初探》，呼和浩特：内蒙古人民出版社1985版，第10页。
2 王洋，“中国音乐审美的文化地理结构研究”，《飞天》2009年第四期第55页。
3 徐渭著《南词叙录注释》，李复波、梁澄宇注释，北京：中国戏剧出版社1989年版，第24、76页。

如下：

> 粗犷豪放的北方，温柔和婉的南方，这些区别在他们各自的语言、音乐和诗歌中都能看到。我们来对比一下陕西乐曲与苏州乐曲的差异。陕西乐曲用一种木板控制速度，声调铿锵，音节高昂而响亮，有如瑞士山歌，使人联想到呼号的风声，似在高山上，似在旷野里，又似风吹沙丘。另一方面，苏州乐曲的低声吟唱，介乎于叹息与鼾声之间，喉音和鼻音很重，很容易使人联想到一个精疲力竭的气喘病人，那习惯性的叹息和呻吟已经变成了有节奏的颤抖。在语言上，我们听到的是北京话洪亮、清晰的节奏，轻重交替，非常悦耳；而苏州妇女则轻柔、甜蜜地唠唠叨叨，用一种圆唇元音，婉转的声调，其强调的力量并不在很大的爆破音，而在句尾拖长了的，有些细微差别的音节。[1]

确实如此，北方土地辽阔，人民仗义豪爽，因此其戏曲也是高亢悠远。比如秦腔的特点便是吼叫。难怪北方的一些剧种，比如京剧，其女子的角色以前也由男演员扮演。下面这首典型的北方民歌也许可以最好地表现这些北方特点：

敕勒川，阴山下。
天似穹庐，笼盖四野。
天苍苍，野茫茫，
风吹草低见牛羊。

对比之下，南方风景秀美，到处青山绿水，人声也趋于轻柔细软，各种戏曲剧种也因此以音色细腻，腔调委婉见长。这就是为什么南方的一些剧种，比如越剧，其男子的角色以前（现在也常有）也由女演员来扮演。以下这首流行的南方民歌也可用来说明这些南方特色：

---

1 Lin Yutang, *My Country and My People* (NewYork: Reynal & Hitchcock, 1935), p. 20. 中译文采自林语堂著《中国人》，郝志东、沈益洪译，上海：学林出版社1994年版，第33–34页。

好一朵美丽的茉莉花！
好一朵美丽的茉莉花！
芬芳美丽满枝桠，
又香又白人人夸。
让我来把你摘下，
送给别人家。
茉莉花啊茉莉花！

二、中国传统戏曲剧目介绍

在当代中国舞台上仍有很多传统戏曲剧目在上演。这些剧目深受欢迎，因此便构成了很多当代中国戏曲剧团的保留剧目。不过中国戏曲传统剧目作为一个整体，则是一个很大的资料库。没有数据显示其中到底有多少个戏曲。所以以下只是对一些剧种中最有代表性或最流行的戏曲剧目，包括现代剧目，做一个简要的介绍。[1]

（1）京剧

搜孤救孤

此剧取自纪君祥的元杂剧《赵氏孤儿》，描写了赵氏孤儿惊心动魄的复仇经过。

故事发生在春秋时期(公元前770—公元前476)。据说晋灵公荒淫无道，大夫赵盾屡屡进谏都不听。后来晋灵公被赵盾的弟弟赵穿杀死。之后，到了晋景公时期，他的宠臣屠岸贾与赵盾的儿子赵朔不和。因此，屠岸贾便以赵盾杀了先前的晋灵公为借口，图谋将赵氏满门抄斩。赵朔的妻子是庄姬公主，她躲避进王宫中，生下一个儿子，由赵氏门客程婴伪装偷带出宫。抄杀赵氏全家之后，屠岸贾听说公主生了一个儿子，但在

1 不包括前一章中已作过介绍的一些经典戏曲曲目。

王宫内却搜查不到，于是便下令如果十日内不交出孤儿，他就要把国内所有的同龄婴儿都杀死。程婴于是同赵家另一门客公孙杵臼商议，决定前者舍子，后者献身，救下孤儿。多年以后，孤儿赵武长大成人，诛杀屠岸贾，为赵家报了仇。

此京剧剧本又名《八义图》，1933年第一次在舞台上上演。

玉堂春

故事发生在明代。吏部尚书之子王景隆冶游烟花，认识了北京的名妓苏三，花名玉堂春。二人一见钟情，发誓要白头偕老。苏三让王景隆发奋学习，考取及第。她也同时许诺不再接客。但当王景隆钱财用尽后，便被老鸨赶出大门。王走之后，苏三矢志等待，拒不接客。无奈之下，老鸨只好将她卖给富商沈燕林为妾。沈将苏三带回他在山西洪洞县的老家。

沈燕林常年在外经商。他的妻子皮氏与邻居赵昂私通。看到丈夫将一个漂亮的女子带回家，皮氏部分出于嫉妒，想要谋害苏三。有一天她给苏三准备的一碗下了毒药的面条，不想，却被丈夫沈燕林吃下。沈当场死亡。邪恶的皮氏随即将苏三告上官府，称其谋杀。而县官在接受了皮氏的贿赂之后，也匆匆判决苏三死刑，并将她押解到太原复审，等候执行。

另一方面，王景隆二次进京赴考。最后考上进士，被任命为山西巡按，也来到太原。复审时，王惊讶地看到苏三的案子。他于是微服私访，见到了苏三。经过大量的调查，以及同事的帮助，王景隆最后洗清了苏三所有的不白之冤，两人最终得以团圆。

由于情节起伏跌宕，唱词曲调优美，所以该剧在中国极其有名，脍炙人口。

白蛇传

这出戏描写峨嵋山上的白蛇精和青蛇精，因为羡慕人间生活，化身

为少女白素贞和小青。他们在杭州西湖游玩时，邂逅书生许仙，互生爱慕，经小青撮合成亲。但金山寺的法海和尚却不满他们的结合，试图破坏其婚姻，于是便严词恐吓许仙。许仙受惊，听信谗言，离家出走金山寺。白素贞了解这些之后，赶到金山寺，向法海索要她的丈夫，并与法海大战，但却败走断桥。之后，由于小青从中斡旋，许仙回心转意，与白素贞和好如初。但法海之后又前来用强力拆散两人，并将白素贞镇压在雷峰塔下。于是小青又求助于天将，将雷峰塔烧毁，从而救出白素贞。许仙和白素贞最终团圆并从此过上幸福生活。

该剧是中国四大民间传说之一。剧本主要根据冯梦龙（1574—1646）的短篇小说《白娘子永镇雷峰塔》。很多其他剧种也都有关于这一故事的剧本，但往往剧名不同。20世纪50年代，中国剧作家田汉改编此剧，用了现在的剧名。自那以后，常演的京剧都是用田汉的剧本。

(2) 昆剧

十五贯

故事原出于冯梦龙的《醒世恒言》，清代剧作家朱素臣将其改编为传奇《双熊梦》。20世纪50年代，据朱素臣的传奇改编成了昆剧《十五贯》。由于《十五贯》的演出在全国的巨大成功，这出剧实际上使当时日渐衰落的昆剧得到了新生。这个故事也被改编为其他一些剧种，如京剧、粤剧、秦腔，还在1956年拍成电影。

故事发生在明代。屠夫尤葫芦借得十五贯铜钱，对他的继女苏戌娟戏称是卖她到别人家为婢女所得到的钱。苏戌娟信以为真，连门也未关，便深夜逃离投亲去了。尤葫芦的邻居娄阿鼠是一个赌徒，那天晚上正缺钱，便溜进尤葫芦家，盗走十五贯钱，并杀死尤葫芦灭口。另一方面，熊友兰身带十五贯铜钱前往常州办事，途中遇到苏戌娟，两人同行。衙门差役见两人同行，而且又带十五贯铜钱，以为是嫌犯，便将他俩带往无锡县衙门。无锡知县未经调查便宣判苏、熊死刑，而常州知府及江南巡抚都轻信知县，唯有监斩官况钟发觉事有蹊跷，要求缓期执行，但被告

之不许。况钟不为所动，再据理力争，要求缓期半个月，并甘愿冒丢官之风险。最后，况钟亲去无锡微服私访，终将真相大白于天下。

玉簪记

这是明代戏剧家高濂（约1573—约1620）所作的传奇，讲述道姑陈妙姑与书生潘必正的恋爱故事。金人南侵宋朝，少女陈娇莲于逃亡途中与家人失散。附近一个道观的观主收留陈娇莲为道姑，为她取法名叫陈妙姑。观主的侄儿潘必正恰好因为科考落榜而留住在观内。经过一系列的波折，潘必正与陈妙姑倾心相恋，私订终身。但观主却怕有碍道观名声，因而硬逼潘去临安应试，而且不能与陈妙姑道别。妙姑在必正的船启程之前赶到，赠送给潘一枚碧玉鸾簪，而潘也回赠了陈一枚白玉扇坠，作为信物。剧终潘必正考试中举，潘陈两人从此结为连理。

此剧以词语典雅华美著称，尤其是将青年男女在恋爱中的心理描写得淋漓尽致。其情节也被其他剧种改编，盛演不衰。

(3) 越剧

红楼梦

此剧根据曹雪芹（1724—1764）著名的同名小说改编。戏剧从林黛玉来到她的外祖母家贾府开始，写黛玉与其表兄贾宝玉一见如故。在大观园里，两人意趣相投，私下里一起偷读《西厢记》，并互相交流自己的想法。他们之间的爱情也与日俱增。

贾宝玉的父亲贾政希望儿子遵从封建传统，学习经书，为家里带来功名利禄。可是宝玉却偏偏蔑视这些东西。绝望之下，贾政痛打贾宝玉。而林黛玉则同情宝玉，前来看望他，但却产生了误会。多愁善感的黛玉于是去葬花、赋词，以抒发其孤寂苦闷。听到黛玉的赋词，宝玉向她吐露了爱意。

另一方面，为了贾府的利益，贾母、管家王熙凤等人决定要宝玉与其表姐薛宝钗成婚。他们对宝玉耍了一个计谋：表面上许诺宝玉，说他娶

的是黛玉,但私下里却让他与遮掩得严严实实的薛宝钗成婚。不幸的是,消息走漏,让黛玉知晓,如晴天霹雳,使她孱弱的身体更加不堪一击。黛玉焚毁其诗稿,悲愤而死。宝玉于婚礼中得知真相时,不顾一切奔出去见林黛玉。在黛玉灵前,宝玉嚎啕痛哭、悔恨无尽,决定离开家去当和尚。

祥林嫂

这是根据鲁迅(1881—1936)的短篇小说《祝福》改编的现代越剧。祥林嫂年轻守寡,不愿再嫁。她逃离婆家到鲁四老爷家帮工。数月后她被发现抓住,抢至山中被逼与猎户贺老六为妻。不过,她的再婚生活倒还和谐,婚后还生了一个儿子叫阿毛。然而,好景不长,不久贺老六即贫病而死,而阿毛又被狼叼走。祥林嫂悲痛万分,没有办法,只得重回鲁家帮工。但因为她守了两次寡,所以这次老爷和乡亲都嫌弃她。于是,祥林嫂去当地的土地庙中赎其"罪孽"。然而她仍然被老爷从鲁家撵出,沦为乞丐。几年以后,在一个除夕之夜,她终于死于风雪之中。

该剧最早于1946年由南薇(1921—1989)编导上演,于20世纪60年代与70年代分别经过了几次修改。由于该剧在舞台上的成功,它在1948年和1978年被两次拍成电影。

(4) 沪剧

罗汉钱

该剧根据现代作家赵树理(1906—1970)的短篇小说《登记》创作。20世纪50年代初,中国的包办婚姻仍很普遍,特别是在农村。年轻男女自由恋爱、结婚的非常少见。该剧写的就是发生在1950年这一背景下的故事。张家庄青年男女李小晚与张艾艾相恋。作为爱情信物,小晚送艾艾一个罗汉钱,而艾艾则回赠小晚一个戒指。但他们的婚姻请求却遭到了村长的反对,因为他认为青年男女自己找对象名声不好。艾艾的母亲绰号叫小飞蛾。她偶尔发现了女儿的罗汉钱,于是回忆起她二十多年前一段痛苦的日子。那时候她与一个叫保安的青年相恋，但是最后被父母逼着与现在的丈夫张木匠成婚。为了不让女儿也像她当年那样被村民们非议，为流言蜚语所伤，小飞蛾决定跟他丈夫一起去东王庄为女儿另择姻缘。没想到在那儿她听到人们议论她的冷言恶语，使她事未成便愤而归家。最后，在艾艾女友燕燕的劝说下，她与丈夫商定，最终将艾艾许配给小晚。

该剧剧本于1952年出版，同年10月17日首演于北京。1956年上海电影制片厂还将其拍成了电影。

(5) 评剧

花为媒

员外王少安之子王俊卿和他的表姐李月娥青梅竹马，一往情深。王少安寿诞之日，李月娥随其父母前去祝寿。两人重又见面，分外高兴，相互赠送香罗帕为其爱情信物。但受俊卿母亲之托，媒婆阮妈却去向张朋之靓女张五可提亲。俊卿坚持要娶表姐李月娥而不想提与张五可之亲事。于是受俊卿母亲之托，阮妈又去找李月娥的父亲李茂林说亲，但李茂林也以中表婚为理由而拒绝了这门婚事。与此同时，俊卿见难与月娥成婚，忧虑成病，而张五可却深爱俊卿的一表人才，亟愿结此良缘。为解脱此窘境，阮妈于是设计让俊卿表弟贾俊英替俊卿去相亲。张五可在花园里见到贾俊英之后，虽然怨恨俊卿拒婚，但却与贾一见倾心，并送他红玫瑰定情。结婚当日，俊卿听说新娘为李月娥，疾病顿愈，而张五可也与贾俊英喜结良缘，皆大欢喜。

该剧为评剧的经典剧目，取材于清代蒲松龄(1630或1640—1715)的《聊斋志异·寄生》，编剧为评剧的创始人成兆才(1874—1929)。由于备受欢迎，长春电影制片厂还于1963年将其拍成了电影。

(6) 黄梅戏

天仙配

农夫董永很贫穷,但非常孝顺。为了凑足钱埋葬父亲,他卖身为奴,在傅员外家做工。玉皇大帝的小女儿七仙女为之感动,私自下凡,并以槐树为媒,与董永结为夫妇。婚后他们一起到傅家做工。七仙女并以她精湛的纺织手艺,成功地把董永三年的契约缩短为一百天。期满之后,夫妇俩正准备离开傅家回去,没想到玉皇大帝命令女儿立刻返回天庭,否则将严惩董永。此时七仙女已有身孕,于是只好在那棵槐树下与董永忍痛相别。

此故事最早见于干宝(?—336)的《搜神记》。剧作家陆洪非(1923—2007)改编成黄梅戏,又名《百日缘》、《槐荫树》,1955年拍成电影。

(7) 豫剧

花木兰

北魏时期(386—534),北边柔然部落首领突力子侵犯边疆地区。朝廷征召大批年轻人来保家卫国。皇上的命令来到了花弧的家。花弧有一个儿子叫花木力,一个女儿叫花木兰。花木兰觉得父亲年事已高,而弟弟又太小,所以决定用弟弟的名字替父从军。在军队里的十二年,木兰骁勇善战,还帮助贺元帅智擒了部落首领突力子,从而结束了边疆的战事。贺元帅非常喜欢木兰,要求朝廷封官晋爵,还将其爱女许配给木兰成婚。但木兰什么都不要,只要了一匹好马,骑着回家乡见父母,并换上了女儿装。朝廷封木兰为尚书郎,贺元帅则带着很多礼物,亲自上门来看望木兰。当他惊奇地发现木兰原来是一个女子时,禁不住连声夸赞木兰真是个伟大的巾帼英雄。

该传说最早记载于乐府诗《木兰辞》,由著名豫剧演员常香玉(1923—2004)的丈夫陈宪章(1917—2000)改编成豫剧演出。1956年拍成电影,由常香玉扮演花木兰。

（8）晋剧

打金枝

唐代宗（726—779）将女儿升平公主许配给汾阳王郭子仪（697—781）的第六个儿子郭暧为妻。郭子仪花甲寿诞之日，子女纷纷前往祝寿，唯独升平公主不去，引起人们议论纷纷。郭暧怒而回到王宫，打了他妻子升平公主。公主遂向其父母哭诉，要求皇上惩罚郭暧的所作所为。与此同时，郭子仪则将儿子捆绑起来一起上殿向皇帝请罪。唐代宗宽宏大度，不但没有听女儿所言，而且还给郭暧加了封。沈皇后也安慰女婿、斥责女儿。之后，小夫妻消除前嫌，和好如初。

该剧为晋剧的经典剧目，1955年拍成电影。

（9）淮剧

女审

陈世美、秦香莲为夫妇。陈世美离家赴京城赶考。陈世美走后，长久音信全无，因此秦香莲携带她的儿子女儿去京城寻找丈夫。没想到陈世美考中状元之后，做了入赘驸马。此时陈世美拒不认他的妻子儿女，还派侍卫想谋杀三人灭口。秦香莲带子女逃离京城，在路上遇到一个老人。老人带他们到解元山练习武艺。

若干年以后，秦香莲母子都练成一身好本领，投军退敌，智勇双全，屡建奇功，被封为都督。回到京城，秦香莲见到陈世美，将其拘留，并亲审陈世美三项罪名：不孝父母、停妻再娶、杀妻灭子。陈世美自恃为皇帝的女婿，拒不认罪，反而指秦香莲犯上。此时，王丞相带圣旨来到，命令秦香莲马上释放陈世美，同时，御林军也包围了都督府，欲以武力进行威胁。秦香莲忍无可忍，斩杀陈世美，然后带其子女杀出京城，重回解元山。

该剧为传统淮剧剧目，1960年拍成电影。

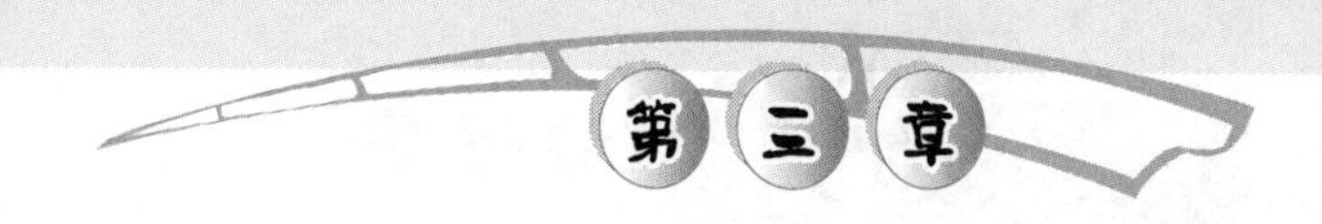

(10) 莆仙戏

春草闯堂

相国李仲钦的女儿李半月有一天在丫环春草陪伴下去华山进香。途中,受到吏部尚书之子吴独纠缠。义士薛玫庭恰好在场,见义勇为,搭救半月。混乱中吴独被薛玫庭的一个仆从打死。吴母自恃官高权重,欲强迫知府胡进杖杀薛玫庭。另一方面,春草关心薛玫庭之安危,赶到府衙,得知薛即将受刑,便愤而闯入公堂,阻止其执行。当被问及缘由之时,春草一时情急,称薛玫庭为相府姑爷,使胡进不敢动刑。春草回到相府之后,以大义晓之李半月,说服其假意认薛为她的丈夫。但相国李仲钦得知女儿与薛玫庭的意图之后大怒,发书信给知府胡进,令其取薛玫庭首级进京报功。春草设计从信使处截得书信,改动文字,使这封书信成了婚书。胡进见信大喜,火速大张旗鼓,送相国贵婿上京完婚。同时,消息传开,京城及各省官员也都纷纷送礼致贺,连皇帝也赐予贺喜御匾。事已至此,李相国只得将错就错,认薛玫庭为婿。

该剧从旧戏《邹雷霆》改编而来,由陈仁鉴(1913—1995)执笔,1960年首演。

(11) 河北梆子

蝴蝶杯

该剧在各种梆子剧种中广泛流传搬演。源出清代花部乱弹一部作品,作者已不可考。此剧在陕西、山西、河北、河南等地极为流行,剧中某些段落如《藏舟》在那儿几乎家喻户晓。该剧的前半部也叫《游龟山》。

故事发生在明朝嘉靖年间(1522—1566)。两湖总督卢林的儿子卢世宽带家奴游龟山,因买鱼纠纷将渔夫胡彦打死。江夏知县田云山的儿子田玉川正巧也游龟山,路见不平,遂打死卢世宽。卢林四处追捕凶手。田玉川逃至江岸,恰巧遇上胡彦的女儿胡凤莲。凤莲把玉川藏在舟中脱险。玉川心生感激,临别时在舟中将一个蝴蝶杯送给凤莲,作为其婚约。[1]卢林搜查不到田玉川，便想加罪于他的父亲田云山。胡风莲则闯堂鸣冤，救出田云山。之后，卢林受命出征南蛮，但战事受挫为敌所困。正在此时，田玉川为避官府追捕改名雷全州亦逃亡至此，遂将卢林救出，并助其反败为胜。卢林将女儿许配给田玉川。全剧以田玉川一夫二妻结束。

(12) 川剧

黄金印

该剧又名《金印记》，源自明代早期苏复之所撰写的同名南戏。

故事发生在战国(公元前475—221)时期。苏秦(?—公元前284)年少时落魄，屡次参加科考都不成功。因此他受尽了家人和亲友的羞辱，甚至连他母亲都不以他为儿子，嫂嫂也不认他为弟弟。于是，苏秦开始日夜发愤苦读，头悬梁，锥刺股。他的艰苦努力终于给他带来了荣誉。经过多年努力推行他的“合纵”攻秦的战略，他最终被拜为六国的宰相。当苏秦衣锦还乡之时，母亲为他清扫道路，而他的嫂嫂则长跪在路旁。昔日嘲讽苏秦的人，现在都前来阿谀奉承。该剧极大地讽刺了社会上的人情冷暖、世态炎凉。

(13) 湖南花鼓戏

刘海砍樵

刘海砍樵的传说在北宋年间(960—1127)便已流行，到清代中期已经基本演变成了今日戏曲本的模样。该剧情节很简单，但一些曲调却不仅在湖南非常盛行，而且在全中国都非常流行。

根据传说，刘海是一个孝顺的儿子，每天上山砍柴为生，侍奉老母。有一个老狐狸精在山中修炼多年，已成半仙，所以化身成一妇人形，取名

---

1 蝴蝶杯是传说中的一种陶瓷酒杯。当酒斟满酒杯时，可以看见杯中一只蝴蝶在翩翩起舞，而当酒喝完时，则蝴蝶亦消失离去。因为有此奇特功能，所以在古代，人们将蝴蝶杯作为传家之宝或作为男女定情之物。制作这种蝴蝶杯的工艺久已失传，1979年，山西一个村子里发现了一个蝴蝶杯实物，所以现在人们已经可以据此重新制作这种蝴蝶杯了。

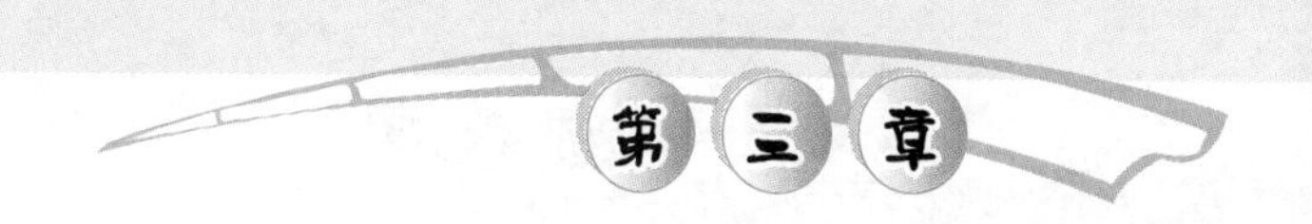

为胡秀英。秀英见刘海日复一日上山，爱其勤劳，便告诉刘海，愿结连理。没想到刘海感到踌躇。他告诉胡秀英，自己为一贫穷樵夫，家中还有老母要侍奉。但胡秀英甘守贫贱，还愿意帮他照料老母。于是两人便以“柳树为媒，山作证”，结成恩爱夫妻。

（14）秦腔

三滴血

该剧为秦腔的代表剧作，取材于纪昀（1724—1805）的《阅微草堂笔记》，由剧作家范紫东（1878—1954）创作，首演于1921年。1958年经过修改后，由西安电影制片厂在1960年拍成电影。

周仁瑞为山西五台县人，在陕西韩城县经商。其妻在生下一对孪生子后不久去世。周仁瑞无力抚养两个儿子，便将次子卖给李三娘为嗣，取名李遇春，而自己则带着长子，取名周天佑。不久仁瑞经商折(shé)本，于是携带儿子天佑回乡。周仁瑞的弟弟周仁祥怕天佑日后继承家产，不认其为侄。兄弟俩涉讼公堂。县令晋信书为一腐儒，以滴血之法（取两当事人之血，滴入盆中看其是否相融合）判断天佑与仁瑞非亲子关系。于是父子失散。

另一方面，三娘抚养遇春长大。遇春与三娘的亲生女儿李晚春的感情日久弥深。三娘也有意让他们成亲，但尚未成婚，三娘病故。当地财主阮自用垂涎晚春已久，借吊唁之机，挑起讼端，以拆散晚春与遇春之姻缘。县令晋信书又以滴血之法拆散晚春、遇春，并将晚春判给阮自用。花烛之夜，晚春将阮自用灌醉，逃出阮家，去寻找遇春。遇春得知晚春已逃出阮家，也离家去寻找晚春。他在路上与周天佑邂逅，两人相貌一样，同感惊异，很快便结为金兰之好，且一起投军，因立功而受封得官。

与此同时，周仁瑞寻找他的儿子，在路上与遇春奶娘王妈相遇。两人都不服衙门断案，遂同去县衙质对。晋信书招来周仁祥父子，再用滴血之法试验。不料，父子之血不融，使晋信书先前的判断大受打击。正在此时，军中大帅接受周天佑、李遇春请求，问罪晋信书屡判屡误。此时晚春也赶到。于是，父子、夫妻终于团圆，而晋信书则遭罢官。

（15）粤剧

搜书院

该剧据说是发生在清朝雍正、乾隆年间（1722—1795）的一段动人故事，由杨子静（1913—2006）、莫汝城（1926—2009）及林仙根编写。因为广受欢迎，1956年拍成电影。

故事发生在海南岛。一天，镇台小姐在放风筝。线断，风筝飞走，落入琼台书院，为学生张逸民拾得。小姐的丫环翠莲前往书院索取。张逸民在风筝上题诗一首，然后交还。在交谈中，张对翠莲在镇台家所遭受的苦难深表同情。另一方面，镇台夫人见风筝上所题的诗，便怀疑翠莲行为不端，于是打算将她赠送给道台为妾。得知消息后，翠莲女扮男装，深夜出逃。在路上，翠莲遇到书院老师谢宝。听说翠莲之遭遇，谢宝带她入院。在学院里，翠莲与张逸民幸福重逢。

因为丫环在逃，镇台率兵来搜书院。鉴于情况紧急，张逸民与翠莲只得向谢宝吐露真情，乞求帮助。谢宝被他们的真挚爱情所感动，决定救翠莲，将她藏在轿底。谢宝出去见镇台，以不见道台手谕为理由，拒绝搜查书院。无奈之下，镇台派兵围住书院，自己则同谢宝一起去面见道台。路过竹林时，谢宝有意从坐轿里下来，与镇台步行去见道台。谢宝的侍从见他们两人走远，便将翠莲放出，找到张逸民。两人远走高飞，寻找自由。

（16）二人转

蓝桥会

该剧起源于《庄子》中的一则故事。元代剧作家李直夫亦写过杂剧《尾生期女淹蓝桥》，但已不传。这部爱情悲剧又名《水淹蓝桥》，是二人转剧目中有代表性的一部。

蓝瑞莲与魏奎元为青梅竹马，长大以后决定终生相与厮守。但蓝瑞莲的父亲贪图钱财，逼迫女儿嫁给了老财主周玉景。瑞莲在周家吃尽了苦。一天，蓝瑞莲去井边打水，巧遇魏奎元。瑞莲向魏奎元诉说了婚后在周家的悲惨遭遇，于是两人约定当晚半夜在蓝桥相会，私奔他乡。

当晚，魏奎元应约先来到蓝桥。他没有见到心上人，倒发现暴雨突至，山洪暴发，马上就要冲到蓝桥。为了让蓝瑞莲知道他来过，魏奎元立刻将衣服脱下，系在桥栏上，自已则随即被洪水卷走。蓝瑞莲做完家务，赶到蓝桥，只见魏奎元的衣服还在。推知魏奎元已被洪水吞噬，蓝瑞莲亦纵身跳入水中，以死践约，生死相随。

讨论题：

1. 在当代中国，戏曲的地理分布是怎样的？北方戏曲与南方戏曲大致上有什么不同？
2. 中国的传统戏曲一般喜欢表现哪些题材或主题？

第四章

中国戏曲与中国文化

中国戏曲是中国文化的产物。因此，学习中国戏曲就必须了解它在中国文化以及中国社会中所发挥的种种功能，了解由中国文化发展而来的戏曲它独特的表演特色，以及与中国文化和中国戏曲的发展密不可分的中国剧场的演变。

一、中国戏曲的社会功能

中国戏曲从一诞生起就一直有着两种形式的演出：一种是为帝王、朝廷官员以及某些富豪家族的演出。这种演出有时是由教坊乐人、宫廷乐部伶人或官僚贵族蓄养的家伶来完成的，有时则是从地方伶人剧团中召应。这种召应在元代被叫做“唤官身”，而从晚清开始则称为“堂会”。自然，在这种场合，观众少，其观看的目的也比较简单——节日庆典或宴请宾客，但是处于这种场合的小规模的观众，却可能对演剧的质量有较严格的要求。因此，一般来说，这种演出比较认真，质量较好，而且也很循规蹈矩。另一种演出则是商业化的，面向大众的，在公共场所进行，在寺庙进行，观众显然比较多，因此演出会附和观众的喜好。由于这种场合下的观众可能来自各行各业，而且来观看的目的也并非一致，所以这种演出并不能保证演出质量，因为演员为了生存需要必须要照顾到观众情绪、兴趣的波动变化。因此，这种演出不一定会循规蹈矩，而且有时演出秩序也会比较紊乱、嘈杂。

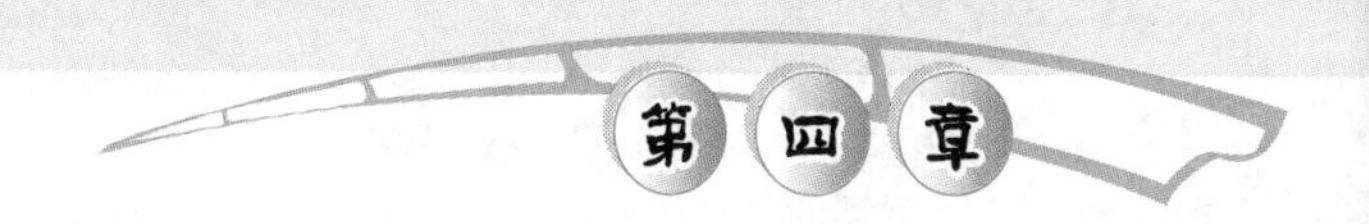

在以下对戏曲社会功能的讨论中，我们会对这两种演出情况都加以考虑，特别是后者，因为商业化的、面向大众的演出是戏曲发展中最主要的一种演出形式。很多社会功能都跟这种演出形式有关。

(1) 作为娱乐工具

在第一章里我们谈到中国戏曲的起源仍然是有争议的。所以虽然我们不能说戏曲的诞生就是出于娱乐的需求，但很明显，其中一个主要功能在各个时期都与娱乐有关系，不管是供帝王百官消遣还是供普通百姓娱乐。《松江府志》就记载了一条有趣的轶事，说明代名医秦景明有一次被叫去为某一位方知府看病。秦景明带了两名优伶随行。到了之后，秦景明先让优伶演唱了两支曲子。方知府听了优美的曲子，心情有所转变，面容也改善了。于是秦景明再给他诊断开药，不久他的病就好了。[1]这恐怕是戏曲娱乐功效一个最生动的例子。但是，戏曲的娱乐功效总是如此吗？戏曲还提供些其他什么样的娱乐？

作为一种大众消遣工具，戏曲演出是一种社会性的活动，对观众产生直接、即时、而且是强有力的影响。因此，戏曲所提供的娱乐及影响会超出戏曲本身所表现的内容。要了解中国戏曲的社会功能，或者它提供的娱乐及影响，我们就必须考虑戏曲活动所赖以存在的环境与场地。在过去，中国戏曲常常在一些节日期间演出，或在农闲时演出。人们从四面八方赶来观看，得到消遣，获得娱乐。此外，出于风俗习惯，人们也借此机会互相交流、进行社交，甚至谈论生意。因此，很自然，戏曲在这种情况下演出常常会人声嘈杂，而演员与琴师则不得不提高嗓门，打开乐器音量，使大家都能听到。这就是为什么现代人会觉得中国戏曲这么喧闹，因为他不习惯于这种演出情境。也因为有这种氛围，我们可以想象得到这种演出场所也常会沦为是非之地：吵架谩骂、打情骂俏，甚至偷盗，时有发生。很明显，所有这些都是源自于娱乐。再者，因为观众来自

1 蒋星煜著《以戏代药》，上海远东出版社2007年版，"自序"，第1页。

各行各业，出身背景各不相同，所以有些人会有低级趣味，而有些剧团也为迎合他们的口味而演出一些格调低下或具有淫荡，色情内容的戏曲。这有时又会形成一种恶性循环，因为那些演员本来在社会上就是被看不起的，而戏曲本身也是文人所不屑一顾的。庸俗的演出则使社会上的人们更看不起这些演员和戏曲。宋代胡寅（1098—1156）的下列评论也许就表达了当时典型的文人对戏曲的观点：

> 词曲者，古乐府之末造也。[1]古乐府者，诗之旁行也。诗出于离骚、楚辞，[2]而离骚者，变风变雅之意，[3]怨而迫、哀而伤者也。[4]其发乎情则同，而止乎礼义则异。名之曰曲，以其曲尽人情耳。方之曲艺，犹不逮焉；其去曲礼，则益远矣。然文章豪放之士，鲜不寄意于此者，随亦自扫其迹，曰谑浪游戏而已也。[5]

因为文人自己也不把他们为戏曲而作的词曲，看做是传之久远的事，所以他们想到什么就写什么，甚至可以随意抛弃。这样的写作本身虽然无可厚非，但其结果有时却是令人感到惊奇的：比如，元代杂剧的一大特点就在于它反映了元代文人内心深处对社会的看法、想法，毫无保留，一泻千里，因为很多文人写作时根本没有任何顾忌，他们所感觉到的、所想要的，全部都通过手中的笔，流露了出来。所以王国维（1877—1927）才视元代戏曲为"最自然的文学"，而这也正可以说明为什么大部分元杂剧都没有存留下来。[6]

---

1 乐府诗特指汉代（公元前206年—公元220年）一些佚名的民谣歌曲，用乐府之名是因为汉武帝于公元前120年左右正式设立了一个管理音乐的宫廷官署，名叫"乐府"，其职责之一就是收集编纂全国各地的民歌，因此就用"乐府"这个词来表示这些早期的民谣歌曲。

2 "离骚"为著名诗人屈原（约活动于公元前300年前后）所作的抒情长诗。西汉刘向（约公元前77年—6年）将屈原的诗作以及其他人仿效的作品收辑成书，名为《楚辞》。因此"楚辞"一词以后便用来表示这一类的诗歌。

3 "风"、"雅"为中国最早的一部诗歌总集《诗经》中两种不同类型的诗歌音乐。《诗经》共包含三种类型的诗歌音乐，第三种为"颂"。

4 孔子提倡对世事持中庸的态度，因此他认为任何事趋向极端都是不可取的。参考《论语·八佾》："《关雎》乐而不淫，哀而不伤。"

5 胡寅，"向薌林酒边集后序"，载《景印文渊阁四库全书》，第1137册第547页。

6 王国维著《宋元戏曲考》，姚淦铭、王燕编《王国维文集》，中国文史出版社1997年版，第1卷第389页。

由此看来，中国戏曲的娱乐功能便导致了这样一种错综复杂的场面：戏曲肯定给不同的人带来不同的娱乐享受，而这种娱乐本身对某些人来说是欢乐愉快的，而在另外的人看来则可能是非道德的，或淫荡的。这就是为什么数百年来总有官员学者大声疾呼，不断要求禁演这些所谓的"淫戏"。朱熹（1130—1200）的学生陈淳（1153—1217）提交给当时的大理寺丞傅伯成（1143—1126）以下这样一份文书，就说明了保守者面对宋代蓬勃兴起的戏曲活动时所持的反对态度：

> 今秋自七八月以来，乡下诸村，正当其时，此风在在滋炽。其名若曰戏乐，其实所关利害甚大：一、无故剥民膏为妄费；二、荒民本业事遊观；三、鼓簧人家子弟玩物丧恭谨之志；四、诱惑深闺妇女出外动邪僻之思；五、贪夫萌抢夺之奸；六、后生逞斗殴之忿；七、旷夫怨女邂逅为淫奔之丑；八、州县一［按：应为二］庭纷纷起狱讼之繁，甚至有假托报私仇，击杀人无所惮者。
>
> 其胎殃产祸如此，若漠然不之禁，则人心波流风靡，无由而至，岂不为仁人君子德政之累……[1]

显而易见，戏曲的娱乐是多种多样的。不过，当戏曲作为娱乐工具时，它常常会使人产生戒备之心。

(2) 作为祭祀的一部分

戏曲活动经常是在祭祀活动时进行。事实上，很多学者论证中国戏曲源自于祭祀。宗教祭祀时，巫师与驱魔师模仿神灵，迷狂般地叫喊，歌舞。当这种活动从娱神转变为娱人时，最初的戏曲就诞生了。[2]所以有些戏曲是经常在宗教祭祀时上演的（比如以假面舞蹈的傩戏，一些关公

---

1 陈淳著《北溪大全集》卷47，载《景印文渊阁四库全书》第1168册第876页上。

2 参看王国维著《宋元戏曲考》，载《王国维文集》第一卷第309-310页；黄天骥、康保成主编《中国戏剧形态研究》，第8页；又见龙彼得，"中国戏剧源于宗教仪典考，"王秋桂，苏友贞译，《中外文学》1979年第7卷第12期第158-181页。

戏如《关云长大破蚩尤》,或目连戏),而且在一些戏曲里也插进了祭祀的场景,比如宋南戏《张协状元》的第十六出中有李大公主持的祭祀来祈求神对张协与贫女婚姻的裁决,或元杂剧《桃花女》第一折中则介绍了道教拜北斗的礼仪。[1]但是我们须注意,不同的戏曲在相同的场合演出可能会取得相同的效果。同样,同一出戏在不同场合上演则可能会产生不同的效果。所以表演场合是戏曲演出效果的关键。

1986年,在山西潞城县一个农民家里发现了《迎神赛社礼节传簿四十曲宫调》。它为我们了解戏曲祭祀表演提供了宝贵的资料。对这一资料的研究表明,很多源自元杂剧或南戏的戏曲在迎神赛社上演出,而且因为这些戏曲表演就是祭祀中的一部分,所以会有很多村民参加演出。有些祭祀表演和舞蹈会有多达上千村民参与。[2]此外,参与的村民演员也明显地把表演当作是半真实的祭祀,因为在《五关斩将》的表演中,

> 关公骑马过五关斩六将,不是在一个舞台上演出,而是骑马奔驰在村巷中,过一关换一个舞台,连续登上五个舞台才演完全剧。[3]

很明显,这种戏曲演出的功能一般便是在村寨里驱除邪灵,并祈福于天。

另一方面,节庆时期,或庙会、佛寺道观开光时也常有戏曲演出。此外,戏曲演出还用于祈雨、丧葬、祝寿或还愿等场合。在特定的场合会选择一些特定的戏曲来进行表演,因为这些戏曲具有其特定的祭祀意义。[4]比如,朱有燉(1379—1439)的《瑶池会八仙庆寿》便常用来在祝寿会上演出,而目连戏则常为祈愿者所喜爱。

从演出者的角度来看,他们也有他们行内的一些宗教仪礼。比如,

---

1 参看荣世诚著《戏曲人类学初探:仪式、剧场与社群》,广西师范大学出版社2003年版,第2页;倪彩霞著《道教仪式与戏剧表演形态研究》,广东高等教育出版社2005年版,第65-80页。

2 冯俊杰,“赛社:戏剧史的巡礼”,《中华戏曲》1987年第3期,第191页。

3 张之中,“队戏、院本与杂剧的兴起,”《中华戏曲》1987年第3期,第160页。

4 参看倪彩霞著《道教仪式与戏剧表演形态研究》,第152页。

当这些演员初到一地演出或当一个戏台新搭建成之时，会表演一些仪礼祭祀，称为“破台”、“祭台”、“净台”或“镇台”。表演的最后一天，也会举行一些仪式，叫做“扫台”或“送台”。[1]除此之外，以前在戏曲正式演出之前或演出之中，也常常会有一些哑剧表演。这些哑剧表演称之为“跳加官”。演出时，“一演员，身著蟒袍，脸带白面具，手持朝笏进场。他一言不发，只随着乐器的敲击蹦跳于台上，好像难以控制住他的兴奋。他慢慢地对观众展示一卷轴，上书‘天宫赐福’或其他吉祥语。下场前，他以手指日。”[2]这些祭祀都很明显的是演员们在演出前所作的驱邪、祈福。从这里可以看到，一场正式的戏曲表演会含有多么复杂的祭祀功能！

元明之际，有很多所谓的“度脱剧”。元代的度脱剧大约占元杂剧总数的十分之一。这些度脱剧的剧情一般总是这样的：一位道家祖师爷发现人间某人有仙缘，于是便去让他皈依。但他的最初努力却总是遇到顽强抵抗。于是祖师爷不得不使其陷入险境，甚至绝境，这人才被逼着看到人世间安逸与追求之空虚，而最后决定皈依祖师爷。学者们对这一类的戏剧看法不一。比如，在廖奔与刘彦君看来，马致远的度脱剧“与其说他们热衷度脱是出于对天堂的向往，不如说是出于对现实的失望。”[3]日本的田仲一成则将这类戏曲看成是“庆祝剧的一种”，这种庆祝剧则“是在富裕家族的个人祭祀的场合中演出的。”[4]而荷兰籍美国汉学家伊维德（Wilt Idema）则认为这类戏曲“来自于丧葬祭祀，再现死亡与再生，意在引导死者灵魂上升至天堂。”[5]如果这些度脱剧真是在那些祭祀的场合上演，则其必然会成为祭祀的组成部分，从而发挥作用。

这些度脱剧中还有一个现象似乎使很多学者感到诧异：即其包含在皈依过程中的暴力行为。举个例子，在马致远的《马丹阳三度任风子》一

---

1 参看《道教仪式与表演形态研究》一书第182–187页中的详细列表。

2 龙彼得，“中国戏剧源于宗教仪典考，”第172页。

3 廖奔、刘彦君著《中国戏曲发展史》，山西教育出版社2000年版，第二卷，第275页。

4 田仲一成著《中国演劇史》，东京大学出版会1998年版，第132页。中文译文见云贵彬、于允译《中国戏剧史》，北京广播学院出版社2002年版，第130页。

5 Wilt L. Idema, *The Dramatic Oeuvre of Chu Yu-Tun (1379—1439)* (Leiden: E. J. Brill, 1985),p.67。

剧中，屠户任风子最终决定抛弃妻子儿女，将他自己的亲生儿子摔在地上摔死，以皈依道家真人马丹阳。这一无情举动无疑是为了显示任风子与尘世的一切决裂，包括其家庭成员。这当然是符合全真教派的教义的。事实上，虽然这些戏曲并非没有任何夸张，但那些痛苦、险情乃至死亡则不过是剧中所设计出来考验被度脱者的意志的。这就像在现代西方的一些大学的兄弟会里，在新会员被接纳为其正式成员前，必有一段考验期，其中便不乏体力与精神上的痛苦磨炼。

中国戏曲的祭祀功能是有目共睹的，有时称其为迷信，有时则视其为一种民俗。而且一直以来就有数不清的皇帝朝廷禁令，取缔涉及神灵的演出，比如四大天王戏、佛戏或一些圣贤戏等。[1]

为什么帝王政权要过问涉及祭祀的戏曲活动呢？其一，在中国历史上，祭祀和仪礼一直是一项重要的国事，因为这些祭祀是与上天建立联系的，作为"天之子"，皇帝每年都会亲自主持一系列祭祀活动，祈祷国运隆昌或君权长久等。帝王政权不会愿意与别人分享其祭祀权，因为它认为这一般是属于帝王的权利，尤其是如果祭祀会影响广大民众之时。有了祭祀权，皇帝便觉得他是上天意志的代言者，更有权统治其子民。其二，当大批民众在祭祀中进入迷狂状态时，或被居心叵测者所鼓动时，祭祀时上演的戏曲亦毫无疑问可以引起迷信，制造混乱或甚至于导致伤残死亡。据历史记载，元代朝廷于1350年征召了二十六万民伕去治理黄河。民伕中有一个叫韩山童（1351年卒）的，看到周围民伕因官府腐败而怨愤四起，便私下里用石头凿刻出一个独眼石人，并在其背部刻写上这几个字："莫道石人一只眼，此物一出天下反。"[2]韩山童将石人埋在第二天民伕要开挖的河道下，结果正如预料之中："掘者得之。遂相为惊诧而谋乱。"[3]元末一支主要的农民起义军红巾军就是这样揭竿而起的。此例

1 见王利器辑录《元明清三代禁毁小说戏曲史料》（增订版），上海古籍出版社1981年版，第4–5页，第19及35页。

2 叶子奇著《草木子》，中华书局1959年版，第50页。

3 同上书，第51页。

说明了迷信之重要以及出于政治目的而操纵迷信的做法。戏曲作为大众娱乐的一种形式,当然会在其演出中为传播这种种神话、迷信而起重要作用,因此也便必然会遭到官府的禁止了。

(3)作为教育、政治及意识形态的工具

中国文学常常带有说教、道德及功利的倾向,而且在文学创作中也向来没有"为艺术而艺术"的倡导。早在汉代(公元前206—公元220)的《诗大序》中,便把《诗经》中的"风"里的诗[1]说成是"上以风化下,下以风刺上。"[2]这以后便成为文学批评中所谓的"美刺说",它的意思就是文学或用来彰表贤明的人及其言行或讽刺不义之人与事。因此,宋代周敦颐(1017—1073)所提出的"文以载道"便成为以后鉴赏文学创作的一个重要标尺[3]。无怪乎日本著名汉学家吉川幸次郎(1904年—1980年)在他的《中国文学史》中指出,中国文学的七个显著特点之一便是其"对政治的强烈关注"。[4]

中国戏曲作为中国文学的一部分,虽然常常被用于娱乐与祭祀,但也常用做各种教育与政治的工具。举例来说,中国戏曲里常有所谓的"插科打诨",其目的一般是活跃一下剧场气氛。但是,因为这种科诨源自于古代优孟传统,伶人以其喜剧性的对话来讽谏皇上官僚,所以这些插科打诨经常含有对官僚及其政权的讽喻或暗含着批评。一个明显的例子便在元代(1271—1368)关汉卿的杂剧《窦娥冤》里。第二折,有如下的一段:

[净扮孤引祗候上诗云]　我做官人胜别人,告状来的要金银。若是上司当刷卷,在家推病不出门……

1《诗经》的"风"里的诗歌都是民歌,作者现在已不可考。
2 阮元校刻《十三经注疏》,北京:中华书局1980年版,第一册第271页b。
3 参看周敦颐著《周子通书》,上海:上海古籍出版社2000年版,第39页。
4 吉川幸次郎述,黑川洋一编《中国文学史》,東京:岩波書店1974年版,第25页。

[张驴儿拖正旦卜儿上云]	告状！告状！
[祗候云]	拏过来。
[做跪见孤亦跪科云]	请起。
[祗候云]	相公，他是告状的，怎生跪着他？
[孤云]	你不知道，但来告状的，就是我衣食父母。[1]

这一段显然是插科打诨，夹在谋害与庭审这两个严肃的段落之间以笑一笑，轻松一下。这里重要的是州府太守作为一个权威人物，竟然也成了取笑的对象（向其原告下跪），而司法体制则也成了攻击的目标（向观众显示司法追求的是钱财，而朝廷调查则奈何不了司法官）。这些都没有公开批评，也没有明确的不满语调，而是以间接的、喜剧性的演出来完成。这样就将一般被认为是严肃、有尊严的人与事贬到熟悉、滑稽的地步，因而表达对元代朝廷的鄙视、讥讽与批评。

因为戏曲演出的公众效应，它有时也被用来揭丑，让历史上的一些贪官污吏或作恶多端者臭名远扬，从而起到揭露和遏制这些社会恶行的作用。周密（1232—1298）的《癸辛杂识》中便记录了这样一件发生在元初浙江温州的事。

当地一个叫祖杰的僧人积累了大量不义之财，于是贿赂结识了京城里的官员。他居住在一个非常奢华的江心佛寺里。一天，一个叫俞生的人因为不堪科役来寺里做僧人。正巧当地州府跟祖杰关系密切，于是便托他访寻美人。祖杰物色到一个，但却因为她太漂亮，所以便让她留在寺里供自己享用，致使这个女人不久就怀上孕了。但因为有众人议论，祖杰便又把她嫁给俞生的儿子作为妻子，不过之后他自己还常去找她。俞生不堪忍受邻人的嘲笑，于是就携带她去别处以躲避祖杰。祖杰听说之后大怒，派人砍伐俞生家的坟木以寻衅。俞告到地方官府，却反而被杖打。再告到廉访司，而祖杰则叫人把弓刀武器事先藏在俞家，然后诬告俞生私藏军器，于是俞又被杖打。俞生咽不下这口气，要去京城寻求

1 臧晋叔编《元曲选》，北京：中华书局1958年版，第1507页。

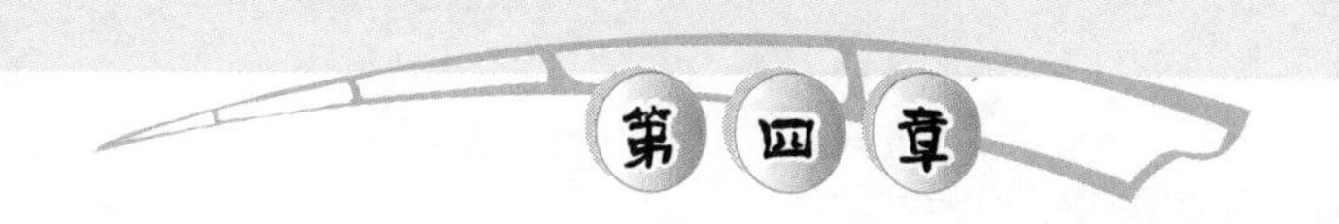

正义。祖杰得知后，便派遣彪悍家仆数十人，将俞一家老小抓住，用小船载至偏僻的地方，全部溺死。事发之后，官府来传唤祖杰，祖杰过了两个多月才到府。而在押以后，祖杰仍然拒不认罪，还叫人携带很多钱财去行省京城求援。“旁观不平，唯恐其漏网也，乃撰为戏文，以广其事。后众言难掩，遂毙之于狱，越五日而赦至。”[1]这段史实明白无误地表明了戏曲在将罪犯绳之以法中所起的重要作用。可惜的是，该剧本没有流传下来。

另一方面，皇帝与历代宫廷也经常用戏曲表演来为其歌功颂德，或在外国宾客之前弘扬国家的长治久安，繁荣富强。比如，明代朱有燉所写的不少歌颂花卉的戏就常作此用。“朱有燉在给这些戏写的序中不止一次地强调，只有在太平盛世，花草才能达到最美，才能被充分欣赏。这样，欣赏花草也便意味着，鉴于当朝皇上的恩惠，而对太平盛世的庆祝”。[2]更多其他戏曲则是对道德善行的讴歌。有大约一半左右的南戏是关于婚姻的。比如元代最有名的五个南戏《琵琶记》、《荆钗记》、《刘知远白兔记》、《拜月亭》和《杀狗记》，就都是关于婚姻和家庭伦理的。这些戏或者歌颂男女之间在历经生活中的跌宕起伏之后仍然保持着的忠贞爱情（如前四个南戏），或者教导家庭成员之间孝悌之重要（如最后一个南戏）。我们也许可以简要地检视一下最早的一部关于赵贞女故事的南戏的演变，来说明戏曲演出在教育上所起的作用。

南戏《赵贞女》或《赵贞女蔡二郎》在宋代一定广为流行，因为著名诗人陆游（1125—1210）在他的一首诗里这样描述过这个故事的演出：

斜阳古柳赵家庄，
负鼓盲翁正作场。
死后是非谁管得，

1 见周密著《癸辛杂识》，载《文渊阁四库全书》，第1040册第133b-135a页。亦可参看刘壎著《水云村稿》卷4中的“义犬传”，载《文渊阁四库全书》第1195册第371-373页，叙述略有不同。

2 L. Idema, *The Dramatic Oeuvre of Chu Yu-tun* (1379—1439), p.94。

满村听说蔡中郎。[1]

南戏《赵贞女》戏文没有流传下来，其情节大致如此：书生蔡伯喈与贤惠女子赵五娘婚后去京城参加科举考试。中榜及第之后，蔡伯喈被封了官，娶了高官的女儿做妻子，并抛弃了原配妻子赵五娘。长久得不到蔡伯喈的消息，赵五娘背负琵琶一路乞讨进京寻夫。见到五娘，蔡伯喈不但拒不相认，而且还让他的马把五娘踹死。蔡伯喈最终在暴风雨中遭雷殛，作为他忘恩负义、冷漠无情的报应。这出戏显然是谴责书生在功成名就之后，对原配背信弃义的行为。这种情况在当时有可能是比较普遍的。而且因为此剧的广泛流行与其影响，它可能因此而损害了一些官员的形象。这些官员很可能也与剧中的蔡伯喈有相同的经历。因为这个缘故，这出南戏曾经一度被官方禁演。[2]到元末明初，剧作家高明则将其大幅改动，写成著名的《琵琶记》。《琵琶记》描写蔡伯喈忠孝，有良心，不再是一个邪恶不忠、抛弃妻子的人，而是一个最后娶了新妻，但同时又迎回旧妻的丈夫。这一结局让每个人都满意。剧作者在戏的一开始便自豪地说："不关风化体，纵好也徒然。"[3]确实，高明改编过的戏宣传对父母的孝敬，对上级的忠诚，以及对所爱之人的忠贞。一言以蔽之，是一个"全忠全孝蔡伯喈[4]"。由于这出戏所具有的道德影响力，据说有人把它进呈给明太祖朱元璋(1328—1398)。朱元璋看后说："五经、四书[5]，布、帛、菽、粟也，家家皆有；高明《琵琶记》，如山珍、海错，贵富家不可无"。[6]这同一个故事，经过不同修改，经历了官方禁演和官方推荐，其影响力与道德上的功能在这里是不言而喻的。

当然，对戏曲的接受也常常受到意识形态的影响，视一时一地社会

---

1 陆游著，钱仲联校注《剑南诗稿校注》，上海：上海古籍出版社1985年版，第4册第2193页。

2 参看祝允明的《猥谈》，《说郛续》卷46，载陶宗仪等编《说郛三种》，上海：上海古籍出版社1988年版，第10册第2099页。

3 钱南杨校注《元本琵琶记校注》，上海：上海古籍出版社1980年版，第1页。

4 同上。

5 五经指的是《诗经》、《书经》、《易经》、《礼记》与《春秋》；而四书则指的是《大学》、《中庸》、《论语》与《孟子》。

6 参看徐渭著《南词叙录》，载《中国古典戏曲论著集成》第三册，第240页。

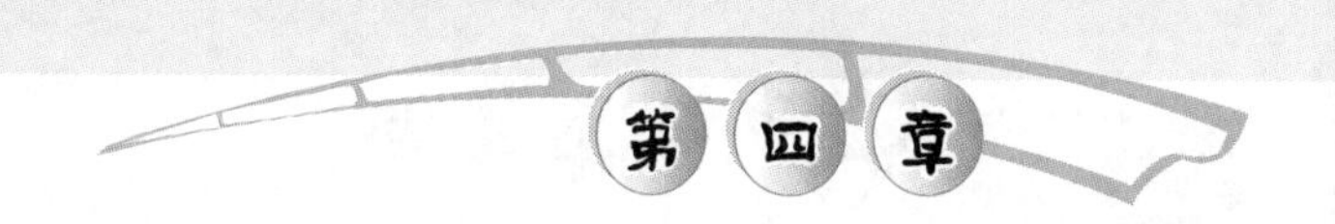

价值观之不同而不同。不过，无论如何，如上所述，戏曲的功能与影响是不容忽视的。实际上，历史上一些流行曲目潜在的对文化的影响与教育作用是经常被关注的，而且有时还被有意识地加以利用。从这个角度来看，历史上不断发生的官方对某些戏曲的禁演，对另外一些曲目的鼓励与推荐，则可被视为官方意识形态与其欲压制的其他思想间的一种张力。明代儒士陶石梁曾这样说过：

> 今之院本即古之乐章也。每演戏时见有孝子、悌弟、忠臣、义士，激烈悲苦，流离患难，虽妇人牧竖往往涕泗横流，不能自已。旁观左右，莫不皆然。此其动人最恳切、最神速，较之老生拥皋比讲经义，老衲登上座说佛法，功效更倍。[1]

因此在中国历史上不乏文人官宦建议修改某些剧目以利道德说教，就像高明在《琵琶记》里所做的改编一样。但是意识形态的运作颇为复杂。戏曲在讴歌道德伦理，作为官方教化工具的同时也会宣扬一些流行的潜移默化影响人的思想意识。这种思想意识之一便是妇女形象的塑造，以及对妇女形象的表现。中国社会从整体上来说在过去的两千年里都是由男性统治的，话语权也是由男性来掌握的。这便影响到妇女在文学艺术中形象的塑造。男子沙文主义的思想在人们的头脑里是根深蒂固的，所以很多时候便习以为常，以为女人的形象就是如此，天经地义。这就是为什么有些作者公开声称同情妇女，但在他们的剧作中仍能找到丑化妇女的例子，或起码是歪曲妇女形象的例子。

我们可以用关汉卿杂剧《救风尘》第二折一开始中的一段插科打诨来作为一个例子。这是纨绔子弟周舍的独白，从他的角度讲述他陪伴新娘宋引章回家的经过。宋引章在轿子里把自己剥的"精赤条条的在里面打筋斗" 引起观众谑笑。[2]这可能是周舍对歌妓品行的恶意中伤，但同时

---

1 刘宗周著《人谱类记》卷下，载《文渊阁四库全书》，第717册，第234页。
2 臧懋循编《元曲选》，第197页。

也可以看做是当时的世俗对妓女和歌妓的一种流行的厌女观。同样道理,描写宋引章套被子出丑的那一段科浑也是充满夸张的,而且是从男性角度对妇女不会针线活的讽喻。

另一个例子来自于佚名的元杂剧《鸳鸯被》。情节如下:洛阳府尹李彦实受左司劾奏,被召进京。因为赴京盘缠不够,所以向当地的财主刘彦明借了十个银子,许诺回来之后当即付清本金加利息。一年过去后没有李的消息,刘彦明大怒。他以此为借口要娶李彦实的漂亮女儿李玉英,并叫附近一个道庵里的道姑当媒人去说亲。玉英无力还债,于是便答应当晚去道庵面见刘彦明成亲。玉英还叫送去一床绣有鸳鸯的被子给她的未婚夫作为信物,并说被子到哪儿,她便去哪儿成亲。但当晚事有不巧,刘彦明去时被巡夜兵士当窃贼抓捕去官府。而与此同时,年轻书生张瑞卿则正好来庵中过夜。与张瑞卿共度良宵之后,玉英同意嫁给张。张瑞卿则第二天即去京城赶考。之后,玉英因为婚约失诺被罚在刘彦明的酒店里做苦工。还是张瑞卿和玉英的父亲李彦实回来之后,才把玉英从奴役中解救出来。

该剧旨在描写李玉英与书生张瑞卿的婚姻,可是剧中实际上是把男女幽会作为重点来为男性提供关注,迎合了男性窥视的倾向,同时又将玉英作为一个性商品提供给两个争夺她的男人。其二,玉英将其自身许诺给第一个夺走她童贞之身的男人,这再次确认了"妇女从一而终"的封建教条,从而使她处于被支配或"身无主"的地位。最后,玉英的父亲作为父权制的代表,戏一开始离开,而在结尾时才返回。他的现身是意味深长的,因为这意味着离开了家长,问题与混乱便接踵而生,而随着他的归来,一切又回归有序、平静。[1]

台湾学者曾永义在检阅了一系列的中国戏曲作品之后曾评论说:"我国戏曲起于民间,以伦理教化和喜庆娱乐为目的;……因此所表现的

---

1 参看傅鸿础,"Historicizing Chinese Drama: The Power and Politics of Yuan Zaju" 加州大学洛杉矶分校1995年博士论文,第228–238页的详细讨论。

最多不过是一些传统的宗教信仰和儒家思想。”[1]这些信仰与思想不仅包括值得称颂的道德品行，也包括一些旧式的封建思想和价值观，而这些东西则正是女性研究很好的课题。揭示这些封建意识形态是以何种方式表现出来，并重复加以申述，从而为观众所潜移默化，这同时也是在表现戏曲在意识形态这一重要领域内的功用。

二、中国戏曲的表演特点

(1) 整体特色

亚里士多德将古希腊悲剧定义为“对行动的模仿”。[2]这个对以后西方戏剧颇有影响的模仿理论，导致了西方戏剧从人物塑造到舞台演出等方方面面的写实主义的倾向。中国戏曲则与西方戏剧的写实主义特征截然不同，它从来没有提出过，也未曾尝试过，要像事物的本来面目一样去加以精心模仿。相反，中国戏曲在本质上是表现主义的。正如在第一章里所讨论过的那样，中国戏曲源自于古代的歌舞。因此，它从不以叙述一个具体的故事，或创作出引人入胜的情节为其主要目的。中国戏曲总是将故事叙述与歌舞结合起来，使戏曲表演成为一种综合性的艺术，能为观众提供各种形式的娱乐。正因如此，中国戏曲擅长于抒情，而不善于叙事。

我们可以以元代杂剧作为例子，因为许多现代中国地方戏曲如京剧就仍然保留着不少它的特色。王国维在评价宋元戏曲时就曾经特别赞扬过元代杂剧中的曲词，说：“元剧最佳之处，不在其思想结构，而在其文章。”[3]这里的文章指的就是元代戏剧家所写的曲词。在王国维看来，元

---

1 曾永义，“我国戏剧的形式和类别，”载《中外文学》月刊，1974年第2卷第11期，第16页。

2 Aristotle, *Poetics*. trans. Malcolm Heath (London: Penguin, 1996), p.10.

3 王国维著，马美信疏证《宋元戏曲史疏证》，上海：复旦大学出版社2004年版，第177页。

杂剧中“关目之拙劣，所不问也；思想之卑陋，所不违也；人物之矛盾，所不顾也。彼但摹写其胸中之感想”，于是写出来便成了剧中的曲词。[1]

其他时期的戏曲也是这样，强调戏曲中之歌舞。因此观众来看戏并不是来听一段故事，因为这故事也许观众早已熟悉。他们来是来看演出，或者是来看某一个演员对这个故事的理解和演绎。正因如此，有些学者将中国的戏曲结构称为“曲体结构”，而另一些则将其视为“剧诗”或“戏剧体诗。”[2]不管是用什么术语，其意思都是想说明中国戏曲强调的是诗、歌之美，而不是首先表现扣人心弦的戏剧情节与冲突。与其注重戏剧性，中国戏曲则更重视其音乐性。现代戏剧理论家齐如山（1875—1962）曾言简意赅地指出，在中国戏曲里“有声必歌，无动不舞……绝对不许写实”[3]。

因为有以上这些特点，所以在中国戏曲里现在就有一个有趣的现象：有些戏曲里的一些个别折子段落，特别是一些精彩有名的段落，常常可以单独抽出来为观众演出。这些折子或段落往往是演员在唱功或做工上可以一展身手之处。这些折子或段落的演出就被称为“折子戏”。现在这些折子戏比那些全本戏更受欢迎，就是因为观众可以在短时间内欣赏到那些全本戏里的某些精彩的歌舞片段。

(2) 具体特点

以绝大部分的传统中国戏曲而言，一场戏曲演出一般总会有歌、舞表演。前者包括所谓的“唱”与“念”，而后者则涵盖俗称的“做”与“打”。艺术表演的这四个方面是一个演员的基本功，必须掌握。以下将一一讨论这四项基本功的具体含义，另外也将谈及中国戏曲的其他特点，比如

---

1 王国维著，马美信疏证《宋元戏曲史疏证》第177页。

2 参看洛地著《戏曲与浙江》，杭州：浙江人民出版社1991年版，第55页；张庚等主编《中国戏曲通论》，上海：上海文艺出版社1989年版，第140页；及朱颖辉，“张庚的‘剧诗’说”，载《文艺研究》1984年第1期第73–84页。

3 齐如山著“国剧的原则”，载《齐如山全集》（八卷本），台北1964年版，第3卷，第4页。

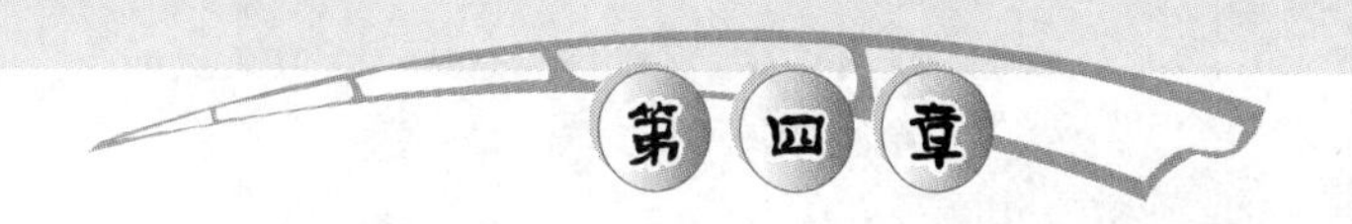

角色、脸谱、服饰以及舞台道具。

A. 唱与念

广义上来说,中国戏曲中所有的声音都被视为歌唱,因为引吭高歌无疑是唱歌,但戏曲中的独白、念诗或对话也都需要遵循很严格的节奏韵律,而它的声调与快慢,则视人物角色与其在剧中的情形而定。此外,所有"说"的话都得跟着锣鼓的击点节奏,时而拉长,时而快速,从而形成一种具有抑扬顿挫、吟咏而成的"话白"。正因为进行戏曲话白有这么多的讲究,所以戏曲界有句俗语,叫"千斤话白四两唱",足见这些"话白"在中国戏曲表演中的重要性了。

同样,因为愤怒、担忧、后悔、哭泣、大笑、愤恨,甚至咳嗽所发的声音都要有些歌唱的成分。以咳嗽为例子,视人的性格、场合以及音乐伴奏的不同,可以有百余种不同的咳法。[1]唯一的例外是丑角的话白,有时就是用现代北京话念的道白,不过其目的则只是以出戏规来博取观众一笑而已。

歌唱是中国戏曲中最重要的成分,用来表现人物的性格、情感,也用来塑造一些具体的戏剧场景。正因为中国戏曲中歌唱成分是占第一位的,所以人们有时把演戏叫做"唱戏",而把看戏叫做"听戏"。

B. 做与打

一般来说,戏曲里所有的动作都带有舞蹈的成分。这是因为以上所述中国戏曲里不能有写实这样一条原则的缘故。因此,舞台表演包括演员的面部表情,其手、眼、身体的移动以及脚步的走法,这一切都必须严格遵照一定的程式。就以舞台上走路的步法为例,这叫"台步",与人们

---

1 齐如山著《国剧的原则》,第3页。

日常在街上走路的步子大不相同。舞台上所走的台步必须随着音乐的伴奏,或随着锣鼓的击点节奏而行,以表明这是程式化的舞蹈步伐。于是,青年男子有青年男子的台步,年轻女子或老年妇女则也有他们自己相应的台步。他们所展现的并非现实中不同人的走法,而是要让那些台步显得美观、优雅,让观众们喜欢。"演员所呈现出的走路的姿态也具有深意。贵妇人走路优雅尊贵,仪态万方;打情骂俏者穿着艳丽服装,走路一摇一晃,仿佛是在调情;士卒将领步伐坚毅;儒士书生踱着方步,略有所思;跳梁小丑走路慌慌张张;而官宦人家则是高视阔步。"[1]所有其他的动作,如骑马、用浆划船或喂鸡等,都遵循同样的原则,即使其在舞台上美观优雅。由于这个原因,我们可以看到演员在舞台上绕一个圈子便表示从一个地方走到另一个地方。睡觉则总是伏在桌上,因为简单地躺下而卧在舞台上便会显得不雅,不美观。同样道理,要表现生病,男子总是呕吐,而女子十之八九是腹痛,因为这样的做工在舞台上比较雅致,"摆得出去。"[2]

另一种包含一系列在舞台上做格斗动作的做工叫武打,这是一种杂技般的格斗,表现的是古代战争与打斗的程式化了的舞蹈动作。武打有两种:一种是徒手或带武器的格斗,另一种则是翻筋斗。它们都是表现人物的勇武,或者是将激烈的战斗变为观众所欣赏喜爱的场景。

C. 角色

中国戏曲的一个独特之处便是角色的使用。不像西方戏剧里以某一演员来演一个具体的人物,中国戏曲创造出了一些人物角色,并以演员在演出中扮演某一角色。这种戏剧演出的来源及缘由众说纷纭。有

---

1 黄琼玫著*Classical Chinese Plays*,台北:美亚书版股份有限公司1971年版,第24页。

2 参看齐如山著"国剧的原则",载《齐如山全集》第3卷,第4–5页。

的把它归咎于印度梵剧的影响,[1]而有的则认为这"是重视人的共性、忽视人的个性的东方文化的必然结果"。[2]虽然角色的划分在不同的剧种中会有所不同,但一般来说都具有以下四种基本角色:生、旦、净、丑。其中每一种基本角色又可以细分为若干组更具体的小角色,而各有其不同的特点。为让演员演好角色,每一角色的方方面面都有很细致的规定,所以演员得刻苦学习多年才能演好一个角色。由于演一个角色需要有大量的训练,所以演员在他的演出生涯中一般只专演一个角色。以下将讨论京剧的角色,它代表了大部分中国地方剧种的普遍规则。

1. 生角

生角为男性主要角色,可细分为三个分角色:武生(武士)、小生(青年男性)和老生(老年男性)。这几个角色并非是互相排斥的,可以兼容。武生一角一般都穿戴织锦图案繁多的衣服,背后常插有四面五颜六色的三角小旗。这些小旗叫做"靠旗",象征着军队里的令旗。他可以扮演武士或将军,衣服的颜色则显示他的性格特征与他的社会地位。而且,一般来说,武士头盔的装饰越多、越复杂,则表明他越有权威。至于小生,在古代的中国戏曲或早期的昆曲中,小生并不一定带有年龄较小的意味。但在京剧中,小生一角便指的是年轻的主角,可以是一个年轻书生,一个年轻王子,或一个普通的年轻人。小生一角作为儒雅俊悦的青年,不戴髯口,以他悦耳的唱腔与优雅的扮相来打动小姐的芳心。年轻儒生还常头戴方巾,或手执纸扇,所以这种人物角色

---

1 参看许地山,"梵剧体制及其在汉剧上的点点滴滴,"载郑振铎编《中国文学研究》,上海:商务印书馆,1927年版,下册第26–28页;黄天骥、康保成主编《中国古代戏剧形态研究》,郑州:河南人民出版社2009年版,第315–330页。

2 傅谨著《中国戏剧艺术论》,太原:山西教育出版社2003年版,第236页。

也分别叫做“巾生”或“扇子生”。老生一角则是一个典型的中国人:老实、忠厚、博学而又有点迂腐。不管是一个贫穷的书生还是一个骁勇的武将,老生一角都必须在道白唱做时做到字正腔圆,绝不可以有半点差错。这是因为不同于小生的刚健活泼,老生必须有庄重、典雅的风度,而其做工则需沉稳、圆熟而又不失权威性。这是符合其年龄特征的。

2. 旦角

旦角可再细分为六个分角色,不过其中最常见的是花旦、青衣/正旦以及老旦。花旦扮演的常常是美丽动人的闺秀,活泼、泼辣或者是举止放荡,卖弄风情的女子。花旦一角的表演强调动作敏捷、伶牙俐齿,尤其是眼神犀利,腰腿灵巧,常常会使观众倾倒,迷恋其中。与其性格相符,花旦穿戴的服装,颜色鲜艳,头饰时髦,珠宝闪烁。青衣一角则性格比较收敛,缄默寡言。她娴静庄重的举止,经常保持着的低垂目光,以及小心谨慎的碎步是儒家贤妻良母的典型妇道。与花旦穿戴不同,青衣的服饰较朴素,颜色素雅。实际上,“青衣”这一名称就是由于演员常穿素色衣服戴白色腰带的缘故。青衣表演以唱为主,所以青衣演员在剧中唱功繁重。老旦一角则表现的是老年妇女,可以是贫穷土气的佣人或者是尊贵优雅的皇室成员。老旦的角色需要演员表现沉稳的性格举止,沉实的念白以及具有高亢的唱腔。

3. 净角

净角行当,也叫花脸,扮演任何有突出特征的男性人物,比如勇敢、正直、鲁莽或者奸诈之人。净角脸上都画脸谱,而这些脸谱则区分其不同

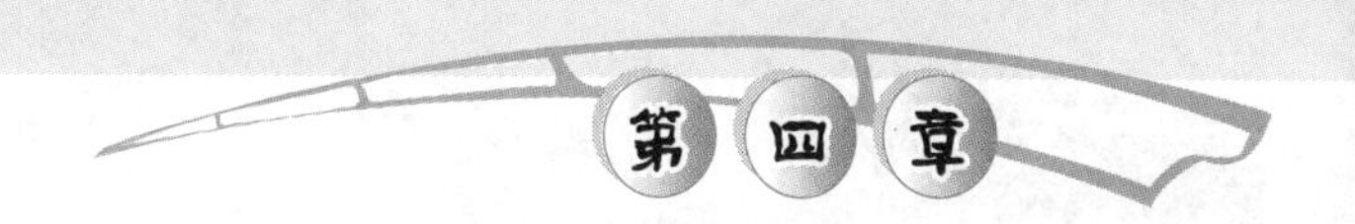

的个性。一般来讲，红脸表示忠勇有正义感的人物；黑脸表示正直、真挚或粗莽的人；白脸表示奸诈阴险的人；黄脸则表现的是凶暴残酷的性格；紫脸代表某些勇武而静穆，有决断的人物；而蓝脸则表示凶猛、特别是固执、桀骜不驯的人物。[1]净角可以再进一步细分为“大花脸”与“二花脸”两种行当。前者以唱功为主，唱起来如雷贯耳，气度恢宏。所以当大花脸演员起唱时，周围的墙都因他的声响而震动。而后者则着重在做工，强调演员在舞台上的一招一式。

4. 丑角

丑角基本上就是舞台上的小丑角色。因为丑角鼻子上眼皮上都涂有一块白粉，所以也称为“小花脸”。丑角使用日常语言，可以在舞台上扮演种类繁多的人物。有的是心地善良、语言幽默的人物，有的则是奸诈刁恶、吝啬卑鄙的小人。丑角又可分为武丑和文丑。前者精通杂耍及各般武器，而后者则善于插科打诨，让观众捧腹大笑。不管扮演什么人物，丑角都是为在紧张的情节发展中以滑稽形式来调节一下气氛。

D. 脸谱

与古希腊戏剧所用的面具不同，传统与现代中国戏曲不用面具，而用脸谱。不过，据说早期中国戏曲也用面具。那个时候的面具背后横插

---

1 参看齐如山著《国剧艺术汇考》，载《齐如山全集》第6卷第237–263页；黄殿祺著《中国戏曲脸谱》，北京工艺美术出版社2001年版，第160–161页。

着一根小竹棍,演员以口衔住面具进行表演。因为当时的演员只需要舞蹈,而乐曲则是由别人来唱,所以他可以戴面具表演。久而久之,歌唱与舞蹈慢慢地被结合在一块儿,由一个演员来表演。因为他唱的时候,不可能同时用嘴衔住面具,所以人们就开始将面具画到演员的脸上去,成为脸谱了。[1]

如同中国戏曲里所有其他成分,脸谱也是非常具有象征性的。它代表着人物的性格、神情,而并非表现其真实的面貌、色相。一般来说,脸谱贬多褒少。因此,好人,正人君子都是素脸,而凶残、奸猾、背信弃义者,他的脸上则涂满了各种光亮的颜色与各种条纹。邪恶的人一般会在他脸上涂上白粉,这是因为邪恶奸险的人往往不显示出其真面目,所露出的只是他的虚假嘴脸。正因如此,我们可以看到人物越邪恶,他脸上所涂白粉的面积也就越大。[2]

E. 戏装

中国戏曲里形形色色的戏曲服装可能会使观众,特别是外国观众,产生两个错误的推断:一个是演员所穿的各个时代的衣服真实地反映了那个时代的服装;如果不是,这些戏服则可能是随意设计以悦人耳目。事实上,中国戏曲里的戏服完全不是历史上某一朝代服装的准确复制,也并不讲究地区与季节上的差别。因此,演员演戏里某朝代某人穿的就不一定非是那个时代的衣服,同样,他穿的服饰也不一定是那个地区或那个季节人们所穿的典型服装。但是尽管这样说,我们仍然必须看到中国戏曲里戏服的穿着是有非常严格的规定的,所以戏曲界有一句俗话,说演员“宁穿破,不穿错”。

同中国戏曲的其他元素一样,戏服是通过服装的样式、色彩、花纹、

---

1 参看齐如山,“脸谱”载《齐如山全集》,第6卷,第240–241页。
2 参看齐如山,“国剧的原则”,载《齐如山全集》,第3卷,第10页。

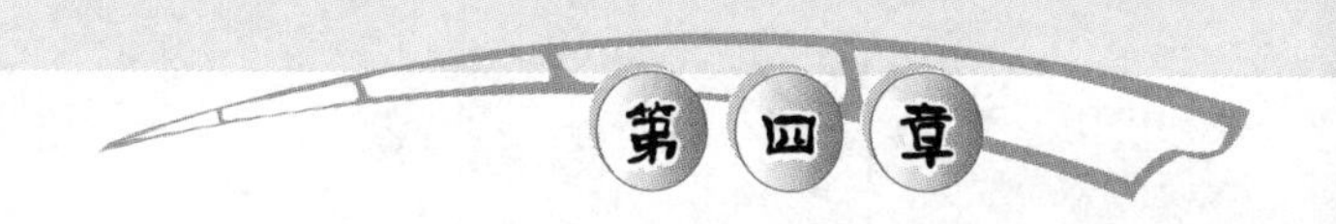

质料以及穿着这五种途径来向观众传达所要表现的内容的。[1]以头饰为例,武士所戴的就与官员不一样;同样道理,皇帝与大臣都可以穿所谓的蟒袍,但其不同的颜色则可以把他们区别开来。[2]一般而言,黄色为皇帝或皇室成员所用;红色则表示忠厚正义;而绿色象征威严庄重;褐色或灰色为老年男女所用;而黑色则表示粗犷直率。因此,就官员的蟒袍来说,地位高而正义凛然的官员穿红蟒袍,忠良有功的大臣穿绿蟒袍,年老的臣子穿白蟒袍,而性格粗犷刚烈的官员则常穿黑蟒袍。

中国戏曲服装里另一个极具吸引力的就是文官或其他非武装人员经常穿的,带有又长又宽的白色加长袖。这种加长袖叫做"水袖",因为演员甩舞水袖以表达他的各种情感时,看起来就像水波在流动。男用的水袖大约长一尺左右,而女用的水袖则在二到三尺之间。在个别特定剧目中,旦角的水袖甚至可达两米以获取一些特殊的效果。水袖的舞动本身就是一门艺术。一个有经验的演员可以用它来表达人物丰富复杂的思想感情,揭示人物变化多端的心理活动。

F. 舞台道具

舞台道具在传统中国戏曲术语里被称为"砌末"或"切末",在使用中也是具有高度象征性的。其主要道具,一桌二椅,在不同摆设之下,"它们有时代表它们自身,有时又代表山、楼、桥、船、床等一切具有一定高度的景物"。[3]因此,演员在舞台上用马鞭便表示是骑马,艄公手上的船桨便表明是用船行走。同样,小旗上画鱼和水波则宣示风雨、海上的波浪

1 详见张庚、郭汉城主编《中国戏曲通论》,第471–475页。

2 "蟒"字在中文里是"蟒蛇"的意思。据明代沈德符(1578—1642)所记,这种蟒袍跟皇帝的龙袍很相像。正统(1436–1449)初年,明英宗要赏赐一件龙袍给一个外国元首。他身边的很多大臣都觉得不应该用皇帝的服装去赐给一个异族人,于是就把龙袍上的龙减去一个爪子,称之为"蟒袍"。从此,戏剧界便有一个规矩:只有皇帝可以穿带有五个爪子的龙袍,其他人则只能穿带有四个爪子的蟒袍。参看《万历野获编》,北京:中华书局1959年版,第三册第830页;或齐如山《国剧艺术汇考》,载《齐如山全集》第6卷第172页。

3 张庚、郭汉城主编《中国戏曲通论》,第489页。

或洪水，而一块用两个竹竿支撑起来的黑布或蓝布，上面用白线画上城门或城堞，则表示是城墙。

传统中国戏曲的舞台道具大多在本质上是不写实的。比如，舞台上用的蜡烛表示光亮的来源，但并不点亮。红灯笼也是如此，一般只是用红布做一个像灯笼的外罩而已。虽然舞台道具不必求其逼真，但必须求其美。因此，中国戏曲舞台道具是很重视装饰的。比如，马鞭用丝穗，船桨用彩画，而车旗则是要用刺绣。这一切都体现了以装饰求美观的原则。另一方面，设计舞台道具也是为了能使这些道具可以很容易地成为舞具。总而言之，传统中国戏曲中的舞台道具都具有三个功能："组织动作的空间，暗示、描绘动作的环境，表达动作的情绪和意义"。[1]

目前，受到西方戏剧的挑战，很多中国戏曲也开始使用一些花哨写实的道具，有些甚至借用多媒体来提高戏剧效果，不过这些现代创新在不少中国戏曲学者看来仍然是颇有争议的。

三、中国剧场的演变及影响

中国戏曲经历了长时期的演变。同样，中国的剧场也经过了长期的转变才成为今天这样的剧场。

(1) 早期的戏台形式

在传统中国戏曲里其实没有像古希腊剧场或伊丽莎白剧场这样的剧场概念。这种概念是近代才有的。这是因为早期的中国戏曲并没有一个固定下来作为戏曲表演的场所。它常常跟其他一些民间活动，如宗教祭祀、官方或私人庆典、集市娱乐一起进行，所以便利用任何空间进行表演：如庙宇、宫廷、私人住宅或集市市场。因此最早的舞台就只是一块

1 张庚、郭汉城主编《中国戏曲通论》，第495页。

供表演的空地而已，各种各样的观众聚集在一起，随心所欲地观看。之后，为了方便观看，人们垒土筑台，这些戏台便叫做“平台”或“露台”。隋唐之前以及隋唐(581—907)年间，情况大致如此。这是因为当时中国戏曲还正处于胚胎期，大量流行的娱乐活动还只是百戏。而对百戏表演来说，一个空旷的平台便已大致能满足当时的需要了。

虽然在汉代(公元前206—公元220)的文献中就可以找到最早的在平台上进行戏曲表演的记载，但是直到唐代(618—907)，人们才开始搭建所谓的“看棚”，这样观众在观看表演时就可以不怕日晒雨淋。另外还搭建所谓的“乐棚”，使露天表演成为有顶盖的演出。这标志着戏台设计和建筑上的一个进步。有顶盖的戏台不仅能遮日头挡风雨，而且还能造成回音，提高演出的音响效果。这种有顶盖的戏台方便了戏曲演出，但却限制了百戏中的一些需要开放性场地的表演。因此这些有顶盖的戏亭的出现也标志着中国戏曲正在走向独立和成熟。

久而久之，那些临时性搭建的带有看棚的平台渐渐地被更永久性的建筑所替代。这些建筑称为“舞亭”，常建在庙宇之内。这是因为当时流行的如百戏歌舞等一些娱乐活动仍然常常作为宗教祭祀的一部分进行表演。舞亭是一种四方形的亭式建筑，有四根台柱支撑屋顶。因为它四周没有墙，完全开放，所以观众可以从任何一面来观看演出。

(2) 戏曲成熟期的戏台

中国戏曲在宋金之际达到其成熟期。同时，中国剧场也在此时演变成“瓦舍”、“勾栏”。此类剧场在之后约四百年间成为中国戏曲典型的剧场，直到明代初期才有所改变。宋朝的勾栏剧场是一种封闭的棚木结构，顶部有盖。观众席三面环绕戏台由里往外，逐级升高。这种剧场很明显是为商业性演出而设计建筑的，而且因为戏曲活动在金元时期已经变得更为活跃、流行，所以这种剧场在这两个时代也就更为普遍。元杂剧《蓝采和》里就对勾栏剧场有很好的描绘。陶宗仪(1316—?)的《南村辍耕录》里还记录了松江府一处勾栏剧场在演出中所发生的一次坍塌事故，导致了四十二人死亡。[1]

另一方面，舞亭类建筑在元代也有所改进，在戏台的后方加了一堵墙，完成了从四面观看到前台三面观看的过渡转变。这大部分是因为戏曲本身发展的缘由。宋代之前，戏台上上演的常常是百戏歌舞之类的节目，这些节目无需对着某个特定的方向表演，观众也没必要选择特定的方位观看。而当宋代杂剧兴起，取代百戏歌舞时，杂剧显然是朝着某一个方向表演，所以观众也便需要跟着从某个方向来观看，因此便产生了三面观看的剧场了。这种戏台跟以前的戏台比起来实际上有三个优点：首先，将观众安排在前面观看，演员可以更好地迎合观众的观看需要，而不是像以前那样得照顾前后左右的观众。其二，面向前面一个方向的演出还可以提升剧场的音响效果，使演出更吸引人。第三，将戏台一面封闭，使台上形成后台，以利于演员上下场、休息、换装或做其他一些事情。

宋元时期繁荣兴盛的勾栏剧场标志着商业性的中国剧场的正式建立。它的鼎盛时期是在北宋末年，然后又经过南宋、元朝的盛行，之后才进入明朝初年。但到明代中叶，勾栏剧场便销声匿迹了。这恐怕与当时北曲杂剧的消亡不无关系。

(3) 酒楼里的戏曲表演

虽然勾栏剧场明朝中期便已经销声匿迹，但戏曲表演却仍然在继续。宋元时期便已有了酒楼表演，此时酒楼便逐渐取而代之，成为戏曲表演的场所。人们去酒楼吃饭喝酒，同时也欣赏包括歌舞、戏曲表演在内的各种娱乐。起初，这些酒楼并没有固定的戏曲表演，它们所做的无非是提供场所，供客人叫来戏班演出。酒楼本身也并不一定对这些戏班

---

1 参看隋树森编《元曲选外编》，北京：中华书局1959年版，第971–980页；陶宗仪著《南村辍耕录》，北京，中华书局1959年版，第289–290页。

收取场地费,戏班的费用则完全由客人支付。但当酒楼表演日益兴旺之后,酒楼里的戏曲表演就渐渐固定下来了。人们也逐渐开始把这些酒楼叫做“戏园子”或“戏馆”,这表明这些酒楼已经从本来是供人吃饭喝酒的场所,演变成为主要是提供娱乐的一种剧场。当然,当时并非所有酒楼都是如此。而且因为这些酒楼仍然提供酒饭,所以那时其他人仍然可以进来吃饭,免费看戏。根据一些资料,在清初盛京(今日沈阳市)一个地方就有近千家提供这种戏曲表演的酒楼。[1]当然,设备良好,专门提供戏曲表演的酒楼便少得多。比如,在京城北京,我们现在知道的这样一些知名的酒楼就只有“太平园”、“碧山堂”、“白云楼”和“四宜园”、“明月楼”等。

(4) 茶园里的戏曲表演

清朝乾隆期间(1736—1796),北京的茶园生意开始兴盛起来。茶园里提供茶、瓜子及一些小点心,但不提供酒饭。由于茶园没有酒楼那么嘈杂,便很快替代后者成为戏曲表演的固定场所。这些茶园在提升戏曲效果上做了一些改进。这包括将观众席与戏台整体包容在一个全封闭的空间里以不受气候的干扰。其二,这样一个封闭的空间也提高了音响效果,提升了整体的演出效果,使演员得以全神贯注于其演唱和做工,推动了表演艺术的进步。其三,这些茶园第一次将观众席分区,按区收费。茶园剧场里最好的座位叫做“官座”,可能是因为这些座位常为达官富豪所坐,因此叫这个名称。“官座”是在二楼楼厅靠近戏台左右的一些座位。至于茶园剧场的演出,一般每天都会有剧目表张贴在外面,让人们知道每场演出的内容。一般来说,茶园剧场不出售入场券,而是在观众都坐定之后,收取茶费。当时北京的茶园剧场迅速影响了全国的其他城市,特别是上海、天津、苏州、广州等沿海城市。在这些地方,茶园剧场在清朝末年如雨后春笋般地出现了。

---

1 参看《清实录》,北京,中华书局1985–1987年版,第七册第472页上。

(5) 宫廷戏台

在回顾中国剧场的演变时,我们应该明了中国戏曲常在三个不同的场地演出:宗教庙宇、民间与商业剧场,以及宫廷剧场。我们已经讨论了前两个场地,所以下面就简要地检视一下宫廷剧场的情况,特别是清代的宫廷剧场,有些今天依然保存着。

戏曲一直是历代帝王官宦所喜爱的娱乐活动之一。帝王官员们倚仗着宫廷的资源,常常将其戏曲表演的场所建造得比庙宇或民间剧场更精致。不过,从汉代直到清朝,戏曲表演一直都是在殿堂大厅里进行的,这主要是因为传统中国戏曲的演出并不需要十分复杂的设备。换句话说,虽然中国各朝皇帝可以建立一些专门的戏曲教坊,但是直到清朝为止,各朝各代都一直没有建立起一种固定的专业剧场。

清代的时候,情况起了变化。清朝的皇帝皇后都是戏迷,特别是慈禧太后(1835—1908)。有了皇室的支持,清朝宫廷设计建造起了一种三层式的非常精致复杂的专业大戏台。中国传统戏台不管是平台还是露台,都是一层的,从地面到戏台台面一般高度在七到八米左右。而清代建造的这种三层式大戏台则高达二十多米。每层戏台都有自己的名称:最上一层叫"福台",中间一层名为"禄台",而底层则叫做"寿台"。清宫内一共建造了四个这样的大戏台。在这种大戏台上可同时上演表现天堂、地狱等不同领域的戏曲。

(6) 剧场布局的改变

清朝中期,当茶馆戏园刚用于戏曲表演时,剧场的座位前都有一长条桌子,上面放着茶杯和小点。观众围在桌旁,相对而坐,戏台则在其侧面。他们闲谈着,喝着茶,吃着点心,想看表演时,便侧过身子去看。另外,因为在当时还没有电,所以剧场里普遍用的是灯笼,而不是电灯。渐渐地到了清末,受到西方剧场的影响,中国剧场,特别是上海的一些剧

场,便发生了变化。他们改变了座位的安排,观众开始不再相对而坐,而是面对戏台。而且剧场里也开始用电灯照明,另外也开始用脚灯来为表演制造特殊灯光效果。至于座位的分级,直接置于戏台之前的座位开始受到了青睐,因为那儿离戏台很近,观众可以看得更清楚,更好。经过了这些改变与完善,中国的现代剧场便由此诞生了。

(7) 中国传统剧场的特性

一般来说,中国的传统剧场有三大特性。

首先,西方剧场对观众是封闭性的。舞台上的表演,对观众而言,在法国古典艺术批评家狄德罗(1713—1784)看来,是由一想象中所谓的"第四堵墙"隔开的,以此来造成一种现实的幻觉。传统的中国剧场则不同于西方剧场,它对观众是开放的,其戏台的三面在演出中是对观众开放的,可以进行互动。台上的表演不应与台下观众分隔开。由于传统中国戏曲从不追求写实,所以观众来剧场基本上就是为观赏、细细品味演员所展现的精湛技艺。他们边吃边喝,还互相谈话,甚至在演出进行中还在场子里走来走去。显而易见,剧场的气氛是很随便的,观众在演出中可以随时随地大声地喝彩或喝倒彩。中国剧场以及中国戏曲的开放性也反映在以下事实中:西方剧场里只有舞台上是用灯光照亮的,而传统的中国剧场却与此不同,它的戏台上与观众区都照得通亮,以此方便以上所提到的一系列戏台表演与观众的互动。

第二,中国建筑通常坐北朝南。诸如北京四合院式的房屋建筑,北屋总是被认为是最好的,为主人所用,左右厢房则居其次,而位于南面的屋子则为宾客所用。传统中国剧场则正好相反:其建筑总是坐南朝北,或者避开朝南的最佳方位而朝向东西。不过,其戏台则总是正对主要的建筑物。这是因为戏台以前用于祭祀礼仪或为其主人提供娱乐,因此必须处于从属地位。所以在这里,光从建筑设计上便可以看出传统中国戏曲低下的社会地位。

第三，就建筑本身而言，传统中国戏台也有其独特之处。戏台一般是用两根或四根台柱来支撑其硕大的尖顶，尖顶四角则饰有向上卷起的长长的飞檐。尖顶不仅使戏台适合于祭祀仪礼，而且还可以造成回声，增强戏曲演出的音响效果。在台柱子上则一般会写上一些对联，表明戏台所处的具体环境，或者是歌颂当下的社会风气。另外，在戏台建筑里的任何一个地方，包括梁枋、墙壁、天花板上，都会刻着或绘着精美的五彩艺术装饰。这样的戏台建筑，再加上那些卷起的飞檐，就把一个传统的中国剧场装点得富丽堂皇。

讨论题：

1. 中国戏曲都有哪些社会功能？这些社会功能是总是存在的，还是在某些时候有些功能比另外一些更显得突出？为什么会如此？
2. 中国戏曲的本质是表现性的。如何用中国戏曲的一些表演特点来说明这一点？
3. 你觉得中国戏曲里的哪些特点是跟西方戏剧非常不同的？
4. 说明中国的剧场是如何演变的。评论一下中国剧场里的一些有趣或者独特的地方。

第五章

中国主要戏曲剧种介绍与欣赏

一、京剧介绍

清朝后半期，京剧形成并成熟于当时的都城北京，因此中文叫京剧。但严格地说，京剧应当英译为Chinese national drama，因为“京剧”一词里的“京”字并非确指北京这个城市本身，而是表示“京城”的“京”，指首都。因此，京剧并不是“北京的戏曲”，而是“京城的戏曲”，比北京本身具有更多的含义。正如“昆剧”也并非表示昆山市的戏曲，而却指的是来源于昆山，并在那儿得到发展壮大的一个剧种。

我们在前几章里已经讨论过，在中国传统戏曲里，唱腔、音乐是最重要的组成成分。京剧源于徽戏与汉戏的唱腔，并吸取其他剧种如昆曲、秦腔以及京腔等的成分发展而成。比如，京剧的两大唱腔系统，西皮和二黄，便分别来自汉剧与徽剧。自从1840年左右即清道光二十年京剧诞生以来，它已发展成为一个将传统戏曲艺术中的唱、念、做、打进行了高度艺术结合的全国性剧种。而且由于京剧鲜明的民族特性，高度的戏曲艺术成就，以及丰富的传统中国戏曲遗产，它已经成为当今中国最有影响，也最有代表性的剧种。

京剧产生于北方，并在北方发展。它的两个主要来源徽剧与汉剧也是北方剧种。因此，京剧保留着很多北方音乐、北方唱腔以及北方的习性。举例来说，京剧中的做与打都是铿锵有力，大度豪迈，气宇轩昂，很

容易博得观众一阵阵掌声。至于其戏曲唱腔，它属于所谓的“板腔体”。板腔体在唱腔中以押韵对句形式出现，所以戏曲唱腔的长度与节奏都比较自由，适宜于表现高亢激愤与悲苦的情绪。京剧中所使用的伴奏乐器一般是一组小型的打击乐器和声乐乐器。前者包括一个小鼓与一块小板，这两件东西是整个乐队的灵魂，每个演员在演唱中或在台上所做的任何其他动作都得严格按照鼓点和板眼的指挥。至于后者，其主要的乐器叫做“京胡”，是一个小小的带两根弦的胡琴，音色高亢。此外还有月琴和三弦。月琴是四根弦的形似吉他、半梨形的弹拨乐器，而三弦则是三根弦的弹拨乐器。这些乐器在一起演奏，就使得京剧的唱段听起来特别铿锵有力，富有气势。

因为中国封建社会里对妇女的歧视，所以在清代一般禁止妇女上台跟男子一起演戏。有时，甚至不让妇女去剧场看戏。因此在清朝同治(1862—1875)末年、光绪(1875—1908)初年以前，京剧里一直没有女演员。一出戏里所有的行当角色都由男的来演。[1]发展最完全，也最值得关注的是由男演员来担当的旦角，后代也叫做男旦。因为有这种戏曲实践，所以京剧里便有全国最有名的专工旦角的男演员。比如，四大名旦即包括梅兰芳(1894—1961)、程砚秋(1904—1958)、尚小云(1900—1976)和荀慧生(1900—1968)。

京剧拥有众多的艺术流派，而每一个流派都以其创始者的姓氏命名，因为他在某一戏曲角色上展示了精湛、令人羡慕的技艺。以“四大名旦”为例。梅兰芳创立了京剧梅派艺术，它综合了青衣、花旦以及刀马旦等旦角的不同表演方式，致力于使京剧在唱、念、做、打四项艺术上都臻于完美。梅兰芳还在京剧的其他方面如音乐、服饰，甚至舞台灯光上都作了不少创新和发展。梅派艺术在舞台上创造出了一系列令人难忘的善良、温柔或者华贵、典雅的女性形象。

由程砚秋创立的程派艺术，通过它具有特色的唱腔，尤其是其略有共

---

1 参看马少波等主编《中国京剧史》，北京：中国戏剧出版社1999年版，第282–293页。

鸣的发音，特别适合塑造遭遇悲惨、具有外柔内刚性格的社会中下层妇女的形象。

尚派京剧艺术则是由演员尚小云所创立。它以表现女性角色的刚性美而著称。其唱腔刚健有力，具有自己的特色，再辅之以对比鲜明的节奏，深受不少观众的喜爱。

与尚派形成对比的是荀彗生创立的荀派艺术。它强调表现人物心理，表现旦角唱腔与舞蹈上的妩媚娇婉。因此荀派特别擅长表现天真、活泼、妩媚而热情的少女形象。

显而易见，京剧的每一个流派都有其自身特色，使它不同于其他流派，也使它适合于表演某一个特定角色。因此，同一出戏里的同一个人物，假如由不同流派的演员来演的话，便会表现出不同流派的种种特色。

《霸王别姬》选段

此剧演绎了汉朝（公元前206—公元220）开国皇帝刘邦（公元前256—公元前195）与自封为西楚霸王的项羽（公元前232—公元前202）在著名的垓下之战中的一段历史轶事。

刘邦采用谋臣张良、陈平之计，撕毁了和平协议，突袭项羽。项羽有勇无谋，刚愎自恃，听信李左车的劝告。李左车原为赵国谋臣，但现在却是刘邦大军的统帅韩信（？—公元前196）派来引诱项羽中计的。项羽不顾众将与其爱妃虞姬的劝阻，决计起兵迎战汉军，率军直入九里山中，方才发现中了韩信的计谋，大兵被困在垓下。

京剧《霸王别姬》共有九场。以下段落选自第八场。韩信吩咐其部下在项羽军营四周学唱楚国民歌。项羽兵士听到四面楚歌后，思乡心切，厌战情绪高涨，于是大批逃走。项羽觉得这是天将灭亡楚国，开始悲观。以下便是剧中的高潮。虞姬陪伴项羽饮酒歌唱，还拔剑起舞，为他解忧。当听说敌军发起了又一轮进攻，虞姬唯恐项羽为了她而耽误了自己的行动，于是持项羽所佩之剑自刎。之后项羽领残兵出阵，战败，也于剧末自刎。此剧本为著名京剧艺术家梅兰芳中期经常演出的代表剧目之一。

在剧中，项羽的角色一般由净角（花脸）来扮演，而虞姬一角则一般由青衣来扮演。

第八场[1]

（八宫女引虞姬上。）

虞　姬（唱“西皮摇板”）

自从我随大王东征西战，
受风霜与劳碌年复年年。
恨只恨无道秦把生灵涂炭，
只害得众百姓困苦颠连。

（四御林军、二大太监引项羽上。）

项　羽（唱“散板”）

枪挑了汉营中数员上将，
纵英勇怎提防十面的埋藏；
传将令休出兵各归营帐。

二太监：大王驾到。

---

1 中国戏剧家协会编《梅兰芳演出剧本选集》，北京：中国戏剧出版社1961年版，第116页–124页。

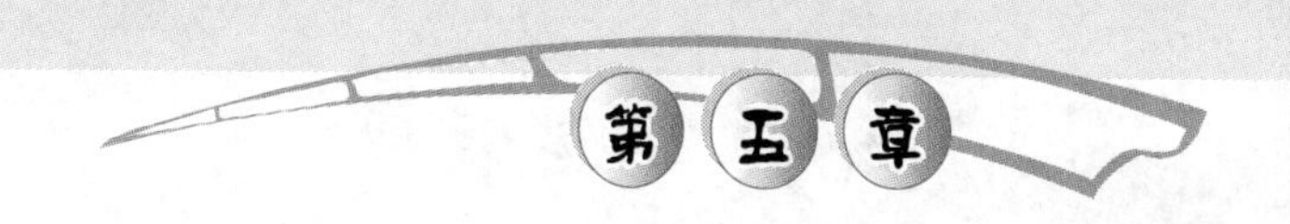

(四御林军、二大太监分下。虞姬上前关切地上下打量项羽,迎入帐中。)

虞　姬:啊,大王!

项　羽(接唱)此一番连累你多受惊慌。

虞　姬:啊,大王,今日出战,胜负如何?

项　羽:唉!枪挑了汉营数员上将。怎奈敌众我寡,难以取胜。此乃天亡我楚。唉!非战之罪也!

虞　姬:兵家胜负,乃是常情,何足挂意。备得有酒,与大王对饮几杯,以消烦闷。

项　羽:有劳妃子!

虞　姬(向宫女)看酒!

八宫女:是。

项　羽(唱"原板")

今日里败阵归心神不定。

虞　姬(接唱)劝大王休愁闷且放宽心。

项　羽(接唱)怎奈他十面敌如何接应!

虞　姬(接唱)且忍耐守阵地等待救兵。

项　羽:唉!(接唱)

没奈何饮琼浆消愁解闷—

虞　姬:大王!(接唱"摇板")

自古道兵胜负乃是常情。

项　羽(伸欠)嗯!

虞　姬:大王身体乏了,帐内歇息片刻如何?

项　羽:妃子你要警醒了。

虞　姬:遵命。—你等退下。

八宫女：是。

(项羽入帐，八宫女分下。初夜，虞姬持灯出帐巡视，进帐，四更夫分上。巡更分下。)

(二更。[1])

虞　姬：看大王醉卧帐中，我不免去到帐外闲步一回！(唱“南梆子”)

看大王在帐中和衣睡稳，

我这里出帐外且散愁情。

轻移步走向前荒郊站定，

猛抬头见碧落月色清明。

看云敛晴空，冰轮乍涌。好一派清秋光景。

众　兵(内)苦哇！

虞　姬：月色虽好，只是四野具是悲愁之声，令人可惨！只因秦王无道，兵戈四起，群雄逐鹿，涂炭生灵；使那些无罪黎民，远别爹娘，抛妻弃子，怎的教人不恨！正是：

千古英雄争何事，赢得沙场战骨寒。

汉　兵(内唱“楚歌”)

堂上撇得双亲在，

朝朝暮暮盼儿回！

(三更。)

(四更夫巡更上。)

1 在古代中国，夜晚时间分成五更，由更夫敲更鼓，或鼓楼击鼓告知。晚上七点到九点为一更，九点到十一点为二更，十一点到凌晨一点为三更，一点到三点为四更，而三点到五点则为五更。

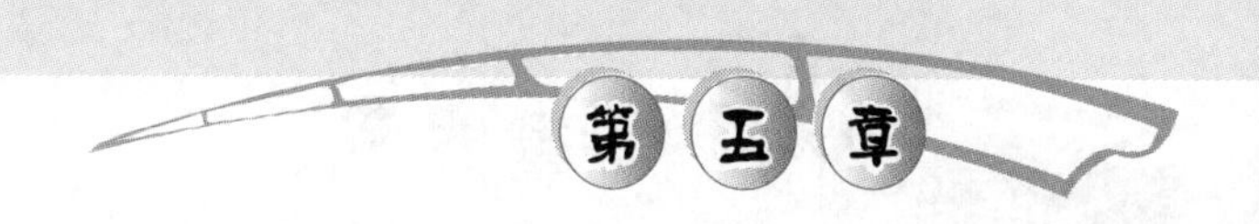

更夫甲：伙计们，你们听见没有？

众　　：听见甚么？

更夫甲：四面敌军所唱的歌声，跟咱们家乡的腔调儿一个味儿，这是怎么回子事呀？

众　　：是啊，不明白是怎么回子事呀？

更夫甲：我明白啦，这必是刘邦占了楚地啦，招来的兵都是咱们的乡亲；所以，他们唱的都是咱们家乡的腔调儿，你们说是不是？

更夫乙：是，这可怎么好哇！

更夫丙：不碍，咱们大王爷有主意。

更夫丁：得啦，大王爷有甚么主意！天天除了饮酒以外，一点儿主意也没有。

更夫甲：是啊，你说的不错。咱们大王忠言逆耳，目不识人；信用李左车，引狼入室，中了人家诱兵之计；这会儿被困垓下，天天盼着楚兵来救。可是，刘邦又得了楚地，后援断绝啦，这可怎么好！

（虞姬偷听。）

更夫乙：要依我看，咱们大家一散，各奔他乡得啦。

更夫甲：哎，别胡说！咱们大王爷的军令最严厉，万一有个差错，那可了不得，还是巡更要紧！

众　　：走着，走着！

（众同下。四更。）

虞　姬：哎呀且住！适听众兵丁谈论，只因救兵不到，大家均有离散之心。哎呀，大王啊大王！只恐大势去矣！（接唱“南梆子”）
适听得众兵丁闲谈议论，
口声声露出了离散之心。

汉　兵（内唱“楚歌”）

田园将芜胡不归，

千里从军为了谁[1]！

虞　姬：呀！(唱“西皮摇板”)

我一人在此间自思自忖，

又听得敌营内有楚国歌声。

哎呀，且住！怎么敌人寨内竟有许多楚国歌声，这是甚么缘故？我想此事定有蹊跷，不免进帐报与大王知道。—啊，大王醒来，大王醒来！

项　羽(惊，按剑出帐)啊？

虞　姬：妾妃在此。

项　羽：妃子，何事惊慌？

虞　姬：适才正在营外闲步，忽听敌人寨内，竟有楚国歌声。不知是何缘故！

项　羽：啊？有这等事！

虞　姬：正是。

项　羽：待孤听来。

虞　姬：大王请。

汉　兵(内唱“楚歌”)

沙场壮士轻生死，

十年征战几人回！

项　羽：哇呀呀……—妃子！四面尽是楚国歌声，莫非刘邦已得楚地不成？

虞　姬：不必惊慌，差人四面打探明白，再做计较。

项　羽：言之有理。—近侍哪里？

虞　姬：近侍哪里？

---

1 注意“里”是中国传统长度衡量单位，但其含义在不同时期相去甚远。现在的标准则是1里＝500米。

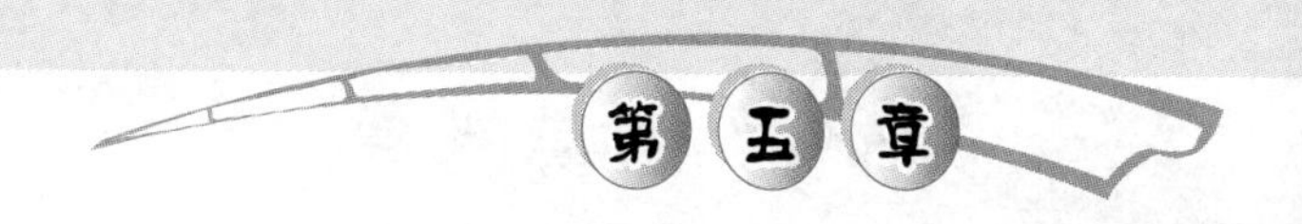

（二太监同上。）

二太监：参见大王，有何吩咐？
项　羽：四面尽是楚国歌声，吩咐下去，速探回报。
二太监：领旨。（同下。）
项　羽：嘿！孤想此事定有蹊跷。
虞　姬：且听近侍一报。

（二太监同上。）

二太监：启禀大王：敌营之中，确是楚国歌声，特来报知。
项　羽：详细打探，再来回报。
二太监：领旨。（同下。）
项　羽：妃子！敌军多是楚人，定是刘邦已得楚地；孤大势去矣！
虞　姬：此时逐鹿中原，群雄并起；偶遭不利，也属常情。稍捱时日，等候江东救兵到来，那时再与敌人交战，正不知鹿死谁手！
项　羽：妃子啊，你哪里知道！前者，各路英雄各自为战，孤家可以扑灭一处，再占一处。如今，各路人马，一齐并力来攻；这垓下兵少粮尽，万不能守；孤此番出兵与那贼交战，胜败难定。哎呀，妃子啊！看此情形，就是你我分别之日了！
（唱“散板”）
十数载恩情爱相亲相依，
眼见得孤与你就要分离。

（马嘶声。）

项　羽：啊，乌骓为何这样声嘶，马童，牵了上来！

（马童牵马上。）

项　羽：乌骓呀乌骓！想你跟随孤家，东征西讨，百战百胜。今日被困垓下，就是你……咳！也无用武之地了！（唱“散板”）
乌骓马它竟知大势去矣，
因此上在枥下咆哮声嘶！

（项羽摆手，示意马童牵马下。）

虞　姬：啊大王，好在垓下之地，高岗绝岩，不易攻入；候得机会，再图破围求救，也还不迟呀！
项　羽：唉！
虞　姬：（强做笑容）啊大王，再饮几杯如何？
项　羽：如此，酒来！
虞　姬：大王请。

（吹打。同入座。）

虞　姬：大王请！

（“急三枪”牌子。同饮酒。）

项　羽：（掷杯）咳！想俺项羽呵！（唱“琴歌”）
力拔山兮气盖世，
时不利兮骓不逝；
骓不逝兮可奈何，
虞兮虞兮奈若何！
虞　姬：大王慷慨悲歌，使人泪下。待妾妃歌舞一回，聊以解忧如何？
项　羽：唉！有劳妃子！

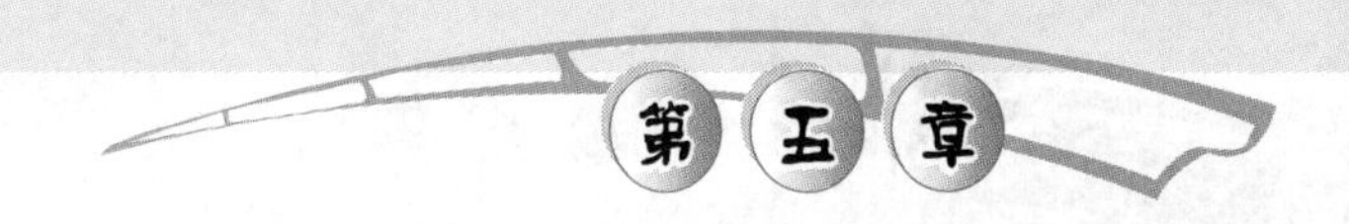

虞　姬：如此，妾妃出丑了！

（项羽凝视虞姬。虞姬强做镇定，避开项羽目光，取剑起舞。）

虞　姬（唱"二六"）

劝君王饮酒听虞歌，
解君忧闷舞婆娑。
嬴秦无道把江山破，
英雄四路起干戈。
自古常言不欺我，
成败兴亡一刹那。
宽心饮酒宝帐坐！

（"夜深沉"牌子。虞姬舞剑。）

项　羽：（苦笑）啊哈哈……

（"扫头"。大太监上。）

大太监：启奏大王：敌军人马分四路来攻。
项　羽：吩咐众将分头迎敌，不得有误。
大太监：领旨。（下）
大太监：（上）八千子弟兵具已散尽，特来报知。
项　羽：再探。
大太监：领旨。（下）
项　羽：妃子啊！敌兵四路来攻，快快随孤杀出重围。
虞　姬：哎呀，大王啊！妾身岂肯牵累大王。此番出兵，倘有不利，

且退往江东，再图后举。愿以大王腰间宝剑，自刎君前，免得挂念妾身哪！

项　羽：这个……妃子你……不可寻此短见。

虞　姬：唉，大王啊！（唱“哭相思”）

汉兵已略地，

四面楚歌声。

君王意气尽，

贱妾何聊生！

项　羽：哇呀呀……

（内喊声。虞姬惊，向项羽索剑，项羽不与。）

项　羽：使不得，使不得，不可行此短见！

虞　姬：（机智地）大王，汉兵他……杀进来了！

项　羽：待孤看来。

虞　姬：（趁势拔出项羽佩剑）罢！（自刎死。）

（四御林军暗上。）

项　羽：哎呀！——带马！

（四御林军、项羽同下。）

二、昆剧介绍

昆剧，也叫昆曲，为中国最早的戏曲形式之一，已经有六百多年的历史了。其渊源来自于元朝（1271—1368）末年。昆山人顾坚及其他人整

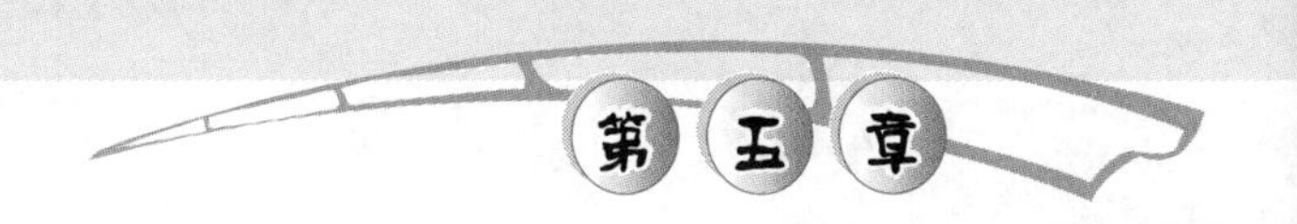

理、改进了当地的南戏音乐，将其取名为“昆山腔”。我们在第二章里提到过，大约在明成化(1465—1487)之后，南戏演变而成为一些不同的戏曲音乐流派，其中最著名的分别是“海盐腔”、“余姚腔”、“弋阳腔”及“昆山腔”。昆山腔吸收一些当地音乐以及南方的民歌发展而成，其演出地点局限于当今江苏东南部的昆山、苏州一带。昆山腔一开始并不太受欢迎，也并不能与其他流派如海盐腔或余姚腔相匹敌。但到了嘉靖年间(1522—1566)，由江西南昌寓居太仓的一名歌唱家、音乐家魏良辅与其他一些戏曲歌唱家及音乐家合作，为昆山腔的音乐作了一些重要的改进。他们以昆山腔的曲调为主，同时吸收了海盐腔和余姚腔的一些特点，还揉进了北方曲调的特色，从而创造出了一种全新的曲调，这种曲调有时被叫做“水磨腔”，它舒徐委婉，雍容美妙，使昆曲马上流行起来了。此外，魏良辅还对伴奏乐器作了改进，将竹笛作为其主要伴奏乐器，使之更适合于演奏这种新创造出来的曲调。这些新的乐器使昆曲的演唱更加具有艺术感染力。

魏良辅对昆山腔确实作出了相当大的改造与变革。但当时这只是流于清唱，并没有与它相匹配的戏曲演出。这种局面一直到梁辰鱼才改变。梁辰鱼是昆山人，他写出了剧本《浣纱记》，使昆曲完成了从清唱到戏曲演出的转变。《浣纱记》是特地为新的昆曲唱腔而写的，所以它的曲词严格遵守昆曲的曲律。该剧演出后一夜成名，也使昆曲影响日隆，传播愈广。昆剧的影响力迅速超过了当时其他一些声腔。到了清朝，其影响甚至远至京城北京，成为皇室官方首肯的一种戏曲，从而雄踞之后的中国剧坛近二百年。

昆曲的表演艺术是非常精致细腻的。昆曲音乐属于所谓的“曲牌体”，其音乐唱段是由一套曲子以某种规则放在一起的。其曲词为长短句式，但严格遵守平仄音律。因此，在昆曲的念白以及声腔演唱中，十分讲究咬字吐音，因为这是演出中最为重要的。不过，与其他戏曲剧种相比，昆曲表演的最大特点则是它的抒情性。这种抒情性是由它的曲调与舞蹈所反映出来的。从音乐方面来看，昆曲强调对声音的控制，发音的

抑扬顿挫以及歌唱的节奏，它的曲调特别婉转缭绕。至于它的舞蹈，昆曲演员的每一个扮相与动作都必须辅之以合适的舞蹈动作，以此来诠释其唱腔的意思，或描写场景，或表达人物的情感，所处的情境等等。

经过长期的艺术提高和改进，昆曲已经形成了一套完美的表演体系。其他很多剧种，包括京剧，都从昆曲中汲取过养分。比如，京剧脸谱中的大多数图案以及技巧就都是从昆曲中演变而来的。因为昆曲的悠长历史及其对其他剧种所起的表率作用，所以它常被尊为“百戏之祖”以及“百戏之师”。2001年5月，联合国教科文组织亦将昆曲列为“人类口述与非物质遗产代表作”。

昆剧里也有不同的艺术流派。与京剧流派所不同的是，昆剧流派以其所在地命名以示区别。因此，流行于江南，特别是上海、江苏、浙江一带的昆剧便统称为“南昆”，而在中国北方如北京演出的昆剧便叫做“北昆”。另一方面，在湖南流行的昆剧则叫做“湘昆”，而在四川一带上演的昆剧则一般称为“川昆”。在昆剧传播过程中它所吸收的当地方言以及当地文化则使得这些昆剧流派在唱腔与唱法上都略不同于彼此。

《牡丹亭》选段

《牡丹亭》为戏曲家汤显祖（1550—1616）所写，它大力歌颂了激情的力量，并且在明代晚期流行的一场关于情与理的哲学辩论中首肯、支持人内心深处的情感。该剧以戏剧化的形式表现了杜丽娘与柳梦梅之间奇特的爱情故事。杜丽娘是太守的女儿，刚满十六岁，而柳梦梅则是来自广州的书生。因为是官宦家庭的独生女儿，所以杜丽娘从小就受到严格的儒家礼教，不能跨出闺门，只能看儒家经书。一个和暖的春日，杜丽娘被丫鬟引诱到了她家的后院花

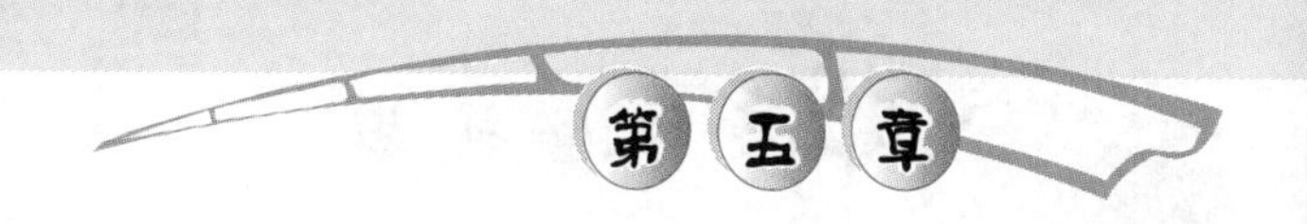

园。在那儿她看到了满园春色,这勾起了她的思春之情。回到屋里,杜丽娘就做起了梦,在梦中与一名叫柳梦梅的书生幽会。此后,杜丽娘便因为情感思念而憔悴忧伤。临死前,她画了一幅自画像,请丫鬟把它埋在花园石下。此时,杜丽娘的父亲得到朝廷提升,要他立刻赶往淮安。于是,他在匆匆上任之前,将丽娘的遗体埋在后花园中一株梅树旁边,并托杜丽娘的私塾教师陈最良以及一位道姑修建一座"梅花庵观"以安置丽娘的神位。

三年以后,书生柳梦梅去京城参加考试,路上得病,便借住在梅花庵观。一天,他闲暇之中走进后花园,偶尔发现了杜丽娘的画像,于是便把它挂在自己的房间里,每天为它祈祷。与此同时,冥间阎王裁定杜丽娘与柳梦梅日后有姻缘,因此便放回杜丽娘的灵魂,让它回梅花庵观看望柳梦梅。两人相会相认之后,每天夜里享受重逢的喜悦。另外,在杜丽娘的要求下,柳梦梅还同意把杜的遗体从坟墓中取出来,以让她起死回生。事成之后,他们俩一起去京城,在那儿柳梦梅一举中榜,成了状元。柳梦梅随后去见杜丽娘的父亲杜宝,但却因为杜宝怀疑他是盗墓者冒名顶替,所以被拘捕受刑。不过,最后结局是完美的:皇帝出来原谅了所有的人。剧终皇帝下御旨,令杜丽娘与柳梦梅正式成婚。

《牡丹亭》全剧共有五十五出,是汤显祖所写剧本中最长的一部。现在已经很少上演全剧,但一般上演全剧得需要二十个小时左右。以下的选段为第十齣,它生动地描写了杜丽娘在自家后花园里看到大好春光后所产生的兴奋与伤感的情绪。她在园中散步时的所思所想,引发了剧中后来所发生的一切。该出戏是《牡丹亭》中最为著名的,也是舞台上最常上演的一出戏。

在这出戏中,杜丽娘一角一般是由闺门旦来扮演,柳梦梅一角是由巾生应工,而杜丽娘的丫鬟春香的角色则是由贴旦来扮演的。

第十龅:惊梦[1]

【绕地游】〔旦上〕
梦回莺啭,
乱煞年光遍。
人立小庭深院。
〔贴〕炷尽沉烟,
抛残绣线,
恁今春关情似去年?

【乌夜啼】『〔旦〕晓来望断梅关,宿妆残。
〔贴〕你侧着宜春髻子恰凭阑。
〔旦〕翦不断,理还乱,闷无端。
〔贴〕已分付催花莺燕借春看。』

〔旦〕春香,可曾叫人扫除花径?
〔贴〕分付了。
〔旦〕取镜台衣服来。

〔贴取镜台衣服上〕

『云髻罢梳还对镜,
罗衣欲换更添香。』
镜台衣服在此。

【步步娇】〔旦〕
袅晴丝吹来闲庭院,

1 汤显祖著《牡丹亭》,徐朔方、杨笑梅校注,北京:人民文学出版社1963年版,第42—50页。

摇漾春如线。
停半晌、整花钿。
没揣菱花,偷人半面,
迤逗的彩云偏。

〔行介〕
步香闺怎便把全身现!

〔贴〕今日穿插的好。

【醉扶归】〔旦〕
你道翠生生出落的裙衫儿茜,
艳晶晶花簪八宝填,
可知我常一生儿爱好是天然。
恰三春好处无人见。
不隄防沉鱼落雁鸟惊喧,
则怕的羞花闭月花愁颤。

〔贴〕早茶时了,请行。

〔行介〕你看:
『画廊金粉半零星,
池馆苍苔一片青。
踏草怕泥新绣袜,
惜花疼煞小金铃。[1]』

---

1 指唐代一藩王将一些小金铃系在红线上,然后把它们缚在一些花梗上。之后,他叫园丁见有鸟来便拉动红线,以赶走鸟,防备其伤害花卉。参看王仁裕等撰《开元天宝遗事十种》,丁如明辑校,上海古籍出版社1985年版,第73页。另一种说法是,古代年轻女子脚上缀铃,就像今日的脚链。这既是为女子好看,也是为了训练其走路而不让脚铃响起—真正的妇女莲步。因此这段话可能指的是这两个小姑娘因为怕踩到花,又怕脚上的铃铛响,所以走起路来,肌肉很紧张,弄得脚都痛了。这里的“小金铃”便是用来喻指姑娘们的脚。见http://www.yuleshow.com/?p=437 (12 Aug. 2011).

〔旦〕不到园林，怎知春色如许！

【皂罗袍】

原来姹紫嫣红开遍，
似这般都付与断井颓垣。
良辰美景奈何天，
赏心乐事谁家院！

恁般景致，我老爷和奶奶再不提起。

〔合〕
朝飞暮卷，
云霞翠轩；
雨丝风片，
烟波画船
——锦屏人忒看的这韶光贱！

〔贴〕是花都放了，那牡丹还早。

【好姐姐】〔旦〕
遍青山啼红了杜鹃，
荼蘼外烟丝醉软。
春香呵，
牡丹虽好，
他春归怎占的先！
〔贴〕成对儿莺燕啊。
〔合〕
闲凝眄，

生生燕语明如翦，
呖呖莺歌溜的圆。

〔旦〕去罢。
〔贴〕这园子委是观之不足也。
〔旦〕提他怎的！

〔行介〕

【隔尾】

观之不足由他缱，
便赏遍了十二亭台是枉然。
到不如兴尽回家闲过遣。

〔作到介〕

〔贴〕『开我西阁门，
展我东阁床。
瓶插映山紫，
炉添沉水香。』

小姐，你歇息片时，俺瞧老夫人去也。〔下〕
〔旦叹介〕

『默地游春转，
小试宜春面。』

春呵，得和你两留连，春去如何遣？咳，恁般天气，好困人也。春香那里？〔作左右瞧介〕〔又低首沉吟介〕天呵，春色恼人，信有之乎！常观诗词乐府，古之女子，因春感情，遇秋成恨，诚不谬矣。吾今年已二八，未逢折桂之夫；忽慕春情，怎得蟾宫之客？昔日韩夫人得遇于郎，张生偶逢崔

氏，曾有《题红记》、《崔徽传》二书。[1]此佳人才子，前以密约偷期，后皆得成秦晋。〔长叹介〕吾生于宦族，长在名门。年已及笄，不得早成佳配，诚为虚度青春，光阴如过隙耳。〔泪介〕可惜妾身颜色如花，岂料命如一叶乎！

【山坡羊】

没乱里春情难遣，
蓦地里怀人幽怨。
则为俺生小婵娟，
拣名门一例、
一例里神仙眷。
甚良缘，
把青春抛的远！
俺的睡情谁见？
则索因循腼腆。
想幽梦谁边，
和春光暗流传？
迁延，
这衷怀那处言！
淹煎，
泼残生，
除问天！

身子困乏了，且自隐几而眠。〔睡介〕〔梦生介〕

〔生持柳枝上〕

『莺逢日暖歌声滑，

---

1 从上下文看来，《崔徽传》当为唐代元稹所写《崔莺莺传》之笔误。

人遇风情笑口开。

一径落花随水入，

今朝阮肇到天台。[1]』

小生顺路儿跟着杜小姐回来，怎生不见?〔回看介〕呀，小姐，小姐!
〔旦作惊起介〕〔相见介〕

〔生〕小生那一处不寻访小姐来，却在这里!

〔旦作斜视不语介〕
〔生〕恰好花园内，折取垂柳半枝。姐姐，你既淹通书史，可作诗以赏此柳枝乎?
〔旦作惊喜，欲言又止介〕〔背想〕这生素昧平生，何因到此?
〔生笑介〕小姐，咱爱杀你哩!

【山桃红】

则为你如花美眷，

似水流年，

是答儿闲寻遍。

在幽闺自怜。

小姐，和你那答儿讲话去。

〔旦作含笑不行〕
〔生作牵衣介〕

〔旦低问〕那边去?

〔生〕 转过这芍药栏前，

1 指传说中的两个人刘晨、阮肇，因迷路入天台山而遇见两个神仙女子的浪漫故事。参看刘义庆著，郑晚晴辑《幽明录》，北京，文化艺术出版社1988年版，第1–3页。

紧靠着湖山石边。

〔旦低问〕 秀才,去怎的?

〔生低答〕 和你把领扣松,
衣带宽,
袖梢儿揾着牙儿苫也,
则待你忍耐温存一晌眠。

〔旦作羞〕
〔生前抱〕
〔旦推介〕

〔合〕 是那处曾相见,
相看俨然,
早难道这好处相逢无一言?

〔生强抱旦下〕〔末扮花神束发冠,红衣插花上〕

『催花御史惜花天,
检点春工又一年。
蘸客伤心红雨下,
勾人悬梦綵云边。』

吾乃掌管南安府后花园花神是也。因杜知府小姐丽娘,与柳梦梅秀才,后日有姻缘之分。杜小姐游春感伤,致使柳秀才入梦。咱花神专掌惜玉怜香,竟来保护他,要他云雨十分欢幸也。[1]

【鲍老催】〔末〕
单则是混阳蒸变,

1 "云雨"常在中国古典文学中用来指男女做爱。

看他似虫儿般蠢动把风情搧。
一般儿娇凝翠绽魂儿颤。
这是景上缘，
想内成，
因中见。

呀，

淫邪展污了花台殿。

咱待拈片落花儿惊醒他。〔向鬼门丢花介〕

他梦酣春透了怎留连？
拈花闪碎的红如片。

秀才才到的半梦儿；梦毕之时，好送杜小姐仍归香阁。吾神去也。〔下〕

【山桃红】〔生、旦携手上〕
〔生〕
这一霎天留人便，
草籍花眠。

小姐可好？　〔旦低头介〕
〔生〕
则把云鬟点，
红松翠偏。

小姐休忘了啊，
见了你紧相偎，
慢厮连，

恨不得肉儿般团成片也，

逗的个日下胭脂雨上鲜。

〔旦〕秀才，你可去呵？

〔合〕

是那处曾相见，

相看俨然，

早难道这好处相逢无一言？

〔生〕姐姐，你身子乏了，将息，将息。〔送旦依前作睡介〕〔轻拍旦介〕姐姐，俺去了。〔作回顾介〕姐姐，你可十分将息，我再来瞧你那。

『行来春色三分雨，

睡去巫山一片云。』〔下〕

〔旦作惊醒，低叫介〕秀才，秀才，你去了也？〔又作痴睡介〕

〔老旦上〕

『夫婿坐黄堂，

娇娃立绣窗。

怪他裙衩上，

花鸟绣双双。』

孩儿，孩儿，你为甚瞌睡在此？

〔旦作醒，叫秀才介〕咳也。

〔老旦〕孩儿怎的来？

〔旦作惊起介〕奶奶到此！

〔老旦〕我儿，何不做些针指，或观玩书史，舒展情怀？因何昼寝于此？

〔旦〕孩儿适花园中闲玩，忽值春暄恼人，故此回房。无可消遣，不觉困倦少息。有失迎接，望母亲恕儿之罪。

〔老旦〕孩儿，这后花园中冷静，少去闲行。

〔旦〕领母亲严命。

〔老旦〕孩儿，学堂看书去。

〔旦〕先生不在，且自消停。

〔老旦叹介〕女孩儿长成，自有许多情态，且自由他。正是：

『宛转随儿女，
辛勤做老娘。』〔下〕

〔旦长叹介〕〔看老旦下介〕哎也，天那，今日杜丽娘有些侥幸也。偶到后花园中，百花开遍，睹景伤情。没兴而回，昼眠香阁。忽见一生，年可弱冠，丰姿俊妍。于园中折得柳丝一枝，笑对奴家说："姐姐既淹通书史，何不将柳枝题赏一篇？"那时待要应他一声，心中自忖，素昧平生，不知名姓，何得轻与交言。正如此想间，只见那生向前说了几句伤心话儿，将奴搂抱去牡丹亭畔，芍药阑边，共成云雨之欢。两情和合，真个是千般爱惜，万种温存。欢毕之时，又送我睡眠，几声"将息"。正待自送那生出门，忽值母亲来到，唤醒将来。我一身冷汗，乃是南柯一梦。忙身参礼母亲，又被母亲絮了许多闲话。奴家口虽无言答应，心内思想梦中之事，何曾放怀。行坐不宁，自觉如有所失。娘呵，你教我学堂看书去，知他看那一种书消闷也。〔作掩泪介〕

【绵搭絮】

雨香云片，
才到梦儿边。
无奈高堂，
唤醒纱窗睡不便。
泼新鲜冷汗粘煎，
闪的俺心悠步亸，
意软鬟偏。
不争多费尽神情，
坐起谁忺？
则待去眠。

〔贴上〕

　　『晚妆销粉印，

　　春润费香篝。』

小姐，薰了被窝睡罢。

【尾声】〔旦〕

　　困春心游赏倦，

　　也不索香薰绣被眠。

天呵，

　　有心情那梦儿还去不远。

　　春望逍遥出画堂，　（张说）

　　间梅遮柳不胜芳。　（罗隐）

　　可知刘阮逢人处？　（许浑）

　　回首东风一断肠。　（韦庄）

三、越剧介绍

越剧也叫“绍兴戏”，因为它发源于嵊县，临近位于浙江省东北部的绍兴，所以叫“绍兴戏”。越剧有大约一百年的历史，是目前中国的第二大剧种。它是上海市以及浙江、江苏、安徽、福建等省的重要剧种。虽然越剧在中国的一些主要城市以及北方的一些省份都有演出，但它的影响主要是在南方。上世纪60年代初越剧鼎盛时期，除了西藏、广东、广西等少数省和自治区以外，几乎全国所有的地方都有专业越剧团活动。据粗略统计，当时大约有280个专业剧团，而业余剧团的数目则更多。[1]

1 参看百度百科“越剧”条目。http://baike.baidu.com/view/16781.htm (29 July, 2011)

1906年春节期间，浙江嵊县农村的六名业余说唱艺人首次登台演出，其说唱艺术主要是依据当地的“落地唱书调”。艺人们和着笃鼓、檀板击节发出的有节奏的“的笃”、“的笃”之声而唱，因此最初被称为“的笃班”或“小歌班”。“小歌班”最初的成员大多是当地农民兼业余演员，他们在农闲期间组织演出。以后，随着“小歌班”的日益欣荣，他们便逐渐组成了专业的“小歌班”，定期在桐庐、富阳、海宁以及杭州等地演出。

但是“小歌班”是在上海才得以繁荣的。1917年春“小歌班”首次来上海演出。因为它善于学习其他剧种如京剧、绍剧等的长处，所以它在唱腔与表演艺术上作了一系列重要的改进和创新，因而进一步提高了它的声誉。“小歌班”这时开始改用“绍兴文戏”这一名称在上海的一些茶园里表演。[1]

最早的“绍兴文戏”的演员都是男艺人。1923年，在嵊县招收并培训了第一批女艺人。第二年，她们在上海作了首场演出。女班艺人掌握了“绍兴文戏”的精髓，她们的演出把唱腔中的温婉柔美推到一个新的艺术高度，因此几乎是一夜成名，随之，在上海滩声名鹊起。相比之下，那些男班艺人，因为后继乏人，便逐渐为女班所替代。从那时起，“绍兴文戏”（日后于1938年改为“越剧”）就一直为女班艺人的天下。直到上世纪五十年代，一些越剧团才开始招收男演员并试验进行男女演员同台演出。不过直到现在，在越剧里还是女演员比男演员多得多。

跟京剧一样，越剧的唱腔也属于所谓的“板腔体”。不过，越剧的唱腔非常清悠婉转，而且优美动听，所以特别适宜于抒情；至于它的表演，经过几代艺术大师的锤炼，也很真切细致，非常适合于抒发情感。中国的第一首小提琴协奏曲《梁山伯与祝英台》（英文有时名为 *The Butterfly Lovers*）就是根据同名越剧的音乐创作的，这绝不是偶然。

与其他戏曲剧种一样，越剧也有众多的艺术流派，每个流派都是以其创立者的姓氏命名的，她一般在唱腔上有卓著的表现。各个越剧流派

1 “文戏”即以唱工、做工为主，而不表演如京剧里武打的戏。

通过其在旋律、节奏以及板眼上的变化与强调不同从而在舞台上展示出不同的艺术形象。越剧中的一些主要流派包括演员袁雪芬(1922年—2011年)所创立的袁派艺术,她专工青衣;演员尹桂芳(1919年—2000年)创立的尹派艺术,她的专长是小生;演员范瑞娟(1924年—)创立的范派艺术,她也以小生为专长;以及演员傅全香(1923年—)所创立的傅派艺术,她则以善演花旦而著称。

《梁山伯与祝英台》选段

梁山伯与祝英台的爱情故事几乎是每一个中国人都熟知的中国四大民间传说之一。这一个故事现在已经被改编成很多戏剧、电视剧、电影,甚至音乐和芭蕾舞。

越剧《梁山伯与祝英台》有时简称为《梁祝》,讲述的是梁山伯与祝英台之间一段凄婉的爱情故事。梁山伯是来自会稽(今绍兴)的书生,而祝英台则是浙江上虞一个富裕人家的小姐。

在旧中国是不提倡女子受教育的。尽管如此,祝英台还是说服其父亲让她女扮男装去就学。在去杭州就读的路上,祝英台邂逅梁山伯,因为后者也去那儿上学。两人相见,情投意合,于是结拜为兄弟。

在学校就读三年,两人同窗同床。日复一日过去,祝英台对梁山伯一往情深,然而,后者对英台的女性表白却一无察觉。一天,英台收到家书一封,要她即速回家。临走之前,英台对师母吐露了自己的心声,并请她做媒。另一方面,梁山伯也依依惜别,相送英台十八里到长亭。一路上,英台一次次暗示山伯她的爱慕之心,可是山伯丝毫没有领会,最后在分别之前,英台只好自称为她的“九妹”做媒,请山伯来她家。之后,山伯在师母处得知真情,欣喜若狂,不久便匆匆赶

到祝家。可是此时英台已被她父亲许配给地方太守的儿子马文才。梁山伯伤心不已，回到家郁郁寡欢，之后便病倒，不久即死于相思。

祝英台出嫁之日，她坚持要在去马家之前去看望一下梁山伯的坟墓。英台身着白色丧服，哭倒在梁山伯墓前。突然，狂风大作，雷电暴雨袭来。随着一声雷响，坟墓裂开，英台纵身跳入墓中，与山伯相伴。暴风雨过后，梁山伯与祝英台则已化为一对蝴蝶，从墓中翩翩飞出。他们自由自在地在空中飞翔，永不再分离。

该剧共有十三场。以下选段为脍炙人口、令人难忘的第四场。这一场讲述祝英台在与梁山伯分别之前想尽方法，使用了一个又一个的比喻来让梁山伯明了她的内心。这一场里的唱腔特别优美婉转，生动地表现了英台未启口明言的对梁山伯的爱慕之心。

在剧中，梁山伯一角一般由小生来扮演，而祝英台一角则是由青衣来扮演。

第四场：十八相送[1]

（景：途次。）

幕后合唱　　三载同窗情如海，
　　　　　　山伯难舍祝英台。
　　　　　　相依相伴送下山，
　　　　　　又向钱塘道上来。

（梁山伯、祝英台、四九、银心上。）

祝英台（唱）　书房门前一枝梅，

1 中国戏剧家协会主编，上海市文化局编辑《中国地方戏曲集成：上海市卷》（上下卷），北京：中国戏剧出版社1959年版，下卷，第577—582页。

树上百鸟对打对。
喜鹊满树喳喳叫，
向你梁兄报喜来。

梁山伯（唱）　弟兄两人下山来，
门前喜鹊成双对。
从来喜鹊报喜信，
恭喜贤弟一路平安把家归。

祝英台　梁兄请。

梁山伯　贤弟请。

祝英台（唱）　出了城，过了关，
但只见山上樵夫将柴砍。

梁山伯（唱）　起早落夜多辛苦，
打柴度日也艰难。

祝英台（唱）　他为何人把柴打？
你为哪个送下山？

梁山伯（唱）　他为妻子把柴打，
我为你贤弟送下山。

祝英台（唱）　过了一山又一山，

梁山伯（唱）　前面到了凤凰山，

祝英台（唱）　凤凰山上百花开，

梁山伯（唱）　缺少芍药共牡丹。

祝英台（唱）　梁兄若是爱牡丹，
与我一同把家还。
我家有枝好牡丹，
梁兄要摘也不难。

梁山伯（唱）　你家牡丹虽然好，
可惜是路远迢迢怎来攀？

祝英台（唱）　青青荷叶清水塘，
鸳鸯成对又成双。

梁兄啊！英台若是女红妆，
梁兄愿不愿配鸳鸯？

梁山伯（唱）　配鸳鸯，配鸳鸯，
可惜你，英台不是女红妆！

银心（唱）　前面到了一条河，

四九（唱）　飘来一对大白鹅，

祝英台（唱）　雄的就在前面走，
雌的后面叫哥哥。

梁山伯（唱）　未曾看见鹅开口，
那有雌鹅叫雄鹅。

祝英台（唱）　你不见雌鹅对你微微笑，
她笑你梁兄真像呆头鹅！

梁山伯（唱）　既然我是呆头鹅，
从此莫叫我梁哥哥。（生气）

祝英台（向他赔罪）梁兄……

银心（唱）　眼前一条独木桥，

梁山伯（先上桥）贤弟，你快过来啊！

祝英台（唱）　心又慌来胆又小。

梁山伯（唱）　愚兄扶你过桥去。

（梁山伯扶祝英台过桥，至桥中心。）

祝英台（唱）　你我好比牛郎织女渡鹊桥。

（梁山伯扶祝英台下桥。四九、银心随之过桥。）

梁山伯、祝英台（合唱）
过了河滩又一庄，

　　　　　　庄内黄狗叫汪汪。
祝英台（唱）　不咬前面男子汉，
　　　　　　偏咬后面女红妆。
梁山伯（唱）　贤弟说话太荒唐，
　　　　　　此地哪有女红妆？
　　　　　　放大胆量莫惊慌，
　　　　　　愚兄打犬你过庄。
祝英台（唱）　眼前还有一口井，
　　　　　　不知井水多少深？（投石井中。）
梁山伯（唱）　井水深浅不关紧，
　　　　　　还是赶路最要紧。

（祝英台要梁山伯照影，遂相扶至井前俯视。）

祝英台（唱）　你看井底两个影，
　　　　　　一男一女笑盈盈。
梁山伯（唱）　愚兄明明是男子汉，
　　　　　　你不该将我比女人！
梁山伯、祝英台（合唱）
　　　　　　过一井来又一堂，
　　　　　　前面到了观音堂。
梁山伯（唱）　观音堂，观音堂，
　　　　　　送子观音坐上方。[1]
祝英台（唱）　观音大士媒来做，
　　　　　　来来来，我与你双双来拜堂。

---

1 中国人认为观音菩萨是大慈大悲，普救众生的菩萨。人们常去观音庙祈子。

(拉梁山伯同跪。)

梁山伯(唱)　　贤弟越说越荒唐，
　　　　　　　两个男子怎拜堂?

走吧!

梁山伯、祝英台(合唱)
　　　　　　　离了古庙往前走，
银心(唱)　　　但见过来一头牛，
四九(唱)　　　牧童骑在牛背上，
银心(唱)　　　唱起山歌解忧愁。
祝英台(唱)　　只可惜，对牛弹琴牛不懂，
　　　　　　　可叹梁兄笨如牛。
梁山伯(唱)　　非是愚兄动了怒，
　　　　　　　谁教你比来比去比着我!
祝英台(唱)　　请梁兄，莫动火，
　　　　　　　小弟赔罪来认错。
梁山伯　　　　好了，快走吧。
祝英台(唱)　　多承梁兄情义深，
　　　　　　　登山涉水送我行。
　　　　　　　常言道送君千里终须别，
　　　　　　　请梁兄就此留步转回程。
梁山伯(唱)　　与贤弟草桥结拜情义深，
　　　　　　　让愚兄送你到长亭。
梁山伯、祝英台(合唱)
　　　　　　　十八里相送到长亭，
　　　　　　　十八里相送到长亭。

(梁山伯、祝英台入亭坐，四九、银心在亭下休息。)

祝英台(唱)	你我鸿雁两分开。
梁山伯(唱)	问贤弟,你还有何事来交代?
祝英台(唱)	我临别问你一句话, 问梁兄家中可有妻房配?
梁山伯(唱)	你早知愚兄未婚配, 今日相问又何来?
祝英台(唱)	若是你梁兄亲未定, 小弟给你做大媒。
梁山伯(唱)	贤弟替我来做媒, 未知千金哪一位?
祝英台(唱)	就是我家小九妹, 不知梁兄可喜爱?
梁山伯(唱)	九妹今年有几岁?
祝英台(唱)	与我同年—乃是双胞胎。
梁山伯(唱)	九妹与你可相象?
祝英台(唱)	她品貌就象我英台。
梁山伯(唱)	未知仁伯肯不肯?
祝英台(唱)	家父嘱我选英才。
梁山伯(唱)	如此多谢贤弟来玉成。
祝英台(唱)	梁兄你花轿早来抬。 我约你,七巧之时——
梁山伯	七巧之时,
祝英台(唱)	——我家来。
幕后合唱	临别依依难分开, 心中想说千句话, 万望你梁兄早点来。

——幕落

讨论题：

1. 谈谈京剧的表演特色。为什么称京剧是中国戏曲的代表？
2. 在京剧《霸王别姬》的末尾，项羽被打败，他和宠妃虞姬一起先后自杀。从什么意义上可以将项羽视为一个悲剧英雄？
3. 说说昆剧的表演特点。为什么把昆曲看做是中国的“百戏之祖”？
4. 怎样看待昆剧《惊梦》一场中杜丽娘所做的梦？它仅仅是一个少女长久被抑压的性心理的显露吗？这一场还可能表达其他文化上的意义吗？
5. 对于越剧的表演艺术，你知道多少？它的表演特点是怎样的？为什么在越剧里女演员比男演员多？
6. 你认为是什么造成了《梁山伯与祝英台》一剧中的悲剧？
7. 人们常常把中国戏曲《梁山伯与祝英台》与莎士比亚的《罗密欧与朱莉娅》相比较。在哪些方面这两出戏可以进行一些有意义的比较？

Chapter One

The Origin of Chinese Drama

The origin of Chinese drama is a matter of much debate in recent history. Some, for instance, have attributed it to ancient shamans and sorceresses; some have considered the early performances of songs and dances as the precursor of Chinese drama; others have referred to the performances of ancient jesters in the court as the beginning of dramatic activities; and still others have proposed various entertainment forms commonly referred to as the "*hundred games* (bǎixì百戏)" popular during the Han dynasty (206 BC—220AD) as the source for Chinese drama... None, however, is persuasive enough to convince the other.[1] We may as well take a look at the issue from the following perspective.

Unlike modern Chinese drama which is usually called 戏剧 (xìjù) because of its inclusion of what is called "spoken drama" (话剧 huàjù) in Chinese, which is an equivalent of Western drama, traditional Chinese drama is usually referred to as 戏曲 (xìqǔ), which includes both play (xì戏) in the western sense of the word and the component of music and songs (qǔ 曲). The Chinese word 戏 (xì) actually stands for two things: one denotes drama proper and the other refers to play, amusements, games or even acrobatics, as included in the aforementioned "*hundred games*" 百戏 (bǎixì). Therefore, to have a better understanding of the origin of Chinese drama, one ought to examine both the tradition of imitation, acting, play

1 For a detailed discussion of various scholarly opinions on the origin of Chinese drama, see Huang Tianji 黄天骥 & Kang Baocheng 康保成 eds. *Zhongguo gudai xiju xingtai yanjiu* 中国古代戏剧形态研究 (Zhengzhou: Henan renmin chubanshe, 2009), pp. 3-19.

performance as well as that of music and songs composed for that purpose.

I. Activities Related to Drama

The earliest activities related to Chinese drama can perhaps be traced to the ancient religious rituals where shamans or sorceresses impersonated gods, ghosts, and other deities in chanting and dancing in their services. The exorcist activities shown in some *nuo* play (傩戏 nuóxì) or *nuo* dance (傩舞 nuówǔ) performed in some country areas in Anhui, Hubei and Jiangxi provinces today still retain traces of those primitive performances. Such a ritual enactment of some simple plots or stories then, although apparently without any conscious thought for artistic performances, provided a prototype for later actors and actresses on stage.

Later on, the court jesters during the Spring and Autumn Period 春秋 (722—481 BC) may have supplied another channel for the development of Chinese drama at its earliest stage. According to Sima Qian's 司马迁 (145 or 135 BC—?) Shǐjì 史记, You Meng 优孟, an entertainer residing in the state of Chu 楚, seeing the unfair treatment borne by the late prime minister Sun Shu'ao 孙叔敖's son and the plight he was currently in, decided to disguise himself as Sun Shu'ao and acted with the latter's manner to see the King of Chu. Greatly surprised at seeing Sun Shu'ao coming back to life, King of Chu wanted You Meng to serve as his prime minister once again. You Meng then remonstrated with the king and succeeded in having him employ Sun Shu'ao's son instead.[1] The real-life disguise and acting for some political purposes mixed up with some pure jokes were often techniques used by those court jesters and entertainers to make veiled mockeries or to convey some advice, which may otherwise be hard to be accepted. Such practice of real-life imitation with dialogs and plots may

1 See Sima Qian, *Shiji,* 3 vols. (Beijing: Zhonghua shuju, 1999), 3:2426.

have contributed to the subsequent birth of drama in China.

Another type of activities that may have contributed to the birth of drama in China is what came to be known as the bǎixì 百戏 (hundred games) mentioned above, which may have originated during the Qin dynasty (221—206 BC) and became popular during the Han. Hundred Games (bǎixì) is a general term that covers a wide variety of entertainments ranging from acrobatics, martial arts, magic shows, songs and dances, all the way to vaudevilles and what was called Horn Butting (jiǎodǐ 角抵). Enactment of a fight between a person and a wild animal was a typical performance for Horn Butting. One such skit titled *Mr. Huang of the Eastern Sea* (东海黄公), recorded in *Xijing zaji* 西京杂记 by Ge Hong 葛洪 (284—364) of the Eastern Jin dynasty, recounts the tragic story of a Mr. Huang, who was a magician and who used to be able to subjugate snakes or tigers with his magic. Toward the end of the Qin dynasty, as the story goes, there emerged a white tiger in the Eastern Sea area and Mr. Huang went again in an attempt to subdue the tiger with his magic. This time, however, because of his advanced age and as a result of his excessive drinking, his magic could no longer overpower the tiger; on the contrary, he was attacked by the tiger and died in the end. Unlike all previous entertainments, this performance of Horn Butting was no longer jesters or entertainers doing impromptu performances, but rather, it was an enactment of some prearranged plot with the characterization, conflict as well as the result all previously planned, as if they were following a play script. Perhaps because of its novelty at the time, *Mr. Huang of the Eastern Sea* was later called into the Han court to be performed for the emperors.

From the above brief survey of the various activities occurring at the early stages of Chinese drama, one can see for oneself that, taken by themselves, perhaps none of the activities mentioned above may be regarded as the origin of Chinese drama: the ritual services performed by shamans and sorceresses indeed had songs and dances, but the content of their services was too sacred, too religiously-oriented and too simplistic to be linked to what one may deem a theatrical plot. On the other hand, the court jesters and other entertainers' performances may have more sophisticated plots or story lines that were derived from the real life, but those performances were mostly done impromptu and were usually not meant to be repeated. The Horn Butting skit *Mr. Huang of the Eastern Sea* does seem to have advanced a step further in that it had an interesting and somehow complicated plot line that could be reenacted again and again similar to a later play script. However, we are not told of any music or songs as an integral part of the skit.

II. Music Related to Drama

In terms of music and songs accompanying theatrical performances, on the other hand, they have enjoyed a long tradition as well. Qǔ 曲 in Chinese is often associated with songs (gē 歌) and poetry because poems were originally meant to be sung or chanted. So *qu* refers to songs as well as to a type of verse for singing. Although music and songs were long in existence early in Chinese history—to accompany dance or to be used in ritual services—they became an integral part of drama fairly late. It was only around the Northern Song and Jin (1115—1234) dynasties when we would see earliest dramas performed together with songs and music used or composed specifically for that purpose. Initially those music and songs for dramatic purposes were mostly taken from some folk songs or music popular at that time. Since those song writers then were familiar with the music, they simply inserted words to such melodies to make new songs. Hence those initial songs were not quite strict with the prosody of their words (verses). But, as time went by, people were no longer familiar with the melodies (as today we have almost totally lost track of the music and

melodies of those dramas). Song writers started to imitate their predecessors' songs by following the prosody of the verses of those songs so as to make new songs. Furthermore, in order to make it easy for subsequent writers to write songs whose verses would fit the melodies, people started to regulate and to specify the prosody of each melody or tune. As a result, later writers no longer wrote new songs according to music, but rather wrote according to the prosody of each melody or tune to produce a new song for a play. Only when those songs for a drama were written according to the regulated prosody for the tunes and verses, and not according to the melodies, could Chinese drama be said to have entered its mature age.

Apparently, just as Rome was not built in a day, as the saying goes, so Chinese drama did not come into being on a certain date. Rather, it is a long process in the making. The variety of ancient ritual services and entertainments we have surveyed here, therefore, were each making some contributions to the making of Chinese drama and each of them may be regarded as a kind of immature form of drama. With the gradual accumulation of those immature drama forms, Chinese drama will finally reach its mature age.

Questions for Discussion:

1. What are the various scholarly views on the origin of Chinese drama? What you think should be the necessary elements of a mature drama?
2. How was Chinese drama different from the Western drama from the beginning? What might have contributed to such differences?

Chapter Two

Development of Chinese Drama

I. Theatrical Activities during the Tang and Song Dynasties

Tang dynasty (618—907) is one of the strong and prosperous dynasties in Chinese history. As a result, the Tang Empire flourished politically, economically, as well as culturally. Many art forms and entertainments underwent rapid development during that time, including the burgeoning forms of drama. The development of those entertainments was, of course, in every way related to official endorsement and even imperial promotion, because, according to historical records, a number of emperors of the Tang dynasty took a fancy to bǎixì 百戏 (hundred games) and sǎnyuè 散乐 (diverse music), a synonymous reference to *baixi*, which incorporated a wide variety of activities such as songs, dances, games, skits, playlets or even acrobatics, etc.[1] Li Longji 李隆基 (685—762), also known as Emperor Xuanzong of Tang 唐玄宗, for instance, was talented in music himself. Good at singing and dancing while he was very little, Li Longji revised and composed a number of musical compositions that are extant today. Soon after his enthronement in 712 AD, Li greatly expanded and reorganized the already existing jiàofāng 教坊 (Royal Academy), which was an official administration for music, dance and theater. Entertainers from various *jiaofang* were often called upon to give performances for the

1 See, for instance, Liu Xu 刘昫, et al., *Jiu tang shu* 旧唐书 (Old Book of Tang), 16 vols. (Beijing: Zhonghua shuju, 1975), 8:2799; or Wang Pu 王溥, *Tang hui yao* 唐会要, 3 vols. (Beijing: Zhonghua shuju, 1955), 1:623.

emperors or other officials. Furthermore, Li Longji founded the líyuán 梨园 (Pear Garden), also a school for music, dance and acting which was physically beside a pear garden, hence the name. Li had three hundred students selected to the school where he himself taught them how to sing and dance. Ever since then, *liyuan* has become another name for theatrical troupes in general and those actors and actresses of traditional Chinese dramas are, as a result, called "children of *liyuan*" (梨园子弟 líyuán zǐdì).

It was amidst such imperial promotion and support during the Tang that various early forms of Chinese drama quickly grew and developed. *Canjun xi* 参军戏 (Adjutant Play) was one of these. It was one of the most popular theatrical entertainments during the entire Tang dynasty. According to one source, it was originally a theatrical mockery of an official (adjutant) corruption during the Eastern Han dynasty (25—220) and subsequently it became a kind of theatrical genre in which two characters performed a kind of modern-day comedy or talk show with one making fun of the other.[1] Inheriting the previous tradition, many such shows during the Tang also aimed at ridiculing official corruption. Because of its popularity in performance, the two characters in such a show gradually acquired fixed role titles on stage: one is called cānjūn 参军 (adjutant) and the other is usually called cānggǔ 苍鹘 (grey hawk). Some scholars believe this marked the beginning of the role types in classical Chinese drama.[2] Adjutant plays were initially performed by two characters whose comic dialogs were simply meant to make people laugh; but, later on, such performances involved more complicated plots, which did not necessarily aim at cracking jokes or making mockeries, and sometimes there appeared more than two characters in a show, even with female entertainers participating.

1 See Duan Anjie 段安节, *Yue fu za lu* 乐府杂录, in *Zhongguo gudian xiqu lunzhu jicheng* 中国古典戏曲论著集成, 10 vols. (Beijing: Zhongguo xiju chubanshe, 1959), 1:49.

2 See Tao Zongyi 陶宗仪, *Nan cun chuo geng lu* 南村辍耕录, in *Jingyin wenyuange siku quanshu* 景印文渊阁四库全书, 1500 vols. (Taipei: Taiwan Commercial Press, 1986), hereafter abbreviated as *SKQS*, 1040:685b; or Liao Ben 廖奔 & Liu Yanjun 刘彦君, *Zhongguo xiqu fazhan shi* 中国戏曲发展史, 4 vols. (Taiyuan: Shanxi jiaoyu chubanshe, 2000), 1:225.

Furthermore, as songs and dances became quite popular during the Tang, adjutant plays also incorporated elements of songs and dances, making them closer to the mature drama forms which were to come during the Song and Jin dynasties.

The performances by court jesters and other entertainers such as the popular adjutant plays mentioned above were mostly dialogs in nature; but, on the other hand, performances with mainly songs and dances also abounded at the time. Some of the well-known plays in this category included Lánlíng wáng 兰陵王 (Prince Lanling), Bōtou 钵头, Sū Zhōngláng 苏中郎 (Inner Gentleman Su) and Tà yáo niáng 踏摇娘 (Stepping and Singing Lady), etc. The last play is particularly worth noticing. It enacted a story about a man named Su toward the end of the Sui dynasty (581-618). Su was a drunkard, ugly and unemployed, but he liked to brag about his having an official title of Inner Gentleman (zhōngláng 中郎). His wife, on the contrary, was beautiful and good at singing and dancing. So, whenever Su got drunk, he would beat his wife, and his wife had no other means but to resort to complaining to their neighbors. The play, therefore, dramatized the funny process by first having a male actor impersonating Su's wife singing and dancing to vent her grievances, and then getting the husband back home to have a brawl with his wife, which would always be hilarious, creating a comic theatrical effect. Audience interacted with the characters during the show, too, by echoing the misfortune given in the wife's songs. The play is worth noticing because of its combination of a simple plot together with songs and dances and also because of its male character impersonating a female role, which created a precedent for later dramas to follow.

Song dynasty (960—1279) marked a transition from a strong and prosperous nation to a weak and conquered one by the Jurchens and Mongols. Its theatrical activities, however, continued, thrived and finally became mature. Along with the economic development and commercial prosperity during the Northern Song period (960—1127), population in some big cities such as Bianjing汴京 (present-day Kaifeng开封) or the Jin 金 capital Zhongdu 中都 (present-day Beijing) increased by leaps and bounds. Rapid growth in population created a need for a great variety of entertainment. In Bianjing and Zhongdu, therefore, there occurred a large number of what were commonly called wǎshè 瓦舍 (pleasure precincts) and gōulán 勾栏 (winding railings). The former generally referred to a district where all kinds of commercial entertainments were provided, whereas the latter meant specifically the places within a *washe* where performances were staged. Previously, comic shows such as adjutant plays focusing on dialogs and other kinds of entertainments that mainly used songs and dances all developed separately. Now with the establishment of so many *washe* and *goulan* where all those entertainments were put together, and, where they must have interacted with one another and learned from each other, soon a new hybrid form of theatrical activities called zájù 杂剧 (variety show) came into being during the Northern Song and Jin dynasties (1115—1234), in which acting and singing started to be integrated and to become a fixed form, while more theatrical role types were created. Moreover, such theatrical activities were often divided into two parts in performance, resembling the later acts in a play. All these suggest that the mature form of Chinese drama was to come soon. Regrettably, however, the ensuing years of war between the Northern Song and the Jurchen in the north not only brought huge damage to economy and to people's livelihood, but also greatly disrupted the cultural establishment and theatrical growth.

The first mature form of drama actually came in the form of what is commonly called nánxì 南戏 (Southern drama), because of its origin from the southern part of China perhaps toward the end of the Northern Song according to some scholars.[1] Because it originated in present-day Wenzhou 温州 (formerly Yongjia 永嘉), Zhejiang province, it was also called

1 See, for example, Xu Wei徐渭, *Nanci xulu*南词叙录, in *Zhongguo gudian xiqu lunzhu jicheng,* 3:239.

Wenzhou zájù 温州杂剧 or Yongjia zájù 永嘉杂剧. Those nánxì plays during the Song dynasty were purely theatrical performances without the mixture of any other entertainments such as acrobatic shows therein. Each play would put on stage a story about a human life in its entirety rather than a slice of it. Because of the flexibility of its performance, a *nanxi* play did not observe the rule of having a fixed number of acts in a play as did the later Yuan *zaju* and it could sometimes run as many as more than fifty acts for a single play. Besides, *nanxi* plays also developed seven role types such as *sheng* 生 (young male), *dan* 旦 (young female), *jing* 净 (painted-face, male roles with strong personalities), *mo* 末 (male), *chou* 丑 (clown), *wai* 外 (extra) and tie 贴 (secondary female), which were somehow related to the role types of the Song dynasty *zaju*, but not quite the same. Those theatrical roles were all taken by male entertainers, including the female roles. In terms of music, because of the growth and popularity of a large number of music forms such as *guzi ci* 鼓子词, *changzhuan* 唱赚 and *zhu gongdiao* 诸宫调 that connected songs together to express more complicated ideas, *nanxi* plays started to make use of such music forms and to use songs and song suites as the most important means in their theatrical performances, which was to narrate a plot development, to express character emotions as well as to portray an atmosphere. The most well-known *nanxi* plays prior to the Yuan dynasty were *Zhang Xie zhuangyuan* 张协状元 (Top Graduate Zhang Xie) and Zhào Zhēnnǚ Cài èrláng 赵贞女蔡二郎 (Zhao the Virtuous Woman and Master Cai the Second).

II. Dramas during the Yuan Dynasty

1. Yuan *Zaju* the Northern Drama

Chinese drama reached its golden age during the Yuan dynasty. Around the latter half of the 13th century and the early part of the 14th century,

especially during the reigns of Emperor Yuanzhen 元贞 and Emperor Dade 大德 (1295—1308), there emerged a sudden burst of dramatic form commonly referred to as Yuan *zaju*. Over a span of no more than a hundred years, there appeared more than a hundred active playwrights producing well over five hundred plays.[1] This impressive outburst of *zaju* from the Chinese soil becomes all the more astonishing if one takes into consideration the fact that it was precisely a historical period of subjugation for the Chinese under an alien rule, a moment when "a sudden aesthetic explosion...should least be expected."[2] There are, of course, several reasons accounting for such dramatic growth. For one thing, during most of the Yuan dynasty, the Mongol rulers abolished the long-established civil service examination system (科举考试) in China, relied upon Mongols and western region ethnic minority people as their most important allies, and appointed them as official administrators to rule China. This greatly hurt the pride of the Chinese literati and reduced their social status. Since they had nowhere to turn to for employment whereby they could make use of their knowledge and talent, they had to write plays in order to make a living. Previously it was simply beneath their dignity to be engaged in playwriting. Secondly, the vast Yuan Empire established by Mongols actually increased political, economic as well as cultural exchanges among different ethnic nationalities within the empire. As Mongols and western region ethnic minority peoples loved songs and dances, they brought in large number of their own songs and dances for court performances during the Yuan, which indirectly encouraged theatrical activities then. Also, the rapid economic development along with trading between various ethnic groups created large cosmopolitan cities like Dadu 大都 (present-day Beijing) and Lin'an

1 According to Zhong Sicheng's 钟嗣成 *Lu gui bu* 录鬼簿, there were 111 playwrights during the Yuan; Fu Xihua's 傅惜华 *Yuan dai zaju quanmu* 元代杂剧全目 includes altogether 737 plays, of which 550 were by Yuan dramatists and another 187 were by anonymous authors during either the Yuan or the Ming period.

2 J. I. Crump, *Chinese Theater in the Days of Kublai Khan* (Ann Arbor: Center for Chinese Studies, The University of Michigan, 1990), p. 3.

临安 (present-day Hangzhou), where there also occurred a need for large number of entertainments. And lastly, perhaps partly because of Mongol rulers' lack of experience in cultural control, the Yuan court generally adopted a relatively loose cultural policy so that the local dramatists could often write and perform whatever they would like without much official censorship. That is why in Yuan *zaju*, one may find such a surprisingly rich and colorful display of content, including poignant attacks on the Yuan court and society.

As a mature form of drama, Yuan *zaju* came with a fairly strict dramatic form for both its prosody and music. A Yuan *zaju* play was usually composed of four acts. If four acts did not have enough room to convey its content, a playwright could add a few songs to form what was called a *xiezi* 楔子(wedge) to be placed either in the beginning of a play or between two acts. In a Yuan *zaju* play, each act mainly consisted of a set of song suites. Songs were the soul of Yuan *zaju* because they were the ones that were mainly used to convey plot development, emotional ups and downs as well as characters' personalities. Each song has two components: music and words. The music was initially taken from some folk songs and as it got popular and used often, its tune stayed on and became somehow fixed. Song writers, therefore, started to add words to the same tune by observing a strict tonal pattern and rhyme scheme specific to each tune. The words of those songs, on the other hand, often referred to as Yuan *qu* 元曲, were different from the poems of Tang and Song dynasties, because in writing a Yuan *qu*, a poet could insert a number of words outside the tonal pattern and rhyme scheme for the sake of more flexibility in performance. Such an insertion of words was commonly called *chenzi* 衬字(inserted words). So, in a Yuan *zaju* play, songs to different tunes were put together to form a song suite, but all the songs in each song suite were in a particular musical key (gōngdiào 宫调), which was not used in the other song suites of the play. Besides, those songs collected in each song suite observed the same rhyme scheme throughout the song suite. As far as performance was concerned, there was usually only one leading actor or actress who sang throughout a Yuan *zaju* play, although the actor or actress could assume different theatrical roles. From here one can also see the importance of singing in *zaju* plays.

Because of the lack of adequate extant literature, we now know very little about playwrights of the Yuan dynasty. Of the hundred or so playwrights of the Yuan, many only had their names known to us. Guan Hanqing 关汉卿 from Dadu 大都 (present-day Beijing), for instance, was the most prominent and well-known. But we only know that, originally holding a minor medical post, Guan liked to have social interactions with many people of the lower social strata, including many of his fellow playwrights of various troupes, actors and actresses, singers and dancers, and even courtesans. Because of his connection with those people, his plays were mostly about love and suffering of ordinary people. The intense passions conveyed in his plays and the strong love and hatred he had for the characters he created are the characteristics of his plays and these have been critically acclaimed ever since his time. A prolific writer, Guan has written more than 60 plays in his lifetime, of which only a dozen or so are extant. Some of his well-known plays include *Dou E yuan* 窦娥冤 (Injustice Done to Dou E), *Jiu feng chen* 救风尘 (Rescued by a Courtesan), *Dan dao hui* 单刀会 (Going to the Banquet with a Single Sword) and *Hu die meng* 蝴蝶梦 (The Butterfly Dream), etc.

Wang Shifu 王实甫 was about contemporaneous with Guan Hanqing and was also one of the top playwrights of the Yuan period. His plays mainly focused on love between young men and young women and he wrote with beautiful poetry and literary gracefulness. His most influential and well-known play was *Xi xiang ji* 西厢记 (Romance of the Western Wing), which dramatizes a love affair between Cui Yingying, a girl from a high official family, and a young scholar Zhang. The love affair between the two and their final reunion, delineated with sympathy and approval, ignites such an anti-feudal sentiment with regard to the marriage practice prevalent at the time that it has become a hit among not only young men and young women, but also people of all walks of life, and there have been numerous versions of the play. Some of the character names in the play such as "*Hongniang* 红娘" have since become household names in Chinese society today. Wang Shifu wrote altogether fourteen *zaju* plays, of which only three are extant.

Other important playwrights of the Yuan include Ma Zhiyuan 马致远, Bai Pu 白朴 and Zheng Guangzu 郑光祖, whose dates are all lost to us now. Together with Guan Hanqing, however, they are usually called "The Four Great Yuan Playwrights (yuán qǔ sì dà jiā 元曲四大家)."

According to Zhong Sicheng's 钟嗣成 *Lu gui bu* 录鬼簿, Ma Zhiyuan also came from Dadu and once held a minor official position in the administration governing the present-day Jiangsu, Zhejiang and Fujian provinces.[1] Ma is known for his plays of *shenxian daohua* 神仙道化 (immortality and Taoistic transformation), which advocate a kind of reclusive escape from a normal social life. Ma Zhiyuan's plays are often praised for its language: natural, unadorned, seemingly effortless, and yet full of laconic evocation. Ma Zhiyuan wrote fifteen plays in all, but only seven are extant. The most well-known plays of his are *Han gong qiu* 汉宫秋 (Autumn in Han Palace), *Yueyang lou* 岳阳楼 (The Yueyang Pavilion) and *Huang liang meng* 黄粱梦 (Golden Millet Dream).

Bai Pu had a well-educated family background. His grandfather, father and his uncle were all highly-regarded intellectuals of the Jin dynasty.[2] However, because he lived in a time period when Jin was overtaken by Mongols, he experienced the fall of a country and the subsequent misfortune of his family early in his life, which had a tremendous influence

1 See Zhong Sicheng, *Lu gui bu* 录鬼簿, in *Zhongguo gudian xiqu lunzhu jicheng*, 2:108.

2 See Zhang Peiheng 章培恒, ed., *Shi da xiqu jia* 十大戏曲家 (Ten Great Dramatists) (Shanghai: Shanghai guji chubanshe, 1990), pp. 2-3.

on his playwriting. Perhaps indignant of what Mongols had done to his country and his people, he declined to serve at the Yuan court during his life lifetime. The sentiments conveyed in his plays are, as a result, mostly disconsolate, and the plays often contain grievous recollections nostalgic of some past events. He wrote altogether sixteen plays, but only Wú tóng yǔ梧桐雨 (Rain on the Paulownia Tree), Dōng qiáng jì东墙记 (Romance of the East Wall) and Qiáng tóu mǎ shàng墙头马上 (Over the Wall) are extant.

Zheng Guangzu was originally from Xiangling in Pingyang 平阳襄陵 in the north and he came to Hangzhou to serve as a petty officer. Upright and aloof in nature, he did not get along with other people there.[1] His plays deal with two themes: historical stories and stories about love between men and women. The language couched in his songs often receives critical acclaim as being beautiful and evocative. Altogether Zheng wrote nineteen plays and eight are extant. His representative plays are *Wang Can deng lou* 王粲登楼 (Wang Can Ascends the Pavilion) and *Qian nu li hun* 倩女离魂 (Qiannu's Ghost Leaves Her Body).

2. Southern Dramas of the Yuan Dynasty

Southern dramas (nánxì 南戏) that originated toward the end of the Northern Song dynasty continued during the time when Yuan *zaju* came into being. However, because of the political and military confrontation between the Southern Song and Mongols, the two drama forms developed in their own ways in the north and in the south respectively with little interaction. As Mongols gradually pushed their forces into the south and finally toppled the Southern Song regime, however, Yuan *zaju* also made its way south where it interacted with Southern drama and hence influenced the latter in various ways.

Southern songs (nánqǔ南曲) and Northern songs (北曲 běiqǔ) were

1 See Zhong Sicheng, *Lu gui bu* , in *Zhongguo gudian xiqu lunzhu jicheng,* 2:119.

different in a number of ways: in terms of music, the former used a pentatonic scale (e.g., the present-day popular southern folk song "A Jasmine Flower 茉莉花" uses such a scale), whereas the latter used a heptatonic scale; the former were initially derived from folk songs for their ease in singing without considering their music keys 宫调,[1] whereas the latter strictly observed the same music key when put in a song suite. As for the words used, those of the former were often quite colloquial, slangy and even a bit vulgar, and they were from common and uneducated folk artists, whereas those of the latter were literary and graceful, strictly observing tonal patterns and rhyming schemes because they were composed by the talented literati.

After encountering the Northern drama—Yuan *zaju*, Southern dramas started to absorb some of the Northern drama's elements: first it became more regulated in its song suites by trying to adhere more regularly to one music key for all the songs in a song suite as was the case in the Northern drama; secondly, it started to use some of the northern rhyme schemes. Previously, since the Southern drama was based on southern dialects, its phonetic base and rhyme schemes were quite different from those of the Northern drama. And finally, in terms of diction used in songs, Southern drama writers also tried to improve on their language, rendering their songs more beautiful and elegant, especially in the case of Gao Ming's *Pi pa ji* 琵琶记 (The Lute).

Because of the literati's initial disdain for the Southern drama, the total number of Southern dramas during the Yuan is hard to get accurately. According to some, there are about sixty to seventy.[2] However, except for a very few plays whose authors we now know for sure, most of them remain anonymous. Toward the end of the Yuan dynasty, with the decline of Yuan *zaju*, the Southern drama gained momentum in its development partly

---

1 See Xu Wei 徐渭, *Nanci xulu* 南词叙录, *Zhongguo gudian xiqu lunzhu jicheng,* 3:241.

2 See, for example, Liao Ben & Liu Yanjun, *Zhongguo xiqu fazhan jian shi* 中国戏曲发展简史 (Taiyuan: Shanxi jiaoyu chubanshe, 2006), p. 88.

because of its improvement and partly because of its flexibility in both its music structure and its length—it could adjust and add songs or song suites at will to suit the need of its content, and the entire length of the play was quite flexible without a limit. Because of these advantages, the Southern drama was able to keep itself alive and develop throughout the Yuan, and finally, surpassed Yuan *zaju* to evolve into some modern dramas today. The representative Southern dramas of the Yuan include *Pi pa ji*, *Jing chai ji* 荆钗记 (The Story of the Thorn Hairpin), *Liu Zhiyuan baitu ji* 刘知远白兔记 (The Story of Liu Zhiyuan and the White Rabbit), *Bai yue ting* 拜月亭(The Moon Prayer Pavilion) and *Sha gou ji* 杀狗记 (The Story of Killing a Dog), the last four being commonly called "The Four Great Southern Dramas (sì dà nán xì 四大南戏)."

Jing chai ji 荆钗记 (The Story of the Thorn Hairpin)

Allegedly written by Ke Danqiu 柯丹邱 from Suzhou during the Song and Yuan period, this play dramatizes the vicissitudes of lives of Wang Shipeng 王十朋, a poor scholar from Wenzhou, who becomes the top candidate at an civil service examination in the capital, and Qian Yulian 钱玉莲, a young lady who marries Wang and chooses to be loyal to him, no matter what happens. She even tries to sacrifice her life to be faithful to her husband. Wang, on the other hand, also treasures his love with Qian and resists all kinds of temptations and pressure to remarry. After a series of events and hardships they each have suffered, the two of them are finally reunited at the end. The play has been immensely popular partly because it praises the everlasting love between the two protagonists in good times and in adverse situations. The play is also praiseworthy for its closely-knit plot structure.

Liu Zhiyuan baitu ji 刘知远白兔记 (The Story of Liu Zhiyuan and the White Rabbit)

The script writer of the play is unknown. Although the title refers to Liu Zhiyuan, Emperor Gaozu of the Later Han 后汉高祖 (895—948), the play is really about his wife, Lady Li the Third 李三娘, who endures untold sufferings and persecutions from her brother-in-law and her sister-in-law, who have tried one way or another to get rid of her so as to be able to inherit everything from their deceased father. It is only after many years when the son of Lady Li the Third is hunting for a white rabbit and chasing it to her village to incidentally meet her that the wife and husband have finally got reunited. The suffering and yet undaunted and faithful figure of Lady Li the Third has won sympathy from people of all walks of life and hence making the play one of the most performed plays in history.

Bai yue ting 拜月亭(The Moon Prayer Pavilion)

Also named *You gui ji* 幽闺记 (Story from a Secluded Boudoir), the play is said to be written by Shi Hui 施惠 of the Yuan and is possibly adapted from Guan Hanqing's *zaju* play of the same title.[1] It narrates a story about a young man named Jiang Shilong 蒋世隆, who accidentally meets, falls in love with, and privately marries Wang Ruilan 王瑞兰, a young daughter from a high court official, while they are fleeing from the Mongol invasion. However, Ruilan's father, upon knowing their marriage, forcibly takes her away from Jiang. Later, it is only when Jiang becomes a top graduate at the civil service examination that the two are finally reunited as husband and wife. Usually considered a comedy, the play extols the heroine's courageous persistence in holding on to her own marriage while resisting her father's marriage plan. The play is often praised for its

1 But since both Zhong Sicheng's 钟嗣成 *Lu gui bu* 录鬼簿 and Zhu Quan's 朱权 *Taihe zhengyin pu* 太和正音谱 do not list the play under Shi Hui, some scholars have disputed the play's authorship as such.

comic plot arrangement and its graceful lyrics.

Sha gou ji 杀狗记 (The Story of Killing a Dog)

Generally considered a play by Xu Zhen 徐畛 of the early Ming dynasty, it narrates a family dispute by two brothers in which Sun Hua 孙华, the elder one, is taken in by two local rascals and hence ill-treats his younger brother Sun Rong 孙荣. Sun Rong's wife Yang Yuezhen 杨月真 tries to bring the elder brother around by killing a dog, wrapping it up with some human clothes and throwing it in front of Sun Hua's house. The different attitudes adopted by the two rascals and Sun Rong towards the treatment of the dog's body make Sun Hua finally realize that blood is thicker than water. While the play obviously advocates Confucian ethics, its language is rather colloquial and unadorned, hence often considered vulgar by later scholars.

Pi pa ji 琵琶记 (The Lute)

Written by Gao Ming of the Yuan and Ming period, the play is based on the previous Southern drama *Zhao Zhennu Cai Erlang* 赵贞女蔡二郎 (Zhao the Virtuous Lady and Master Cai the Second), in which Cai Bojie 蔡伯喈, after he comes out the top graduate at the civil service examination and subsequently marries the prime minister's daughter, refuses to recognize his erstwhile wife in the country and uses a horse to kick her to death instead. Cai is thereafter struck to death by lightening from a thunderstorm. Gao Ming's *Pi pa ji*, however, changes the plot by forcing Cai to remarry by an imperial edict and by having him also welcome back his wife Zhao who comes to the capital to look for him, so that the play ends with Cai marrying two wives happily. *Pi pa ji* also emphasizes the hardships that Zhao has gone through, while her husband Cai is away, and her sense of filial piety toward her parents-in-law. The play is much praised for its moral edification, as the playwright himself rightly claims: "If a play is without moral teaching, even if it is finely written, it is useless (*Bu guan fenghuati, zong hao ye wangran* 不关风化体，纵好也枉然)." And the play has also been generally considered "the Father of Southern Drama" because of its nice plot arrangement as well as its language and lyrics, which are graceful and which closely follow the prosody of the tunes. With Gao Ming's *Pi pa ji*, the literati started to change their long-held attitude of contempt for the Southern drama, which continued to grow and develop and finally replaced the Northern *zaju* plays to become a mainstream genre in Chinese dramatic tradition.

III. *Chuanqi* Dramas of the Ming and Qing Dynasties

The term *chuanqi* 传奇, whose root meaning is "marvelous tales," has been used to refer to different things in different historical periods. During the Tang and Song dynasties, it was used to refer to short stories written in classical Chinese; during the Song and Yuan dynasties, since many Northern *zaju* plays and Southern dramas were based on those early Tang and Song stories, some of them were also called *chuanqi* ; and starting with the Ming dynasty and continuing during the Qing dynasty, this term was used to refer to some lengthy Southern dramas to make them distinct from Northern *zaju* plays.

1. *Chuanqi* Dramas of the Ming Dynasty

During the first 150 years or so of the Ming dynasty, the Northern *zaju* drama continued its performance along with the Southern drama, although they were each limited to their own territories—northern *zaju* plays existed in northern China (roughly present-day Anhui, Shanxi, Hebei, Henan and neighboring provinces) while Southern dramas were active in the south (present-day Zhejiang, Jiangsu, Fujian, Jiangxi, Guangdong and neighboring provinces). However, because of the flexibility of the Southern drama in its performing style, including the prosody of its lyrics, it was able to absorb various local songs and also to adapt itself to many local cultures; hence it quickly spread widely and outshone its northern brethren by reducing the latter's sphere of influence. By approximately the reign of Emperor Wanli 万历 (1573—1619), the Northern drama became very much obsolete. On the other hand, after the reign of Emperor Chenghua 成化 (1464—1487), Southern dramas were getting more prosperous and evolving one after another into quite diverse musical variations of the original Southern drama. According to some historical record, there were altogether fifteen such musical variations, of which *Haiyan qiang* 海盐腔, *Yuyao qiang* 余姚腔, *Yiyang qiang* 弋阳腔 and *Kunshan qiang* 昆山腔 were the most popular musical variations of the Southern drama.[1] Those variations of the Southern drama were mostly confined in the southeastern part of China during the Ming. The *Kunshan qiang* variation, after gradual artistic and lyrical innovations and reformations by some local artists in Kunshan, became the *Kunju* opera 昆剧 during the Qing dynasty and is still performing today.

Although Northern *zaju* dramas were obsolete by late Ming, artists were continuously engaged in writing *zaju* plays. However, greatly influenced by the Southern drama at this time, those *zaju* plays underwent changes in their form and lyrics. Instead of using four acts as a regular Yuan dynasty *zaju* play would, those *zaju* plays of the Ming and Qing dynasties could have as few as just one act such as Wang Jiusi's 王九思 (1468—1551) *Zhongshan lang* 中山狼 (Wolf from Mount Zhongshan) , or as many as more than twenty acts such as Xu Chao 许潮's *Taihe ji* 泰和记 (Tales of Taihe). But the most important change came in music: those *zaju* plays used Northern songs which were intermixed with Southern songs, and some even used all Southern songs. As a result, such *zaju* plays were also called

1 See Liao Ben & Liu Yanjun, *Zhongguo xiqu fazhan shi,* 3: 38.

"the Southern *zaju* plays 南杂剧," because the changes made therein sometimes really blurred the distinction between the traditional *zaju* play and the *chuanqi* 传奇 drama.

There are quite a lot of dramatists who wrote *chuanqi* plays during the Ming. Worth-noting in the first place is Liang Chenyu 梁辰鱼 (1519—1591) from Kunshan in modern day Jiangsu province, whose *Huan sha ji* 浣纱记 (The Story of Washing Silk) was the first *chuanqi* drama written for the newly-reformed *Kunshan qiang* musical variant of the Southern drama. Because of the play' s success and popularity, it subsequently made *Kunshan qiang* a "high-brow" art form or "official music (guānqiāng 官腔)" well above all other Southern drama variants, which were then relegated to the status of "low-brow" art forms or were looked down upon as "miscellaneous music (zádiào 杂调)."

Another dramatist who is worth citing here is Zheng Zhizhen 郑之珍 (1518—1595), who wrote the influential *Mulian jiumu quan shan ji* 目连救母劝善记 (The Story of Mulian Saving His Mother) in more than a hundred acts, which could be performed for three days in a row. Zheng was the first dramatist to have incorporated all the previous folktales about Mulian and to have rendered the entire story in dramatic form. Extremely popular for its performance among ordinary people, the play has become the prototype of the story for all subsequent dramatic adaptations.

Chuanqi drama flourished during the Wanli reign, and Xu Wei 徐渭 (1521—1593) is the forerunner of theatrical creativity in this period. His reputation for his drama rests mainly on the four *zaju* plays of *Kuang gushi* 狂鼓史 (The Wild Drummer), *Yu chanshi* 玉禅师 (The Jade Zen Buddhist Monk), *Ci Mulan* 雌木兰 (The Female Mulan) and *Nu zhuangyuan* 女状元 (The Female Top Graduate), all of which are known under the collective title of *Si sheng yuan* 四声猿 (Four Shrieks of an Ape), which expresses Xu Wei' s grievances and indignation against the reality through his dramatization of variously unusual or even visionary tales. Xu' s

unrestrained spirit conveyed by his plays and the changes he made to the *zaju* forms greatly influenced the subsequent Southern dramas.

Shen Jing 沈璟 (1533—1610), a major figure in the Ming dynasty drama, is best known for his contribution to the rules of prosody (qǔlǜ 曲律) formulated in his *Nan jiugong shisan diao qupu* 南九宫十三调曲谱 (Scores of the Nine Keys and Thirteen Modes from the Southern Drama), which established a standard for songs used in *chuanqi* dramas at the time. He also wrote a number of *chuanqi* plays but few were successful due to his strict adherence to the rules of prosody he himself helped established.

Different from Shen Jing, Tang Xianzu 汤显祖 (1550—1616), the most important playwright and also one of the great men of letters of the Ming dynasty, wrote successful *chuanqi* plays as well as poems. His *Yumingtang si meng* 玉茗堂四梦 (Four Dreams from the Yuming Studio) that comprises *Zi chai ji* 紫钗记 (The Story of the Purple Hairpin), *Mudan ting* 牡丹亭 (The Peony Pavilion), *Handan ji* 邯郸记 (Dreams from Handan) and *Nanke ji* 南柯记 (Dreams from the Nanke State) has brought him immense fame, of which *The Peony Pavilion* is his representative play. Greatly influenced by the philosophical debate between *qing* 情 (feelings/emotions) and *li* 理 (reason/rationalism) during the late Ming, the play strongly advocates *qing* and uses Du Liniang, a beautiful girl of a high official's family, to seek her own beloved man. Such a bold and rebellious action would of course be unthinkable in the feudal society of the Ming. Therefore Tang tried to make this possible only in Du Liniang's dream and in her resurrection back from the underworld after her death. Both artistically and ideologically, *The Peony Pavilion* is considered the best *chuanqi* drama during the Ming period.

In late-Ming history and literature, Ruan Dacheng's 阮大铖 (1587—1645) name should also be mentioned. As an official and politician, he was despised by many for his association with Wei Zhongxian 魏忠贤 (1568—1627), a powerful and yet notorious eunuch of the Ming court. But as a playwright, Ruan has written plays with high artistic attainments. His best-known play is *Yanzi jian* 燕子笺 (The Swallow Letter), a convoluted tale of romance with a happy ending. His skilful use of highly coincidental and unusual plot in the play produces unexpected comic effects, which has won people's praise.

2. *Chuanqi* Dramas of the Qing Dynasty

For quite a long period of time during the Qing dynasty, *chuanqi* drama continued its momentum it gained during the Ming dynasty. However, because of the change of dynasties that again brought in an alien rule of China, the *chuanqi* drama of the early Qing period was often permeated with a sense of lost and with palpable feelings of sadness and nostalgia. There were many dramatists engaged in playwriting at this time such as Wu Weiye 吴伟业 (1609—1671), Li Yu 李玉 (c. 1630), Yang Chaoguan 杨潮观 (1712—1791) and Jiang Shiquan 蒋士铨 (1725—1785), but the most well-known and the most representative playwrights of this period were certainly Hong Sheng 洪昇 (1645—1704) and Kong Shangren 孔尚任 (1648—1718).

Hong Sheng was from Qiantang 钱塘 in present-day Hangzhou of Zhejiang province. Except for a brief period in his youth when he seemed to be aspiring and led a happy life, Hong Sheng's entire life was full of frustration, disappointment and loss, which were partly reflected in his masterpiece *Chang sheng dian* 长生殿 (Palace of Eternal Youth). The imperial love between Emperor Xuanzong of Tang 唐玄宗 and his concubine Yang Yuhuan 杨玉环 is well known in history and there have been numerous stories and plays on the subject. But different from all the previous versions of the story, Hong Sheng chose to dwell on the eternal loss or nostalgia on the part of the emperor for his lost and yet beloved concubine, which takes up the entire latter half of the play. Hong Sheng's is the first play in which the imperial love has been depicted as the love between two ordinary man and woman, hence especially truthful and moving.

Kong Shangren was contemporaneous with Hong Sheng and the two of them were known at the time as "Hong in the South and Kong in the North (*nan Hong bei Kong* 南洪北孔)." Born in Qufu 曲阜 of Shandong province, Kong Shangren lived in Beijing for long, hoping in vain eventually to be promoted by the Qing court. Repeatedly frustrated in his career and unhappy with his official prospect, Kong Shangren turned his energy to playwriting, especially to his *Tao hua shan* 桃花扇 (The Peach Blossom Fan), which uses the love story between the Confucian scholar Hou Fangyu 侯方域 and the courtesan Li Xiangjun 李香君 to reflect politics, especially the root cause for the fall of the Southern Ming dynasty. Because of its political relevance in addition to Kong's talented use of the *Kunqu* form, the play won immense success and it brought Kong instant fame, although it was also this play that shortly afterward brought him political trouble and official demotion. Both "Palace of Eternal Youth" and "The Peach Blossom Fan" are representative *chuanqi* plays of the Qing dynasty.

IV. The Rise of Beijing Opera

During the Wanli period of the Ming dynasty, *Kunqu* drama by its graceful tunes and elegant songs won love and support of the literati and it therefore started to dominate the theater as a sort of "official drama" ever since then. Various other local dramas, however, did not disappear, nor perish, but underwent various changes or transformations. During the early Qing dynasty, therefore, those local dramas gained rapid development. Various Southern dramas characterized by the *Yiyang qiang* music 弋阳腔 gradually came to be called altogether as the *Gao qiang* 高腔 (High-pitched drama). On the other hand, various remnant variants of the disappearing

Northern *zaju* drama in present-day Henan, Hebei, Shanxi and Shandong provinces evolved into what is called the *Xiansuo qiang* 弦索腔 (string music drama), whereas the local dramas in the areas of present-day Shanxi and Gansu provinces came to be known as the *Xiqin qiang* 西秦腔 (Western Qin drama). These varieties of regional dramas and music thrived, influenced each other, competed and combined with one another during the Qing. Their increasing interactions with one another gradually gave birth to some new, hybrid forms of music and drama such as *Erhuang qiang* 二黄腔 and *Xipi qiang* 西皮腔 that evolved from *Xangyang qiang* 襄阳腔 which in turn came from *Xiqin qiang*.

During the Qianlong 乾隆 (1736—1795) and Jiaqing 嘉庆 (1795—1821) period in the Qing dynasty, the increasingly popular regional dramas in various places of the country, which used to be regarded as a form of *zadiao* 杂调 (dramas of miscellaneous music) that belonged to what was named *huabu* 花部 (flowery section) drama, gradually formed a real challenge to the then dominating *Kunqu* drama, which had been deemed by the literati as belonging to what was termed *yabu* 雅部 (refined or graceful section) drama. Despite official intervention and even official prohibition of some of the *huabu* regional dramas, those regional dramas continued to thrive and flourish in many places, whereas *Kunqu* drama rapidly declined. The battle between the *huabu* drama and the *yabu* drama, therefore, ended with the victory for the former.

During the fifty-fifth year of the reign of Emperor Qianlong (1790), one drama troupe in Yangzhou 扬州, which was named *Sanqing ban* 三庆班, was summoned to Beijing to perform plays in celebration of the emperor's eightieth birthday. Originally coming from the Anhui troupe circle specializing in *Erhuang qiang*, the *Sanqing ban* troupe won huge success and gained popular support from people in Beijing for their excellent performances. So they ended up staying in the capital and continuing their performances there. Seeing *Sanqing ban*'s success in Beijing, three other

Anhui troupes went to Beijing and gave performances as well. Together the four Anhui troupes performed and competed with one another, making *Erhuang qiang* the most popular tune in Beijing then.

At the time, the local drama popular in the areas around River Han 汉水 in Hubei province was called *Han diao* 汉调, the precursor of the present-day Hanju 汉剧 (Han drama). Because of its geographical proximity to Anhui, Shanxi and Gansu provinces, *Han diao* was a drama form that developed from absorbing elements from the *Erhuang qiang* of Anhui and the *Xipi qiang* of Shanxi and Gansu. After its birth, therefore, it became quite popular and its own troupes developed rapidly. So, following the footsteps of Anhui troupes, *Han diao* troupes gradually began to make their way to Beijing as well. By about the eighth year to the twelfth year in the reign of Emperor Daoguang 道光 (1821—1851), according to some record, *Han diao* troupes had already established themselves in Beijing and were enthusiastically praised there.[1] As a result, Anhui drama troupes specializing in *Erhuang qiang* and *Han diao* drama troupes that were known for their singing which combined *Xipi qiang* and *Erhuang qiang* music performed in the same city, influenced each other then and sometimes they even performed together on the same stage, which gradually generated a new tune called *Pihuang* tune 皮黄调 that is the main musical tune used in the present-day Beijing opera. After the reign of Emperor Daoguang, Beijing opera formally came into being with a great number of well-known actors and actresses who together pushed Beijing opera to its artistic peak. The well-known Beijing opera artist Mei Lanfang 梅兰芳 (1894—1961) even led a Beijing opera delegation to tour Japan three times and visit the U. S. in 1930, making Beijing opera art known internationally and its beauty and charm have continued today.

1 Su hai an jushi 粟海庵居士, *Yantai hongzhua ji* 燕台鸿爪集, in Zhang Cixi 张次溪, *Qingdai yandu liyuan shiliao* 清代燕都梨园史料, 2 vols. (Beijing: Zhongguo xiju chubanshe, 1988), 1:272.

Questions for Discussion:

1. How has Chinese drama developed since the Tang dynasty? When did the earliest mature drama form start to emerge in China?
2. Although the Yuan dynasty was a relatively short period of time when Mongols ruled China, it is nevertheless regarded as a golden age in the history of Chinese drama. What may have contributed to this theatrical boom?
3. Explain the theatrical form and composition of a standard Yuan dynasty *zaju* play.
4. Explain the rise of Beijing opera during the end of the 18th century and the beginning of the 19th century.

Chapter Three

Chinese Drama

I. Variety and Distribution of Chinese Drama

In China today, there are altogether 34 provinces, municipalities directly under the Central Government, and autonomous regions (including Hong Kong, Macau and Taiwan). In all these regions there are some indigenous drama forms. The following is a list of drama forms indigenous to these areas.[1]

1. Municipalities Directly under the Central Government:[2]

Beijing 北京	*Jingju* 京剧
Chongqing 重庆	*Chuanju* 川剧
Shanghai 上海	*Huju* 沪剧
Tianjin 天津	*Hebei bangzi* 河北梆子

2. Provinces:

Anhui 安徽	*huangmei xi* 黄梅戏, *Huixi* 徽戏, *Anhui mulian xi* 安徽目连戏, *Anhui nuoxi* 安徽傩戏, *Luju* 庐剧,

1 This is mostly based on the appendix to Li Hanfei 李汉飞, *Zhongguo xiqu juzhong shouce* 中国戏曲剧种手册 (Beijing: Zhongguo xiju chubanshe, 1987), pp. 847-981, and Liao Ben & Liu Yanjun, *Zhongguo xiju fazhan jianshi* 中国戏剧发展简史 (Taiyuan: Shanxi jiaoyu chubanshe, 2006), pp. 274-289.

2 The municipalities, provinces and regions listed below are all alphabetically arranged according to their pinyin.

	Fengyang huagu xi 凤阳花鼓戏
Fujian 福建	*Puxian xi* 莆仙戏, *liyuan xi* 梨园戏, *gaojia xi* 高甲戏, *Minju* 闽剧
Gansu 甘肃	*Qinqiang* 秦腔, *Longju* 陇剧
Guangdong 广东	*Yueju* 粤剧, *Chaoju* 潮剧, *baizi xi* 白字戏
Guizhou 贵州	*Qianju* 黔剧, *Guizhou huadeng ju* 贵州花灯剧, *Anshun dixi* 安顺地戏
Hainan 海南	*Qiongju* 琼剧
Hebei 河北	*Hebei bangzi* 河北梆子, *Pingju* 评剧
Heilongjiang 黑龙江	*Longjiang ju* 龙江剧
Henan 河南	*Yuju* 豫剧, *Henan yuediao* 河南越调, *Henan quju* 河南曲剧
Hubei 湖北	*Hanju* 汉剧, *Chuju* 楚剧, *huagu xi* 花鼓戏, *caicha xi* 采茶戏
Hunan 湖南	*Xiangju* 湘剧, *Qiju* 祁剧, *huagu xi* 花鼓戏
Jilin 吉林	*Jiju* 吉剧, *erren zhuan* 二人转
Jiangsu 江苏	*Kunqu* 昆曲, *Huaiju* 淮剧, *Yangju* 扬剧, *Tongju* 通剧, *Xiju* 锡剧, *Suju* 苏剧
Jiangxi 江西	*Ganju* 赣剧, *Yiyangqiang* 弋阳腔, *Yihuang xi* 宜黄戏, *caicha xi* 采茶戏
Liaoning 辽宁	*erren zhuan* 二人转
Qinghai 青海	*Qinghai zangxi* 青海藏戏
Shaanxi 陕西	*Qinqiang* 秦腔, *Shaanxi daoqing* 陕西道情
Shandong 山东	*Lüju* 吕剧, *Shandong bangzi* 山东梆子, *Shandong liuzi xi* 山东柳子戏
Shanxi 山西	*Shanxi bangzi (Puju/Jinju)* 山西梆子 (蒲剧/晋剧), *yangge* 秧歌, *daoqing xi* 道情戏
Sichuan 四川	*Chuanju* 川剧, *Sichuan dengxi* 四川灯戏
Yunnan 云南	*Dianju* 滇剧, *Yunnan huadeng* 云南花灯, *Baiju* 白剧, *Daiju* 傣剧

Zhejiang浙江	*Yueju/Shaoxing xi* 越剧/绍兴戏, *Wuju* 婺剧, *Shaoju* 绍剧, *Huangyan luantan* 黄岩乱弹, *Ouju* 瓯剧, *Hangju* 杭剧, *Yongju* 甬剧, *Huju* 湖剧, *Yaoju* 姚剧, *Muju* 睦剧

3. Autonomous Regions:

Guangxi广西	*Guiju* 桂剧, *Yongju* 邕剧
Nei Menggu内蒙古 (Inner Mongolia)	*erren tai* 二人台, *da yangge* 大秧歌
Ningxia宁夏	*Ningxia daoqing* 宁夏道情
Xizang (Tibet) 西藏	*Zangxi* 藏戏
Xinjiang新疆	*Xinjiang quzi xi* 新疆曲子戏

4. Other Regions:

Hong Kong香港	*Yueju* 粤剧
Macau澳门	*Yueju* 粤剧
Taiwan 台湾	*gezai xi* 歌仔戏

One should note that not all the drama forms in China are listed above. The list only shows the representative or popular drama forms in these regions. According to a survey carried out in 1984, there were as many as 360 drama forms in China at that time. One can observe the following facts along with the distribution of Chinese drama.[1] Although they were the result of a survey done in the 1980s, things stay very much the same at present.

1. Of these 360 drama forms, *Jingju* 京剧 (Beijing opera) was the only national drama that had its influence all over the country, which was

1 The following information is from Hu Zhaoliang 胡兆量, "*Zhongguo xiqu dili tezheng* 中国戏曲地理特征 (Geographical Features of Chinese Drama)," *Jingji dili* 经济地理 20.1 (2000), pp. 84-87.

reflected in the fact that all the provinces, municipalities directly under the Central Government, and autonomous regions had their own professional Beijing opera troupes.

2. There were eight major drama forms that were interprovincial, i.e., plays of these drama forms were regularly performed in more than one provinces. These were *Pingju* 评剧, *erren zhuan* 二人转, *Yuju* 豫剧, *Jinju* 晋剧 and *Qinqiang* 秦腔 in the north, and *Yueju* 越剧 (Zhejiang), *Yueju* 粤剧 (Guangdong), and *Chuanju* 川剧 in the south. There were over 70 professional drama troupes for each one of these major drama forms, which were distributed in different provinces. Together with Beijing opera, there were nine major drama forms in China. In 1984, there were altogether 2,302 professional drama troupes in China, of which 1,299 were drama troupes performing these nine major drama forms, accounting for 56.4% of the total drama troupes in the nation.

3. Some drama forms were influential only within the provinces in which they were active, and each of them may have over 25 professional drama troupes to represent them. These drama forms included Shanxi *bangzi* 山西梆子, Hebei *bangzi* 河北梆子, Shandong *Lüju* 山东吕剧, Henan *quju* 河南曲剧, Anhui *huangmei xi* 安徽黄梅戏, Jiangsu *Xiju* 江苏锡剧, Fujian *Minju* 福建闽剧, Hubei *Chuju* 湖北楚剧 and Hunan *huagu xi* 湖南花鼓戏. There were 341 professional drama troupes representing those nine drama forms in 1984.

4. There were 174 local drama forms each represented by a few professional drama troupes. There were altogether 662 such professional drama troupes with an average of fewer than 4 troupes for each drama form in this category. Of the 174 drama forms here, 92 had only one drama troupe for its performances.

5. There were also many local drama forms without any professional drama troupes for their performances. The number of such drama forms reached 168, accounting for almost a half of the total number of drama

forms in China in the 1980s. Mostly during slack seasons in farming or for some festivities in rural areas were those drama forms performed by some amateur theatrical troupes. Because of their infrequent performance and other reasons, 10 of those drama forms were already lost in the 1980s.

By general consent, China is geographically divided along the Huai River 淮河—Qinling Mountain 秦岭 line into Northern China and Southern China. The geographical differences between the North and the South to a large extent determine the differences between dramas in the North and those in the South.

In Northern China, weather is generally much colder than it is in the South. There are fewer rivers and lakes in the North than in the South. In terms of land, the North has much less arable land but with more expanses of open land and space. As a result, Northern China is generally less densely populated than Southern China, particularly in the northwestern part of China. With less population density in the North, language is more or less unified there and there is less variety of dialects in the North than in the South. Because of all these factors, dramas in the North tend to be loud, sonorous and forceful. These features could also have been influenced by the songs and dances of China's ethnic minority people and its neighboring countries in the north and northwest. For example, Mongolian songs and dances are known for their bold, lively and uninhibited manner.[1] Some scholar has also pointed out that the *yangge* 秧歌 form of drama in the northeast of China tends to have a quick tempo and a short rhythm because actors and actresses of *yangge* need to constantly move and leap for the cold weather there.[2]

By contrast, weather is generally mild in Southern China and there are many rivers and lakes with a lot of rain there. In terms of land, the South

1 Wulanjie 乌兰杰, *Mengguzu gudai yinyue wudao chutan* 蒙古族古代音乐舞蹈初探 (Huhehaote: Nei Menggu renmin chubanshe, 1985), p. 10.

2 Wang Yang 王洋, "*Zhongguo yinyue shenmei de wenhua dili jiegou yanjiu* 中国音乐审美的文化地理结构研究," *Feitian* 4 (2009), p. 55.

has much more arable land and is more densely populated than the North. As a result, there are a lot of dialects distributed even within a small area such as the Yangtze River Delta. In such a geographic environment, people do not have to shout in order to be heard, and the mild and humid climate shape the southern voice, particularly the voice in the southeast coastal area, which is comparatively soft, tender and a bit charming. Such is the general feature of the dramas in the South.

In fact, many men of letters and scholars observed the differences between the Northern and the Southern dramas long ago. Xu Wei 徐渭 (1521—1593), a noted scholar of the Ming dynasty, for example, remarked in his *Nanci xulu* 南词叙录 that "the Northern dramas today are all voices of war for the Liao and Jin regimes in the far north, which are magnificent and yet violent" and "to listen to the Northern dramas will boost one' s morale and make one' s hair stand on end...whereas the Southern dramas are slow and unhurried, fluent and sweet, making one unknowingly smug so as to lose one' s defense..."[1] A more recent scholar Lin Yutang (1895—1976) has described their differences in more concrete terms as follows:

> The raw, rugged North and the soft, pliable South—one can see these differences in their language, music and poetry. Observe the contrast between the Shensi[i.e., Shaanxi] songs, on the one hand, sung to the metallic rhythm of hard wooden tablets and keyed to a high pitch like the Swiss mountain songs, suggestive of the howling winds on mountain tops and broad pastures and desert sand-dunes, and on the other, the indolent Soochow [i.e., Suzhou] crooning, something that is between a sigh and a snore, throaty, nasal, and highly suggestive of a worn-out patient of asthma whose sighs and groans have by force of habit become swaying and rhythmic. In language, one sees the difference between the sonorous, clear-cut rhythm of Pekingese

1 Xu Wei 徐渭, *Nancixulu zhushi* 南词叙录注释, annot. by Li Fubo 李复波 & Liang Chengyu 梁澄宇, (Beijing: Zhongguo xiju chubanshe, 1989), pp. 24 & 76.

mandarin that pleases by its alternate light and shade, and the soft and sweet babbling of Soochow women, with round-lip vowels and circumflex tones, where force of emphasis is not expressed by a greater explosion but by long-drawn-out and finely nuanced syllables at the end of sentences.[1]

Indeed, the Northern land is vast, the people there are gallant and straightforward, and the drama forms there are therefore loud and sonorous like *Qinqiang* whose characteristic is roaring. That is why in some Northern dramas such as Beijing opera, even the female roles are used to be taken by male actors. A typical northern folk song can perhaps best show these northern characteristics:

Down by the Chehleh [i.e., Chile] river,
Beneath the Yin hills,
Like an inverted cup is the sky
That covers the wasteland.
Enormous is the earth,
And the sky is a deep blue;
The wind blows, the tall grass bends,
And the sheep and cattle came into view.[2]

By contrast, the Southern land is picturesque, full of green hills and clear waters, and people' s voice there tends to be soft and gentle; the dramas there, as a result, are known for their tonal exquisiteness and graceful manner. That is also why in some southern dramas like the *Yueju* drama, even the male roles are used to be (and nowadays some of them are still sometimes) taken by female actresses. A popular southern folk song can also be used to illustrate these southern traits:

---

1 Lin Yutang, *My Country and My People* (New York: Reynal & Hitchcock, 1935), p. 20.
2 *Ibid.*, p. 22, original emphasis.

What a beautiful jasmine flower!
What a beautiful jasmine flower!
Fragrant and beautiful, the flowers are all over the branch,
So fragrant and so white that everyone praises.
Let me pick you up and give it to others.
Oh, jasmine flower, jasmine flower!

II. Introduction to the Repertoire of Traditional Chinese Drama

Many traditional Chinese dramas are still performed on contemporary Chinese stage and are popular among people so that they form a repertoire of many modern Chinese drama troupes. The repertoire of traditional Chinese drama as a whole, however, is a large corpus and no statistics are available about the exact number of plays therein. What follows, therefore, is a brief introduction to some of the most representative or popular plays, including some modern plays, for some of the Chinese drama forms.

1. *Jingju* 京剧

Orphan Searched for and Orphan Saved (sōu gū jiù gū 搜孤救孤)

Based on Ji Junxiang's 纪君祥 Yuan *zaju* play titled *The Orphan of Zhao* 赵氏孤儿, this play depicts the soul-stirring revenge by the orphan of the Zhao's family.

The story took place during the Spring and Autumn Period (770—476 BC) when Duke Ling of Jin 晋灵公 was said to be dissolute and unprincipled. Zhao Dun 赵盾, Grand Master of the State of Jin at the time, tried repeatedly in vain to remonstrate with him. Later, Duke Ling of Jin was killed by Zhao's younger brother Zhao Chuan 赵穿. Subsequently during the rule of Duke Jing of Jin 晋景公, his favorite courtier Tu Angu 屠

岸贾 didn't get along with Zhao Shuo 赵朔, Zhao Dun's son, so under the pretext that Zhao Dun indirectly killed Duke Ling of Jin, Tu plotted to kill Zhao's entire family. Zhao Shuo's wife is Princess Zhuangji 庄姬公主, who hid inside the palace and gave birth to a son. Cheng Ying 程婴, a retainer of the Zhao family, smuggled the baby out of the palace in disguise. After killing all the Zhao family members, Tu Angu heard that the princess gave birth to a son. Searching in vain for the orphan of Zhao, he ordered to kill all the babies of the same age in the entire country, if the baby was not submitted in ten days. Cheng Ying then discussed with Gongsun Chujiu 公孙杵臼, another retainer of the Zhao family. They decided that the former would sacrifice his own son, while the latter would gave up his own life in order to save Zhao's orphan. Many years later, after Zhao Wu 赵武, the orphan, grew up, he killed Tu Angu and avenged his family.

This Beijing opera play was also titled *Ba yi tu* 八义图 (A Picture of Eight Righteous Persons), which premiered in 1933.

Yu Tang Chun (玉堂春)

The story is set in the Ming dynasty. Wang Jinglong 王景隆, son of the Minister of Personnel visited an entertainment district in Beijing and met a famous prostitute Su San 苏三 with her professional name as Yu Tang Chun 玉堂春 (Spring in the Jade Hall). They fell in love with each other and vowed to stay together till the very end of their lives. Su San asked Wang Jinglong to be diligent in his studies so he could succeed in his examinations, and she in turn promised Wang that she would not see another client. When Wang ran out of his money, however, he was driven out by the procuress. After Wang was gone, Su San decided to wait for Wang and, therefore, refused to see any client. Without any alternative, the procuress had to sell her as a concubine to Shen Yanlin 沈燕林, a rich merchant, who took her back home in Hongdong county 洪洞县, Shanxi 山西 province.

Shen Yanlin conducted his business away from home year in and year out. His wife Pi Shi 皮氏 and her neighbor Zhao Ang cuckolded him. Partly being jealous of the beautiful girl her husband had brought home, Pi Shi planned on murdering Su. Unexpectedly, however, one day a bowl of noodles with poison that she had prepared for Su was unknowingly eaten by her husband Shen Yanlin, who died instantly. The wicked Pi Shi then sent Su San to the court, accusing her of the murder, and the magistrate, bribed by Pi, hastily sentenced Su San to death and had her sent to Taiyuan for a case reexamination before her execution.

On the other hand, Wang Jinglong went twice to the capital to take the imperial civil service examinations. After he passed the exam as a *jinshi* in the end, he was duly appointed Regional Inspector of Shanxi and also came to Taiyuan. Surprised to see Su San's case in his reexamination, he paid the latter a private visit in disguise. After much investigation and with the help of his colleagues, Wang Jinglong finally cleared all the false charges against Su San and the two were eventually reunited.

Because of the twists and turns of the plot and the moving tunes of some of the songs, the play is extremely popular among the Chinese audience.

Legend of the White Snake (Bái shé zhuàn 白蛇传)

This play depicts a white and a green snake spirits from Mount Emei 峨嵋山, who, out of their admiration for human life, metamorphosed into the forms of two young girls under the names of Bai Suzhen 白素贞 and Xiao Qing 小青. While they were enjoying themselves at the West Lake in Hangzhou 杭州西湖, they ran into a scholar Xu Xian 许仙. Bai Suzhen and Xu Xian fell in love with each other and, acting as a matchmaker, Xiao Qing finally made them come together as a married couple. Monk Fa Hai 法海 from Jinshan Monastery 金山寺, however, wasn't happy with their union and tried to break it up by warning Xu Xian of certain terrifying consequences. Alerted and convinced by Fa Hai's stern words, Xu Xian left his home to go to Jinshan Monastery. Knowing all these, Bai Suzhen rushed to the monastery in demand of her husband. Bai and Fa Hai fought fiercely, but Bai was defeated and had to retreat to the Broken Bridge 断桥. Later, thanks to Xiao Qing's efforts, Xu Xian was brought around, and he and Bai Suzhen were as attached to each other as before. Despite their reunion, however, Fa Hai came to separate the two by force and imprisoned Bai under the Leifeng Pagoda 雷峰塔. Thanks to Xiao Qing again, who, with the help of some heavenly generals, set fire to Leifeng Pagoda and finally rescued Bai Suzhen. Bai and Xu were finally reunited and lived a happy life thereafter.

This is one of the four major Chinese folk tales, and the play is primarily based on Feng Menglong's 冯梦龙 (1574—1646) short story titled *White Lady Eternally Imprisoned under the Leifeng Pagoda* 白娘子永镇雷峰塔 (*Bai niangzi yong zhen Leifeng ta*). Many other dramas also performed this play, but under different titles. In the 1950s, the Chinese dramatist Tian Han revised this traditional play with the current title and since then many Beijing operas have used Tian Han's version.

2. *Kunju* 昆剧

Fifteen Strings of Cash (Shíwǔ guàn 十五贯)

Originally a short story collected in Feng Menglong's *Xing shi heng yan* (醒世恒言 Stories to Awaken the World), the Qing dynasty playwright Zhu Suchen 朱素臣 adapted it into a *chuanqi* play under the title *Shuang xiong meng* 双熊梦. During the 1950s, this story was adapted into a *Kunju* play based on Zhu's *chuanqi* drama. Because of its huge success in performance around the country, the play in fact successfully revived the declining *Kunju* opera then. This story has also been adapted into several other dramas such as Beijing opera, *Yueju* opera 粤剧, *Qinqiang* 秦腔, and was even made into a film in 1956.

The story took place during the Ming dynasty. You Hulu 尤葫芦, a butcher, borrowed fifteen strings of cash and jokingly told his stepdaughter Su Xujuan 苏戌娟 that the money came from selling her to someone else as a maid. Taking this to be true, Su took to her heels in the dead of night to go to her relative, leaving You's door open. You had a neighbor by the name of Lou Ashu 娄阿鼠, who was a gambler. Hard up that night, Lou slipped into You's home, took his fifteen strings of cash and killed You to silence a witness. On the other hand, Xiong Youlan 熊友兰 also happened to carry fifteen strings of cash on his way to Changzhou 常州 on business. He met Su en route and went together. Runners from the court in search of the suspect saw the two of them together with fifteen strings of cash. Taking them as the suspects, the runners took them to the court in Wuxi County 无锡县. Without much investigation, the Magistrate of Wuxi 无锡知县 quickly imposed a death sentence on both Su and Xiong, and the Prefect of Changzhou 常州知府 and the Grand Coordinator of Jiangnan 江南巡抚 both endorsed the verdict. But Kuang Zhong 况钟, an officer in charge of executions, found the case suspicious and asked for a reprieve, but his appeal was initially denied by his superiors. Dauntless at their denial, Kuang Zhong nevertheless provided his arguments and asked for a reprieve of half a month at the risk of being dismissed from his office, should he fail. In the end, therefore, Kuang Zhong went to Wuxi himself in plain clothes and brought out the truth through his skillful and private investigations.

The Story of a Jade Hairpin (Yùzān jì 玉簪记)

This is a *chuanqi* play by the Ming dynasty playwright Gao Lian 高濂 (1573—1620), which dramatizes a romance between a Taoist nun called Chen Miaogu 陈妙姑 and a scholar named Pan Bizheng 潘必正. During the Jurchen invasion of the Song Empire, Chen Jiaolian 陈娇莲, a young girl,

was separated from her family when fleeing from the Jurchen troops. The master of a nearby Taoist temple took her as a nun and gave her a Taoist name Chen Miaogu. It happened that Pan Bizheng, the Taoist temple's master's nephew, was also staying there after he had failed in his civil service examination. After a few twists and turns, Pan and Chen fell in love and stayed together, but for fear of bringing a bad name to the temple, the master forced Pan to leave for another civil service examination in Lin'an 临安 without bidding farewell to Chen. Chen managed to catch Pan before his boat set out and gave him her jade hairpin as a token of her love. Pan in turn also gave Chen a jade fan pendant before he left. The play ends with Pan succeeded in his exam and the two were happily married thereafter.

The play is known for its elegance of diction, especially in its psychological depiction of young man and young woman in love. Its plot has been adapted into other dramas, too, and was very popular among the audience.

3. *Yueju/Shaoxing xi* 越剧/绍兴戏

Dream of the Red Chamber (Hóng lóu mèng 红楼梦)

This play is based on Cao Xueqin's 曹雪芹 (1724—1764) celebrated novel of the same title. It starts with Lin Daiyu's 林黛玉 arrival at Jia House 贾府 —her maternal grandma's home—and formed a close relationship with her cousin Jia Baoyu 贾宝玉 at first sight. In the Grandview Garden 大观园, the two of them found that they had the same interest; together they read privately the play *Xi xiang ji* 西厢记 (Romance of the Western Chamber), exchanged their thoughts freely with each other, and their love for each other, as a result, grew daily.

Jia Baoyu's father Jia Zheng 贾政 wanted his son to follow the feudal tradition of studying classics so as to obtain honor and high official positions for the family, which Baoyu just despised. In despair, Jia Zheng beat Baoyu black and blue, but in sympathy, Daiyu came to comfort him and yet misunderstood him. Sentimental Daiyu went to bury her flowers and composed her poems to disperse her desolation and depression. Overhearing Daiyu's recitation of her poems, Baoyu revealed his love to her.

On the other hand, for the benefit of the Jia House, Grandmother Jia 贾母 and the house manager Wang Xifeng 王熙凤 and others decided to have Baoyu marry Xue Baochai 薛宝钗, another cousin of Baoyu's. They played a trick on Baoyu: ostensibly they promised Baoyu that he was to marry Daiyu, but in secret they had him marry the heavily veiled Xue Baochai instead. Unfortunately, this secret was leaked out to Daiyu, which dealt a heavy blow to her and made her sicker and soon died of grief and anger after burning all her poem manuscripts. When Baoyu came to see the truth during his wedding ceremony, he ran out to see Lin Daiyu in spite of everything. At the bier of Daiyu's coffin, Baoyu cried with endless remorse and decided to leave his home to become a monk.

Sister Xianglin (Xiánglín sǎo 祥林嫂)

This is a modern *Yueju* play based on Lu Xun's 鲁迅 (1881—1936) short story "New Year's Sacrifice (zhùfú 祝福)." Sister Xianglin, a young widow, refused to remarry. She fled her mother-in-law's home and came to work as a maidservant for Fourth Old Master Lu 鲁四老爷. Several months later, she was seized, taken to the mountain and forced to marry He Laoliu 贺老六, a hunter. Their married life, however, turned out to be harmonious and she gave birth to a son named A Mao 阿毛. Their happy life did not last long, however, as He soon died of poverty and sickness while A Mao was taken away by a wolf. The grief-stricken Sister Xianglin had no alternative but to return to Master Lu's home to work. Shunned by the master and the local people this time because she was widowed twice, Sister Xianglin went to a nearby local temple to atone for her "crimes." But she was still kicked out of Lu's home and reduced to a beggar. Several years later, she died on a new year's eve amidst wind and snow.

The play was first written and directed by Nan Wei 南薇 (1921—1989) in 1946 and was put on stage the same year. It went through several revisions in the 1960s and 1970s. Because of its success on stage, it was made into a film twice in 1948 and in 1978.

4. *Huju* 沪剧

The Arhat Coin (Luóhàn qián 罗汉钱)

This play is based on modern writer Zhao Shuli's 赵树理 (1906—1970) short story "Registration for Marriage (dēngjì 登记)." In the early 1950s, arranged marriages were still very popular in China, especially in the countryside. It was very rare that young men and young women would get to love and marry each other all of their own accord. The play was set against such a background in 1950. Li Xiaowan 李小晚, a young man, and Zhang Aiai 张艾艾, a young girl, fell in love with each other in Zhangjiazhuang Village 张家庄. Xiaowan gave Aiai an arhat coin and the latter reciprocated with a ring as tokens of love. Their marriage proposal, however, met strong opposition from the village head who regarded young men and young women seeking their own partners as having bad reputations. Aiai's mother, nicknamed Little Moth (xiǎofēi'é 小飞蛾), discovered her daughter's arhat coin by chance and recalled her bitter days over twenty years ago when she was in love with a young man named Bao'an 保安 but in the end was forced by her parents to marry Carpenter Zhang 张木匠, her present husband. In order not to let her daughter to be subject to the villagers' reproach, rumors and slanders as she had been, Little Moth decided together with her husband to go to Dongwangzhuang Village 东王

庄 to find a suitor for Aiai. To her surprise, Little Moth overheard people there slandering her and she indignantly returned home without agreeing to the business. In the end, persuaded by Aiai's girl friend Yanyan 燕燕, she decided to marry Aiai to Xiaowan after her consultation with her husband.

The play script was published in 1952 and the play premiered on October 17 of the same year in Beijing. It was made into a film by Shanghai Film Studio in 1956.

5. *Pingju* 评剧

Flower As a Matchmaker (Huā wéi méi 花为媒)

Squire Wang Shao'an's 王少安 son Wang Junqing 王俊卿 and his cousin Li Yue'e 李月娥 felt affection for each other since their childhood. On Squire Wang's birthday, Li Yue'e came with her parents to celebrate the occasion and the two were overjoyed at seeing each other again. They exchanged handkerchiefs as tokens of love. Entrusted by Junqing's mother, however, Aunt Ruan 阮妈, a matchmaker, went to propose a marriage with Zhang Peng's 张朋 beautiful daughter Zhang Wuke 张五可. Junqing, however, insisted on marrying his cousin Li Yue'e and refused to marry Zhang Wuke. At Junqing's mother's bidding, therefore, Aunt Ruan went to Li Yue'e's father Li Maolin 李茂林 to propose a marriage but only met with his opposition on account of what he called a "cousin marriage." Meanwhile, anxiety over his now hopeless marriage with Yue'e made Junqing sick, while Zhang Wuke was in deep love with Junqing's personality and talent and looked forward to her union with him. To get out of this impasse, Aunt Ruan tried to have Junqing's cousin Jia Junying 贾俊英 go and see Wuke in his stead. At their meeting in her garden, Wuke was indignant at Junqing's rejection, but she fell in love with Junying nevertheless and gave him a red rose as her token of love. On the wedding day, Junqing got fully recovered on hearing his bride was Li Yue'e, whereas Zhang Wuke also happily married Jia Junying. All was well that ended well.

This is a classic *Pingju* play adapted from the story "Jisheng 寄生" in *Strange Stories from a Chinese Studio* (Liáo zhāi zhì yì聊斋志异) by Pu Songling 蒲松龄 (1630/1640—1715) of the Qing dynasty. The play was written by Cheng Zhaocai 成兆才(1874—1929), the founder of *Pingju*, and it went through several revisions after 1949. Because of its popularity, Changchun Film Studio made it into a film in 1963.

6. *Huang mei xi* 黄梅戏

Marriage with a Fairy (Tiānxiān pèi 天仙配)

Dong Yong 董永 was a poor farmer and yet a filial son. To get enough money in order to bury his deceased father, he sold himself to Squire Fu's family as a laborer. Moved by his filial piety, the Seventh Fairy 七仙女, Jade Emperor's 玉皇大帝 youngest daughter, descended to the earth in private and used a Chinese scholartree as a matchmaker to be married to Dong Yong. After their marriage, they came together to Fu's house to work and the Seventh Fairy used her admiring weaving skill to successfully shortened Dong Yong's original three-year indentured labor to just a hundred days. As the couple got ready to leave the Fu family for home after the expiration of their indenture, however, Jade Emperor ordered his daughter to return to the heaven at once, or else he would inflict a heavy punishment on Dong Yong. Already pregnant by now, the Seventh Fairy had to part very reluctantly with Dong Yong under that Chinese scholartree.

This legend was originally from Gan Bao's 干宝 (?—336) *Sou shen ji* 搜神记 (*In Search of the Supernatural*) and was adapted into the *huangmeixi* play by playwright Lu Hongfei 陆洪非 (1923—2007). Also known as *Bai ri yuan* 百日缘 (Marriage of a Hundred Days) or *Huai yin shu* 槐荫树 (The Chinese Scholartree), the play was made into a film in 1955.

7. *Yuju* 豫剧

Hua Mulan (花木兰)

During the Northern Wei dynasty (386—534), the northern Rouran 柔然 chief Tu Lizi 突力子 invaded the Chinese frontier areas and the court tried to enlist young men in defense of the country. An imperial order came to Hua's home to enlist Hua Hu 花弧, who had a son Hua Muli 花木力 and a daughter Hua Mulan 花木兰. Thinking her father was old and her younger brother Muli little, Mulan decided to replace her father in her brother's name to join the army. During the twelve years of service in the army, Mulan fought bravely and helped Marshal He 贺元帅 capture the tribal chief Tu Lizi by strategy, thus ending the war in the frontier area. Marshal He liked Mulan so much for her valor and her resourcefulness that he asked the court for her promotion and also would like to marry his own daughter to Mulan. Mulan, however, desired none of these and only asked for a good horse to carry her back home to see her parents and to change into her previous girl's attire. Meanwhile the court promoted Mulan to Secretarial Court Gentleman (shàngshūláng 尚书郎), and Marshal He, with a lot of presents, came himself to Mulan's home to see her. Surprised at seeing Mulan as a woman, Marshal He praised her as a great heroine.

This legend was first recorded in a *yuefu* 乐府 poem known as *Ballad of Mulan* 木兰辞. It was adapted into *Yuju* opera by Chen Xianzhang 陈宪章 (1917—2000), husband of the noted *Yuju* actress Chang Xiangyu 常香玉 (1923—2004). It was made into a film in 1956 with Chang Xiangyu acting as Hua Mulan.

8. *Jinju* 晋剧

Beating of a Princess (Dǎ jīnzhī 打金枝)

Emperor Daizong of the Tang dynasty 唐代宗 (726—779) married his daughter Princess Shengping 升平公主 to Guo Ai 郭暧, the sixth son of Guo Ziyi 郭子仪 (697—781), King of Fenyang 汾阳王. During Guo Ziyi's sixtieth birthday celebration, his children all went to celebrate except Princess Shengping, which caused a lot of talk among people. Guo Ai returned to the palace in anger and beat Princess Shengping, his wife now. In tears, Princess Shengping went to appeal to her parents, asking the emperor to penalize Guo Ai for what he did to her. Meanwhile Guo Ziyi had his son Guo Ai tied up and went together to the palace to admit his wrongdoing and asked the emperor for punishment. Emperor Daizong was magnanimous and instead of listening to his daughter, he granted an additional title to Guo Ai in praise of his action. Empress Shen 沈后 also comforted her son-in-law and chastised her daughter. After this, the young couple got rid of their previous resentment to each other and were as good to each other as before.

This is a classic *Jinju* play and was made into a film in 1955.

9. *Huaiju* 淮剧

The Female Judge (Nǚ shěn 女审)

Chen Shimei 陈世美 and Qin Xianglian 秦香莲 were husband and wife. Some time ago, Chen left home for the capital to sit for a civil service examination. Without his news for long, Qin took her son and daughter to the capital to look for Chen only to find that her husband had topped the list of all the candidates and had thereafter been married to a princess. Unwilling to be with Qin now, Chen refused to recognize his wife and children. Moreover, he even sent his guard to try to kill all three to silence witnesses. Qin Xianglian and her children fled the capital and met an old man who took them to Jieyuan Mountain 解元山 where he taught them martial skills.

Several years later, Qin and her children all became very skillful in martial arts, so they joined the army and repeatedly played a crucial role in defeating the invading enemies. Qin was thus appointed Commander-in-chief (dūdu 都督) for her valor and her intelligence. Returning to the capital, Qin met Chen, detained him and tried him herself with three charges: to be unfilial to his parents, to remarry without dissolving previous marriage, and to attempt a murder of his wife and children. Overconfident of his status as the emperor's son-in-law, however, Chen Shimei was defiant of the charges and even countercharged Qin of going against the emperor. At this time, Prime Minister Wang came, bringing an imperial edict ordering Qin to release Chen, and, at the same time, the imperial guards were also surrounding the commander-in-chief's residence, threatening Qin with armed forces. Driven beyond her forbearance, Qin killed Chen and fought their way out of the capital with her children and went back to Jieyuan Mountain.

This is a traditional *Huaiju* play and was made into a film in 1960.

10. *Puxian xi* 莆仙戏

Chun Cao Intrudes into the Court (Chūn Cǎo chuǎng táng 春草闯堂)

Prime Minister Li Zhongqin's 李仲钦 daughter Li Banyue 李半月, accompanied by her maid Chun Cao 春草, one day went on pilgrimage to Mount Hua 华山. En route, Banyue encountered sexual harassment by Wu Du 吴独, son of the Minister of Personnel 吏部尚书. Xue Meiting 薛玫庭, a righteous person who happened to be at the scene, went to help Banyue out of his sense of justice. In chaos, one of Xue's servants killed Wu Du. Counting on their high official status, Wu's mother tried to force Prefect Hu Jin 胡进 to club Xue to death. Concerned about Xue's safety, on the other hand, Chun Cao rushed to the court and, out of indignation at hearing what would happen to Xue, she intruded into the court to stop the execution. When asked about her reason for intrusion, Chun Cao, in a moment of desperation, started to call Xue the would-be son-in-law of the prime minister. Her reply deterred Hu Jin from beating Xue. When Chun Cao returned to the prime minister's residence, she persuaded Li Banyue with reason and succeeded in getting her to falsely acknowledge Xue as her husband. Li Zhongqin, the prime minister, however, was enraged at hearing of her daughter and Xue's intention and sent a letter to Prefect Hu Jin, ordering him to bring Xue's head to the capital for his reward. Chun Cao intercepted the letter from the messenger by strategy and changed its wording so that the letter became one that actually acknowledged the marriage instead. Overjoyed at the letter, Hu Jin quickly sent Xue Meiting as the prime minister's would-be son-in-law to the capital with much publicity. Meanwhile, the news spread far and wide so that officials in the capital and from all other provinces all sent in their presents to congratulate. Even the emperor had a horizontal and inscribed board brought in for the happy union. With all these, Prime Minister Li had to accept the situation and to make the best of it by acknowledging Xue as his son-in-law.

This play was adapted from a previous play titled *Zou lei ting* 邹雷霆 and was written by Chen Renjian 陈仁鉴 (1913—1995). It premiered in 1960.

11. *Hebei bangzi* 河北梆子

The Butterfly Cup (Húdié bēi 蝴蝶杯)

This is a play widely performed by various *bangzi* dramas. It originated from a Qing dynasty *luantan* 乱弹 drama of the *huabu* section 花部 and its author is unknown. The play was extremely popular in Shaanxi, Shanxi, Hebei, Henan provinces and other areas, with some of its scenes such as "Hidden in a Boat (Cáng zhōu 藏舟)" almost known to every household there. The first half of the play is also known as "Touring the Turtle Mountain (Yóu guī shān 游龟山)."

The story took place during Emperor Jiajing's reign 嘉靖 (1522—1566) of the Ming dynasty. General-in-chief of Hubei and Hunan Provinces 两湖总督 Lu Lin's 卢林 son Lu Shikuan 卢世宽 toured Guishan 龟山 (the Turtle Mountain) with his servants and, for a dispute with his purchase of fish, he killed the fisherman Hu Yan 胡彦. It happened that Jiangxia County Chief 江夏知县 Tian Yunshan's 田云山 son Tian Yuchuan 田玉川 was also touring Guishan, and, out of indignation at seeing the bully, he killed Lu Shikuan in turn. Lu Lin tried to capture his son's killer everywhere and Tian Yuchuan fled to a river bank and met Hu Yan's daughter Hu Fenglian 胡凤莲, who hid him in her boat and escaped the search. Out of his gratitude to Fenglian, Yuchuan gave his butterfly cup to Fenglian as a token of their engagement before he left.[1] Unable to find Tian Yuchuan, Lu Lin wanted to punish his father instead. Hu Fenglian rushed into the court to claim Tian Yunshan's innocence. Later Lu Lin was ordered to lead an expedition against the southern barbarians. He suffered some setbacks in battle and was besieged by enemies. At this moment, Tian Yuchuan by

1 A butterfly cup is a legendary porcelain wine cup. When wine was poured into the cup, one could see a butterfly dancing in the cup; but when wine was gone, the butterfly would disappear. Because of its unique feature, it was often regarded as a treasure or used as a token of love in ancient times. The technique for making such cups was long lost until 1979 when a real "butterfly cup" was discovered in a village in Shanxi province and people have succeeded in recreating such cups now.

chance went into exile there under an assumed name of Lei Quanzhou 雷全州 to avoid the court pursuit. He rescued Lu Lin there and helped him win the battle in the end. The latter married his daughter to Tian Yuchuan. The play ends with Tian Yuchuan marrying both wives.

12. *Chuanju* 川剧

The Golden Seal (Huángjīn yìn 黄金印)

Also titled *The Story of a Golden Seal* (Jīn yìn jì 金印记), this comedy originated from Su Fuzhi's 苏复之 Southern drama of the same title written early in the Ming dynasty.

The story took place during the Warring States Period (770—221 BC). When Su Qin 苏秦 (?—284 BC) was young, he was out of luck and repeatedly failed in the civil service examinations. As a result, he was subject to endless humiliations and insults from his family members as well as from his relatives and friends, so much so that even his own mother would be reluctant to call him her son and his sister-in-law would not regard him as her brother-in-law. In view of this, Su Qin resolved to study diligently day and night. He tied his hair with a rope to the beam to keep himself from dozing off when being tired from reading; sometimes he also prodded his thigh with an awl in order to continue studying assiduously. His painstaking efforts finally brought him honor. After years of work pushing for his strategy of what came to be known as "the vertical alliance of states" (hézòng 合纵) against the State of Qin, he was appointed the prime minister of six states then. When he returned to his old home in wealth and honor, his mother was sweeping the road he travelled and his sister-in-law knelt beside the road he passed by. Those who used to sneer at him or mock him in the past all came flattering him and toadying to him now. The play is a good satire on social snobbery.

13. *Hunan huagu xi* 湖南花鼓戏

The Woodcutter Liu Hai (Liú Hǎi kǎn qiáo **刘海砍樵**)

The story about the woodcutter Liu Hai 刘海 was already popular in Hunan during the Northern Song dynasty (960—1127) and towards the mid-Qing dynasty it evolved largely into what its drama version is today. The plot of the play is simple, but some of its songs are immensely popular not only in Hunan alone, but also throughout China.

According to the legend, Liu Hai was a filial son, who went to the mountains everyday to cut and gather firewood in order to make a living and to care for his elderly mother. An old fox spirit was cultivating itself in the mountain for years in order to become an immortal. Since its cultivation had already been halfway done, it assumed a human form as a woman with the name Hu Xiuying 胡秀英. Seeing Liu Hai coming to the mountain day in and day out, Hu Xiuying gradually fell in love with him for his diligence. She approached Liu one day and offered herself as his wife. But to her surprise, Liu Hai was reluctant to marry her because he told her that he was a poor woodcutter with an elderly mother for his support at home. But Hu Xiuying replied that she was willing to be with someone who was poor and was also willing to help take care of his mother. Therefore the two of them were happily married "with a willow tree as their matchmaker and the mountain as their witness."

14. *Qinqiang* 秦腔

Three Drops of Blood (Sān dī xiě **三滴血**)

This is a representative *Qinqiang* play by playwright Fan Zidong 范紫东 (1878—1954). It is based on a story in Ji Yun's 纪昀 (1724—1805) *Notes from Yuewei Thatched Cottage* (yuèwēi cǎotáng bǐjì 阅微草堂笔

记). It premiered in 1921, underwent a revision in 1958 and was made into a film by Xi'an Film Studio in 1960.

Hailing from Wutai County 五台县 in Shanxi 山西 Province, Zhou Renrui 周仁瑞 was doing business in Hancheng County 韩城县, Shaanxi 陕西 Province. His wife died soon after giving birth to two twins. Unable to raise two kids, Zhou Renrui sold the younger one to Li Sanniang 李三娘 as her son with the name she gave as Li Yuchun 李遇春, whereas Renrui himself raised the elder son whose name he gave as Zhou Tianyou 周天佑. Soon afterwards, Zhou Renrui lost money in his business, so he took his son back to his old home. Zhou Renrui's younger brother Zhou Renxiang 周仁祥, however, refused to recognize Tianyou as his nephew for fear that he might inherit his share of the family property later. So the brothers went to the court for a legal decision. County Magistrate Jin Xinshu 晋信书 was very pedantic, who used a method of blood dropping 滴血之法 (i.e., to get one drop of blood from each of the two persons in question into a basin to see if they dissolve into each other) to come to his verdict that Tianyou and Renrui did not have the father-son relationship. Hence the separation of the father and the son.

On the other hand, brought up by Sanniang, Yuchun grew up and became very fond of Sanniang's own daughter Li Wanchun 李晚春. Sanniang also wanted them to be married to each other, but before they could consummate their marriage, she died of illness. A local wealthy lord Ruan Ziyong 阮自用 had coveted Wanchun for long. So he used his condolences as an occasion to launch a law suit against Wanchun and Yuchun's union. Magistrate Jin Xinshu again used his method of blood dropping to separate Wanchun from Yuchun and decided that Wanchun should marry Ruan Ziyong instead. On her wedding night, however, Wanchun made Ruan Ziyong drunk and fled to seek Yuchun. Yuchun, on the other hand, on hearing Wanchun had already fled the Ruan house, also left his home in search of Wanchun. On his way, he met Zhou Tianyou by chance and both were surprised to see each other for their similar appearances. They quickly became good brothers, and together they joined the army and were soon appointed official positions for their meritorious services in the army.

Meanwhile, Zhou Renrui, who was looking for his son, and Mother Wang 王妈, who was Yuchun' s wet nurse, met on the road. Refusing to accept the court' s rulings, both went to question the county magistrate. Jin Xinshu then summoned Zhou Renxiang and his son to the court and used the same method of blood dropping for a test. Unexpectedly, the blood from the father and the son turned out to be indissolvable into each other, which dealt a heavy blow to Jin' s previous verdicts. At this time, the commander in Zhou Tianyou and Li Yuchun' s army at the brothers' request denounced Jin Xinshu for his repeated misjudgments. Wanchun also arrived at this time. Therefore father and son, husband and wife, were finally reunited, whereas Jin Xinshu was duly dismissed from his office.

15. *Yueju* 粤剧

Searching the Academy (Sōu shū yuàn 搜书院)

Written collectively by Yang Zijing 杨子静 (1913—2006), Mo Rucheng 莫汝城 (1926—2006) and Lin Xian' gen 林仙根, this play is based on a moving story said to have actually taken place during Emperors Yongzheng 雍正 and Qianlong 乾隆' s reigns (1722—1795) of the Qing dynasty. For its popularity, it was made into a film in 1956.

The story took place in Hainan Island 海南岛. The Regional Commander' s 镇台 daughter was flying a kite one day. Because its string broke, the kite escaped, fell into Qiongtai Academy 琼台书院 and was picked up by Zhang Yimin 张逸民, a student there. Cuilian 翠莲, the girl servant of the Regional Commander' s daughter, came to the academy to ask for the kite. Zhang Yimin wrote a poem on it before he gave it back to

Cuilian. Meanwhile, in their conversation with each other, Zhang felt very sympathetic towards Cuilian's suffering at the commander's house. On the other hand, seeing the poem on the kite, the commander's wife suspected that Cuilian might have had some dishonorable behavior, so she intended to give her to the Circuit Intendant 道台 as a concubine. Learning this, Cuilian dressed as a man and fled at night. On her way, Cuilian met Xie Bao 谢宝, the teacher at the academy, who took her to the academy after she told him of her misfortune. In the academy, Cuilian was happily reunited with Zhang.

With his servant girl on the run, the Regional Commander led his soldiers to the Academy in search of her. Seeing the situation critical, Zhang and Cuilian had to reveal the truth to Xie Bao, begging him for help. Moved by their true love towards each other, Xie Bao decided to save Cuilian by hiding her underneath his sedan. Going out to greet the Commander, Xie Bao refused to let his soldiers search the academy on account of the commander's failure to show him the order from the circuit intendant. With no alternative, the commander asked his soldiers to surround the academy while he himself and Xie Bao went together to see the circuit intendant. When they passed by a bamboo grove, Xie Bao intentionally stepped down from his sedan and started to walk with the commander to see the circuit intendant, leaving his sedan to his servants, who, after the two left, released Cuilian to find Zhang Yimin. Together they went away to a distant place to find their freedom.

16. *Er ren zhuan* 二人转

Meeting at the Lan Bridge (Lán qiáo huì 蓝桥会)

This play originated from an anecdote in *Zhuangzi* 庄子. The Yuan dynasty playwright Li Zhifu 李直夫 wrote a play titled *Weisheng Qinü yan*

Lanqiao 尾生期女淹蓝桥 (Weisheng and Qinü Swept from the Lan Bridge), which is lost. This tragedy about love, also titled *Shui man Lan qiao* 水漫蓝桥, is a representative play in *er ren zhuan* drama.

Lan Ruilian 蓝瑞莲 and Wei Kuiyuan 魏奎元 were good friends since they were little. When they grew up, they decided to stay together for the rest of their lives. However, Lan's father, greedy for money, forced her to marry an old but rich man Zhou Yujing 周玉景, in whose home, she suffered a great deal. One day, near a well from which Lan Ruilian was asked to draw water, she chanced to meet Wei. After Lan told Wei her immense suffering at Zhou's house after her marriage, they decided to meet at the Lan Bridge at midnight that day and to elope together elsewhere.

That night Wei Kuiyuan kept his promise and came first to the bridge. Instead of meeting his intended, however, he saw a big storm coming with torrents of water rushing down the mountain, which would soon sweep through the bridge. To let Lan know that he had been there, Wei quickly took off his clothes and tied them to a railing of the bridge before he was swept away by the flood. When Lan rushed to the spot after finishing her house chores, she only saw Wei's clothes. Knowing Wei had already been engulfed in the flood, she jumped into the water herself to keep her promise of following him for the rest of their lives.

Questions for Discussion:

1. What is the geographic distribution of dramas in contemporary China? What are the main differences between the dramas in the North and those in the South?
2. What are some of the favorable subjects or themes conveyed in traditional Chinese dramas?

Chapter Four

Chinese Drama and Chinese Culture

Chinese drama is a product of Chinese culture. To study Chinese drama, therefore, one must also study the various functions it is capable of in Chinese culture and Chinese society, the unique performing features of Chinese drama that have stemmed from Chinese culture, as well as the evolution of Chinese theater that is related in every way to both Chinese culture and the development of Chinese drama.

I. Social Functions of Chinese Drama

Since its birth, Chinese drama has been performed on two different occasions: one was the performance for emperors, court officials and certain wealthy families. Such performances of drama were sometimes by actors and actresses kept and trained by the imperial entertainment bureau or by the officials themselves, and sometimes by performers summoned from among local drama troupes. These performances were termed "official calls" (huàn guānshēn 唤官身) during the Yuan dynasty and have been called "home performances" (tánghuì堂会) since the late Qing dynasty. Naturally, on those occasions the audience was relatively small, their purpose for watching was generally simple—to celebrate certain occasions or to entertain some guests—and yet the small audience might have a strict demand on the quality of performances so that, generally speaking, drama performances on those occasions were serious, rather regulated, and with good quality. Another kind of performance was for commercial or public purposes, which would be conducted in public places, in temples, had a larger audience and catered to their likes and dislikes. Because members of the audience might come from all walks of life with their diverse purposes for watching, such performances might not be able to guarantee their quality, for the actors and actresses there might have to follow the swings of mood and interests from the audiences in order to survive. As a result, the performances might be less regulated, noisy, and it is hard to keep the locations for such performances always in good order.

In our discussion of social functions of Chinese drama below, we will take into consideration both occasions, particularly the latter, since commercial or public performances were by and large the primary form of performance for drama in its evolution and many social functions are associated with this kind of performance.

1. As a Tool for Entertainment

Although drama might not have been created specifically for entertainment, since it is still a controversial issue regarding the origin of Chinese drama as was discussed in Chapter One, one of its main functions has obviously been related in various times to entertainment, whether it was the entertainment for emperors and officials or that for ordinary people. *The Gazetteer of Songjiang Prefecture* 松江府志 has recorded an interesting anecdote that the noted physician Qin Jingming 秦景明 of the Ming dynasty was once called upon to see Prefect Fang who was sick. Qin went accompanied by two actors. Upon arrival, Qin first let the two actors sing two songs. Hearing the beautiful songs, the prefect's mood changed and his appearance turned better. Then Qin diagnosed and prescribed medication and soon Prefect Fang got well.[1] This is perhaps the best example showing vividly the entertaining effect of theatrical songs. However, is this always the case? What other kinds of entertainment has drama provided?

In its mass-consumed form, performance of drama is a social activity and it has a direct, immediate, and powerful impact on its audience. Therefore, the entertainment and the influence that drama provides will be more than what the mere content of the drama presents. In studying the social functions or the influence and entertaining effects of Chinese drama, therefore, one has to consider the various performing environments in which the theatrical activities were carried out. In the past, Chinese drama was often performed either at some festivals or during slack seasons in farming when people gathered from far and near to relax and to have enjoyment from the shows. Besides, as was customary of the people then, they also took the opportunity to communicate with one another, to socialize or even to conduct businesses. Naturally, drama performances under such circumstances would often be carried out amidst a hubbub of voices, and performers and musicians, as a result, had to raise their voice or the volume of their musical instruments in order to be heard. That is the reason why Chinese drama would sound so noisy to a modern ear that is unaccustomed to its performing circumstances. And because of these circumstances, one can also imagine that the performing sites might frequently become a locale where certain less honorable behavior or activities such as verbal arguments, name calling, flirtation or even theft might sometimes occur. Obviously all of these went on under the name of entertainment. Also, since audiences came from all walks of life with different backgrounds, some may have come with bad taste, which would then encourage some drama troupes to put on shows in poor taste or plays

---

1 See Jiang Xingyu 蒋星煜, "Foreword," *Yi xi dai yao* 以戏代药 (Shanghai: Shanghai yuandong chubanshe, 2007), p.1.

that may present lewd comment or suggestive behavior so as to cater to their taste. This sometimes formed a vicious circle, for those performers were generally looked down upon in society and drama itself was also widely regarded as a literary genre not worth serious attention by the literati. The vulgar performances only made those performers and dramas more despised in society. The following remarks by Hu Yin 胡寅 (1098—1156) of the Song dynasty may be typical of the literati's view on drama then:

> Songs and song suites [of drama] 词曲 (cíqǔ) were the trivial derivatives of the ancient *yuefu* ballads;[1] the ancient *yuefu* ballads were the crooked form of poetry; poetry came from *Li sao* and *Chu* ci,[2] whereas *Li sao* changed the intentions of the *feng* and *ya* genres of poetry,[3] becoming resenting *and* pressing, sad *and* hurting.[4] They all come from one's emotions and yet they differ in how they end with decency. Those songs are called *qu* 曲 (songs) because they fully express one's emotions, but they are short of what might be called *quyi* 曲艺 (art of songs), and are farther away from what might be termed *quli* 曲礼 (decency for songs). But for those whose essays are bold and uninhibited, they would seldom miss conveying their ideas like this and yet they would destroy what they have created by saying that these

1 *Yuefu* 乐府 ballads referred to some anonymous folk songs of the Han dynasty (206 BC—220 AD). Those folk songs took their name from a government office called *yuefu, i.e.,* music bureau, which was set up around 120 BC by Emperor Wu of Han 汉武帝. One of the duties of this office was to collect folk songs around the country. Hence the term *yuefu* for those early folk songs.

2 *Li sao* 离骚 (Encountering Sorrows), a long lyric poem by the famous poet Qu Yuan 屈原(fl. c. 300 BC), whose poems and a few others' poems following his style were collected by Liu Xiang 刘向 (c. 77BC—6 BC) of the Western Han dynasty under the title *Chu ci* 楚辞 (Songs of the Chu). Hence the term designated for such a genre of poems.

3 *Feng* 风 (airs) and *ya* 雅 (odes) are two genres in the earliest collection of Chinese poems titled *Shi jing* 诗经 (Classic of Poetry), which contains poems of three genres. The third genre is called *song* 颂 (eulogies).

4 Confucius advocated the idea of the mean for virtually everything. Therefore anything that goes to the extreme is considered inappropriate. Cf. "The Master said, The GuanJu ode—joy, but not excessive; sadness, but not to the point of injury." *The Analects of Confucius.* trans. Burton Watson. (New York: Columbia University Press, 2007), p. 29.

were just unconventional and unrestrained stuff for fun.[1]

Because the literati themselves did not regard their writing of theatrical songs as something worth passing down from generation to generation, what they wrote were simply what they felt, which could readily be scratched off. One may not want to find fault with such an attitude for writing, but the end result of such writing was sometimes quite surprising: for instance, one of the salient characteristics of Yuan *zaju* drama is exactly literati's uninhibited pouring forth of their innermost feelings towards society, for many of them wrote without scruples and said what they felt and what they wanted. That is why Wang Guowei 王国维 (1877—1927) would call Yuan *zaju* drama "the most natural literature"[2] and that may also account for the fact that the majority of the Yuan *zaju* plays are not extant.

Therefore, the entertaining function of Chinese drama has resulted in mixed situations as illustrated above. While drama has certainly provided entertainment for various people, the very entertainment itself was joyful and pleasurable for some but may be immoral and licentious for others. That is why for centuries there have always been officials and scholars who have continuously called for a ban on the so-called "immoral" plays (yínxì 淫戏). The following memo presented by Chen Chun 陈淳 (1153—1217), a student of Zhu Xi 朱熹 (1130—1200), to the then imperial minister Fu Bocheng 傅伯成 (1143—1226) is just one of many attempts by the conservatives to stop the theatrical activities which apparently thrived during the Song dynasty:

> This fall, since the lunar seventh and eighth months, many villages in the country are swept up by this type of activities [*i.e.*, drama performances]. They are called plays and entertainments, but in fact

1 Hu Yin, "Xiang xianglin jiu bian ji hou xu 向薌林酒边集后序," in *SKQS*, 1137:547.

2 Wang Guowei, *Song Yuan xiqu kao* 宋元戏曲考 in Yao Ganming 姚淦铭 & Wang Yan 王燕, eds. *Wang Guowei wenji* 王国维文集, 4 vols. (Beijing: Zhongguo wenshi chubanshe, 1997), 1: 389.

they are extremely harmful. First, people are being wantonly fleeced. Second, working people are turned into idle spectators. Third, young men are tempted to become playboys without proper ambitions. Fourth, young women are lured out of their boudoirs and instilled with improper ideas. Fifth, greedy people begin their evil thought of robbery. Sixth, young people are encouraged to resort to violence. Seventh, scandals are created in which unmarried people elope after casual meetings. Eighth, county and prefecture courts are inundated with lawsuits; some even fabricate charges out of some personal grudge and commit murder without any scruples.

These plays and entertainments give birth to so many social evils that, if not outlawed, they can easily sway people and make trouble for the righteous ones running the government...[1]

Obviously, drama can entertain in various ways, but when used as a tool for entertainment, it has often met with wary eyes.

2. As Part of Ritual Services

Drama was often performed during some ritual activities. In fact, many scholars have argued that Chinese drama evolved from ritual services. As the religious rites in which shamans or exorcists impersonated deities or spirits in their ecstatic chanting and dancing turned from entreating and entertaining spirits to performing for and entertaining people, the earliest form of drama was born.[2] That is why there are not only plays which are

1 Chen Chun, *Bei xi da quan ji* 北溪大全集,*juan* 47, in *SKQS*, 1168: 876a. English translation is based on Faye Chunfang Fei, ed. and trans. *Chinese Theories of Theater and Performance from Confucius to the Present* (Ann Arbor: University of Michigan Press, 1999), p. 31.

2 See Wang Guowei, *Song Yuan xiqu kao* 宋元戏曲考, in *Wang Guowei wenji* 王国维文集, 1: 309-310; Huang Tianji 黄天骥 & Kang Baocheng 康保成 eds., *Zhongguo xiju xingtai yanjiu* 中国戏剧形态研究, p. 8; also Piet van der Loon 龙彼得, "Zhongguo xiju yuan yu zongjiao yidian kao 中国戏剧源于宗教仪典考," trans. Wang Qiugui & Su Youzhen, *Zhong wai wenxue* 中外文学 7.12 (1979): 158-181.

often performed during religious rituals (e.g., the so-called *nuo* dramas 傩戏 that feature masked dancing, various plays about Guan Yu 关羽 such as *Guan Yunchang da po Chi You* 关云长大破蚩尤 or plays about the story of Mulian 目连戏) but also ritual scenes inserted in a number of plays such as in Scene Sixteen of the Southern Song dynasty *nanxi* play *Zhang Xie zhuangyuan* 张协状元 (Zhang Xie the Top Graduate), where Li Dagong held a prayer for the deity's verdict on Zhang Xie and the poor girl's marriage, or in the first act of the Yuan *zaju* play *Taohua nü* 桃花女 (The Peach Flower Girl), in which the Taoist ritual of praying for the Plough 拜北斗仪礼 was introduced.[1] One should be aware that a variety of different plays could actually be performed on the same occasion to achieve very much the same effect. Likewise, a single play can be performed on different occasions to achieve different effects. So the performance context is really the key to the effects of theatrical performances.

In 1986, a book titled *Heirloom Booklet Containing Musical Keys of Forty Songs Used in a Program for Spirit-Welcoming Rituals* 迎神赛社礼节传簿四十曲宫调 was discovered in an individual farmer's home in Lucheng county of Shanxi province 山西潞城县, which offers us some valuable information about theatrical performances for ritual services. According to researches on this booklet, quite a lot of plays originated from Yuan *zaju* or Southern dramas were performed during the spirit-welcoming ritual services and since these performances were actually part of the rituals themselves, they involved numerous village people as performers. Some ritual service performance and dance may involve more than a thousand villagers to participate.[2] What is more, the village performers apparently

1 See Rong Shicheng 容世诚, *Xiqu renleixue chutan: yishi, juchang yu shequn* 戏曲人类学初探:仪式、剧场与社群 (Guilin: Guangxi shifan daxue chubanshe, 2003), p. 2; Ni Caixia 倪彩霞, *Daojiao yishi yu xiju biaoyan xingtai yanjiu* 道教仪式与戏剧表演形态研究 (Guangzhou: Guangdong gaodeng jiaoyu chubanshe, 2005), pp. 65-80.

2 Feng Junxie 冯俊杰, "Sai she: xiju shi de xunli 赛社:戏剧史的巡礼," in *Zhonghua xiqu* 中华戏曲 3 (1987), p. 191.

used the performance as a semi-real-life ritual, for in the performance of the play *Wu guan zhan jiang* 五关斩将, for example,

> Riding his horse, Guan Gong 关公 passed through five fortresses and killed six enemy generals. This was not performed on a single stage. Instead, Guan rode his horse galloping through alleys and villages, with one stage changing to another as he passed through different fortresses. The play did not end until he rode onto all five different stages one after another [which were located among various villages].[1]

Apparently the function of such plays is generally to ward off evil spirits from a village or a location so that people there will be blessed for life in the days to come.

On the other hand, plays are often staged on the occasions of festivities, during a temple fair (miàohuì庙会) or during the opening of a Buddhist or Taoist temple. They may also be performed when there is need for rain amidst prolonged drought, for funeral services, for birthday celebration, or to pray for wish-fulfillment, etc. And on all these occasions, specific plays are selected to perform, because each has its own specific ritual purposes to fulfill.[2] For example, Zhu Youdun' s 朱有燉 (1379—1439) *Yaochihui baxian qingshou* 瑶池会八仙庆寿 (Banquet at the Jasper Lake to Celebrate the Eight Immortals' Longevity) was often performed to celebrate longevity, whereas plays about the story of Mulian 目连戏 were a favorite for praying for wish-fulfillment.

From the perspective of performers, on the other hand, they often have some religious rites of their own profession as well. When they first come to a new location to perform or when a new theater is built, for example,

---

1 Zhang Zhizhong 张之中, "Duixi, yuanben yu zaju de xingqi 队戏、院本与杂剧的兴起," in *Zhonghua xiqu* 3 (1987), p. 160.

2 See Ni Caixia 倪彩霞, *Daojiao yishi yu xiju biaoyan xingtai yanjiu* 道教仪式与戏剧表演形态研究, p. 152.

they may often perform some rituals variously called *po tai* 破台 (opening of the stage), *ji tai* 祭台 (sacrificial rite for the stage), *jing tai* 净台 (cleansing of the stage) or *zhen tai* 镇台 (control of the stage). And on the last day of their performance, they may also hold some specific rituals called *sao tai* 扫台 (cleanup of the stage) or *song tai* 送台 (farewell to the stage).[1] Besides, in previous times, in the beginning of or during a theatrical performance, there often occurred some dumb shows called *tiao jia guan* 跳加官 (jump with promotion), in which "an actor with a tablet in his hand came onto the stage in an official robe, wearing a white mask. He didn't utter any word but only jumped to the beat and rhythm of the musical instruments as if he were unable to control his excitement. Slowly, he unfolded to the audience a scroll on which was written the words *tian gong ci fu* 天宫赐福 (Blessings from the Heavenly Palace) or other blessings. Upon exiting the stage, he pointed at the sun with his hand."[2] These rituals are apparently for performers to drive away evil spirits and to pray for deities' blessing on their forthcoming performances. As can be seen now, a regular theatrical performance may have such complex ritual functions.

During the Yuan and Ming dynasties, there were also quite a lot of what are commonly called *du tuo ju* 度脱剧 (religious conversion plays). Roughly, those plays of the Yuan dynasty account for ten percent of all Yuan *zaju* plays. The common plot pattern of those plays is usually that a Taoist master finds someone on earth who is meant for a divine existence, so he goes to convert him or her. His initial efforts at conversion, however, are almost always met with tenacious resistance until he puts the person to jeopardy or even death, which then forces the person to see the futility of all worldly comfort and pursuits and henceforth he decides to follow the master in the end. Scholars have interpreted those plays differently. Liao

---

1 Please see a detailed list of such rituals and what is performed for each in Ni Caixia 倪彩霞, *Daojiao yishi yu xiju biaoyan xingtai yanjiu* 道教仪式与戏剧表演形态研究, pp. 182-187.

2 Piet van der Loon 龙彼得, "*Zhongguo xiju yuan yu zongjiao yidian kao* 中国戏剧源于宗教仪典考," p. 172.

Ben 廖奔 and Liu Yanjun 刘彦君, for instance, look specifically at Ma Zhiyuan's 马致远 conversion plays as "his disappointment with the reality rather than his yearning for paradise."[1] Issei Tanaka 田仲一成 in Japan, on the other hand, regards those conversion plays as belonging to what he calls "a kind of plays of celebration 庆祝剧," which were performed during ritual services for individuals of some rich families,[2] whereas Wilt Idema, a Dutch-American sinologist, considers those plays "evolved from funeral rites reenacting death and resurrection, which were intended to guide the soul of the deceased to paradise."[3] If those plays were indeed performed during those ritual services, then they would certainly have functioned as part of a religious ritual.

One of the elements in most of those conversion plays seems to puzzle many a scholar, *i. e.*, the explicit violence involved in the process of a conversion. For example, in Ma Zhiyuan's *Ma Danyang san du Ren Fengzi* 马丹阳三度任风子, the butcher Ren Fengzi finally decides to follow the Taoist master Ma Danyang by abandoning his wife and dashing his own child to death against the ground. This heartless behavior to one's wife and child was certainly meant to show Ren's resolution in breaking with all worldly affairs, including all one's loved family members, which was in keeping with the doctrine of the Taoist Quanzhen sect 全真教派. In fact, although not without any theatrical exaggerations, these agonies, jeopardy or even death that the initiated had to go through were merely designed to test his will much as in modern day university fraternities in the West, an initiated member often needs to undergo a period of excruciating tests before he can be inducted into the fraternity as a full member.

Chinese drama's ritual function is recognized by all, whether it is

1 Liao Ben & Liu Yanjun, *Zhongguo xiqu fazhan shi* 中国戏曲发展史 4 vols. (Taiyuan: Shanxi jiaoyu chubanshe, 2000), 2: 275.

2 Issei Tanaka 田仲一成, *Chugoku engekishi* 中国演劇史 (Tokyo: Tokyo daigaku shuppankai, 1998), p. 132.

3 Wilt L. Idema, *The Dramatic Oeuvre of Chu Yu-Tun (1379-1439)* (Leiden: E. J. Brill, 1985), p. 67.

called superstition or deemed a folk custom, and there have been numerous imperial and official bans on performances involving certain deities such as the Four Heavenly Kings 四大天王 (*si da tian wang*) or plays about Buddhism or certain saints and sages.[1]

Why should imperial authorities bother about such theatrical involvement with ritual services? For one thing, rites and rituals have been an important national business in Chinese history because they were supposed to establish communications with heaven. As "the son of heaven", therefore, an emperor himself would annually preside over several religious rites to pray for the prosperity of the country or for the everlasting imperial power, etc. The right to conduct rituals, as a result, was not something that the imperial authorities would like to share with others, for they regarded it largely as an imperial right, especially if a ritual may affect a large population. With ritual rights in hand, an emperor felt he could be a spokesman for heaven's mandate and hence be in a better position to govern his people. Secondly, those dramas performed during religious rituals could doubtlessly also invoke superstitions or create disorder or even injuries and deaths when a crowd involved became ecstatic and got easily swayed by people with ulterior motive. According to some historical record, the Yuan court enlisted 260,000 corvée laborers for trying to bring the Yellow River under control in 1350. Among the laborers there was one named Han Shantong 韩山童 (d. 1351), who, seeing his fellow laborers all harbored a lot of grievances and anger because of official corruption at the time, secretly carved out of a stone a man with only one eye and on his back was inscribed these words: "Do not ignore the stone man for having only one eye, for once this thing is discovered, the whole world will be turned upside down 莫道石人一只眼，此物一出天下反."[2] Han then buried

---

1 Wang Liqi 王利器 ed., *Yuan Ming Qing sandai jinhui xiaoshuo xiqu shiliao* 元明清三代禁毁小说戏曲史料, expanded ed. (Shanghai: Shanghai guji chubanshe, 1981), pp. 4-5, 19 & 35.

2 Ye Ziqi 叶子奇, *Cao mu zi* 草木子 (Beijing, Zhonghua shuju, 1959), p. 50.

the stone man underneath the path where the laborers were to open it up the next day, and the result was quite as expected: "[People] who dug up and discovered the stone man were all astonished and awe-stricken so that they informed one another and started to plan an uprising."[1] This was how the Red Turban Army (hóngjīnjūn 红巾军), one of the major peasant uprising forces towards the end of the Yuan dynasty, got started and it evidently showed the importance of superstition and the manipulation of it for political purposes. Drama as a form of popular entertainment certainly played an important role in spreading a variety of myths and superstitions with its ritual performances, and would therefore doubtlessly be subject to various official bans.

3. As an Educational, Political and Ideological Tool

Chinese literature is often didactic, moral and utilitarian, and there has been no advocation of *l' art pour l' art* for Chinese literary creation. As early as the Han dynasty (206 BC—220 AD), *the Great Preface to the Classic of Poetry* 诗大序 already said of the *feng* 风 genre of poems in the *Classic of Poetry*[2] that "the superiors use the *feng* [genre of poems] to transform the inferiors, whereas the inferiors use the *feng* [genre of poems] to satirize the superiors."[3] This later came to be known as "a theory of beautification and thorn (měi cì shuō 美刺说)" in literary criticism, by which is meant that literature is to be used either to laud virtuous people and their conducts or to satirize unrighteous persons and their behavior. Hence the proposition that "literature should convey moral message (wén yǐ zǎi dào 文以载道)" as put forward by Zhou Dunyi 周敦颐 (1017—

1 Ye Ziqi 叶子奇, *Cao mu zi* 草木子., p. 51.

2 What is contained in the *feng* section of the *Classic of Poetry* are all local folk songs, whose authors are not known now.

3 Ruan Yuan 阮元 ed., *Shi san jing zhu shu* 十三经注疏, 2 vols. (Beijing: Zhonghua shuju, 1980), 1: 271b.

1073) of the Song dynasty has become an important tenet in literary creativity,[1] and that is why the noted Japanese sinologist Yoshikawa Kōjirō 吉川幸次郎 (1904—1980) pointed out in his *History of Chinese Literature* 中国文学史 that one of the seven prominent features of Chinese literature was its "strong attachment to politics."[2]

Although often used for entertainment and for ritual services, Chinese drama, as part of Chinese literature, has also been regarded as a great tool for various educational and political purposes. For example, there often have been jesting or comic scenes (chā kē dǎ hùn 插科打诨) in Chinese dramas, whose purpose is generally to enliven the theatrical atmosphere. However, since this practice has evolved from the tradition by ancient entertainers like You Meng 优孟 who remonstrated with kings and officials by his comic talks, those scenes of buffoonery could often contain satire or veiled criticism against officials and the regime to which they belong. A well-known example is from Guan Hanqing's 关汉卿 *zaju* play *Dou E yuan* 窦娥冤 (Injustice to Dou E) written during the Yuan dynasty (1271—1368). In Act II of the play, there is the following scene:

> (Enter the Prefect with his attendant)
> Prefect: I am a better official than others.
> Whoever comes to file a suit will be asked to pay in gold and silver.
> If my superior comes to investigate,
> I will stay at home, pretending to be sick.
> ...
>
> (Enter Donkey Zhang dragging Dou E)
> Donkey Zhang: I've got a lawsuit to file! I've got a lawsuit to file!

---

1 See Zhou Dunyi, *Zhou Zi tong shu* 周子通书 (Shanghai: Shanghai guji chubanshe, 2000), p. 39.
2 Yoshikawa Kōjirō 吉川幸次郎, *Chūgoku bungakushi* 中国文学史, (Tokyo: Iwanami shuten, 1974), p. 25.

Attendant: Bring it here.

(Both Donkey Zhang and Do E kneel. So does the prefect)

Prefect: Please rise.

Attendant: Your Honor, he is the plaintiff. Why do you kneel to him?

Prefect: Don't you know that those who come to file a suit are like my parents who pay for my food and clothing...[1]

This is apparently a scene of buffoonery sandwiched between two serious scenes of an attempted murder and a court judgment for a comic relief. What is significant here is the fact that the prefect, presumably a figure of authority, becomes the butt of laughter (by kneeling to his plaintiff) and the judicial system becomes the object of attack (by revealing to the audience that it aims at money and court investigation cannot really bother the judge). All these are carried out not through open criticism, nor by an explicit tone of disapproval, but rather via an indirect and comic performance that reduces what is commonly regarded as solemn and dignified to a degree of familiarity and ridiculousness. Hence contempt, satire and criticism leveled at the Yuan court.

Because of the publicity of theatrical performances, drama is also sometimes used to publicize evildoings of some corrupt officials and evil people in history, serving both to expose and to curb such social evils. Zhou Mi's 周密 (1232—1298) *Gui xin za shi* 癸辛杂识 recorded such a case in Wenzhou 温州 of Zhejiang province during the early Yuan dynasty.

A monk by the name of Zu Jie 祖杰 accumulated a lot of ill-gotten wealth, with which he bribed and associated with officials in the capital. He lived in Jiangxin temple, a magnificent Buddhist temple. One day, a person named Yu Sheng 俞生, not able to bear the burden of corvee duties, came to be a monk in the temple. It happened that the local prefect was a close friend of Zu Jie's and asked Zu to look for beautiful women. Zu found one

1 Zang Jinshu 臧晋叔 ed., *Yuan qu xuan* 元曲选, 4 vols. (Beijing: Zhonghua shuju, 1958), 4: 1507.

but, because of her beauty, he kept her in his temple for his own and made her pregnant soon. With people gossiping, he then asked Yu's son to marry the woman, but he kept going to her afterwards. Unable to bear neighbors' mockery, Yu took her elsewhere to avoid Zu. At this, Zu flared up and sent his servants to provoke Yu by felling the trees on their graveyard. Yu sued Zu at the local court but only got clubbed instead, and he sued him again to the investigatory official, but Zu had people place weapons in Yu's home and then falsely incriminated Yu by accusing him of hiding weapons instead, so that Yu was flogged again. Unable to swallow the injustice, Yu intended to go to the capital to seek justice. Knowing this, Zu sent dozens of burly men who captured all of Yu's family members. They sent them on a boat to a remote place where they had them all drowned. When this came to be known and the officials summoned Zu for a hearing, it took Zu more than two months to come to the court. And even when Zu was put in custody, he still refused to plead guilty and was busy sending people with money to provincial and capital officials for help. "Bystanders were indignant at this case and, lest he get away with it, they wrote a play to publicize this case. Afterwards because Zu's crime was known to all, he was executed in the jail five days before an order of pardon arrived."[1] This case truly shows the important role a drama has played in bringing a criminal to justice. Unfortunately the play itself is not extant.

On the other hand, plays were often used by emperors and imperial courts in praise of an emperor's reign or to eulogize the prosperity of the country in front of foreign guests whom they entertained. Many plays in praise of flowers by Zhu Youdun of the Ming dynasty, for example, were often used for this purpose. "In his prefaces to these plays, he [Zhu Youdun] repeatedly stressed that only in times of Great Peace could plants

1 Zhou Mi 周密, *Gui xin za shi* 癸辛杂识, in *SKQS*, 1040: 133b-135a. For a slightly different account of the same case, one can also refer to Liu Xun 刘壎's "Yi quan zhuan 义犬传" in his *Shui yun cun gao* 水云村稿, *juan* 4, in *SKQS*, 1195: 371-373.

attain their greatest beauty and be fully appreciated. In this way, the appreciation of flowers comes to mean the celebration of Great Peace due to the reigning emperor's bounty."[1] A greater number of other plays are actually in praise of virtues and morals of various kinds. About a half of the *nanxi* (Southern dramas) plays dramatize the issues related to marriage. The five most well-known *nanxi* plays of the Yuan dynasty *Pi pa ji* 琵琶记, *Jing chai ji* 荆钗记, *Liu Zhiyuan baitu ji* 刘知远白兔记, *Bai yue ting* 拜月亭 and *Sha gou ji* 杀狗记, for instance, are all about marriage or family ethics, which either extol the unswerving love between young men and young women through the ups and downs in their lives (the first four plays), or teach the importance of love and respect between family members (the last play). We can perhaps briefly trace the evolution of one of the earliest *nanxi* plays about Zhao Zhennü赵贞女 in order to illustrate the role of edification that Chinese drama played in its performances.

The *nanxi* play *Zhao Zhennü* or *Zhao Zhennü and Cai Erlang* 赵贞女蔡二郎 must have been a very popular play during the Song period, for the noted poet Lu You 陆游 (1125—1210) thus spoke of the performance of the story in one of his poems:

> In Zhao's Village amidst setting sun and ancient willows,
> A blind old man is performing by a drum.
> Who could judge things right or wrong after one's death?
> For one hears talking about Cai Zhonglang all over the village.[2]

The original *nanxi* play of *Zhao Zhennü* is not extant, but its plot is known: Scholar Cai Bojie 蔡伯喈 went to the capital for a civil service examination after his marriage with a virtuous woman Zhao Wuniang (赵五娘). When he succeeded in his examination and was appointed an official

1 W. L. Idema, *The Dramatic Oeuvre of Chu Yu-tun (1379—1439)*, p. 94.

2 Lu You陆游, *Jian nan shi gao jiaozhu* 剑南诗稿校注, annot. Qian Zhonglian 钱仲联, 8 vols. (Shanghai: Shanghai guji chubanshe, 1985), 4:2193.

position, he married the daughter of a high official and abandoned his former wife Wuniang. Meanwhile, hearing no news from Cai for long, Wuniang, with the musical instrument *pi-pa* on her back, went begging all the way to the capital to look for her husband. On seeing Wuniang's arrival, Cai not only refused to recognize her as his wife, but also sent one of his horses to kick and tread her to death. As a retribution for his ingratitude and heartlessness, Cai ended up being hit by lightening amidst a thunderstorm. This is apparently a play condemning a scholar's faithless betrayal of his former wife after his success in his civil service examinations, which may have been a popular occurrence at the time. Because of its popularity and influence, the play may have hurt the image of some officials who may have had similar experience as Cai Bojie in the play and, as a result, the play was officially banned for a time.[1] Later, during the late Yuan and early Ming dynasties, the playwright Gao Ming 高明 drastically revised the play and wrote his famous *Pi pa ji* 琵琶记 that dramatizes a filial Cai Bojie with conscience, who, instead of being a villainous husband faithlessly abandoning his wife, found a happy ending in marrying a new wife and welcoming back his old one, an ending that seemed to please everyone. The playwright boasted at the beginning of his play: "If a tale does not concern itself with moral ethics, it will not be a good tale, even if it is well-written."[2] Indeed, Gao Ming's revised play propagates the ideas of filiality to one's parents, loyalty to one's superiors and faithfulness to one's loved ones, in a word, "a completely loyal and completely filial Cai Bojie 全忠全孝蔡伯喈."[3] Because of the moral influence of the play, legend has it that when someone presented a copy of the play to Zhu Yuanzhang 朱元璋 (1328—1398), the founding emperor of

---

1 See Zhu Yunming 祝允明, "Wei tan 猥谈" in *Shuo fu xu* 说郛续, *juan* 46, in Tao Zongyi 陶宗仪, et. al. eds, *Shuo fu san zhong* 说郛三种, 10 vols. (Shanghai: Shanghai guji chubanshe, 1988), 10: 2099a.

2 Qian Nanyang 钱南杨, ed., *Yuan ben pi pa ji jiao zhu* 元本琵琶记校注 (Shanghai: Shanghai guji chubanshe, 1980), p.1.

3 *Ibid.*

the Ming dynasty, he remarked after reading it: "The Five Classics and the Four Books are cloth, silk, beans and grain that every household has,[1] whereas Gao Ming's *Pi pa ji* is like delicacies from land and sea that a wealthy and noble family cannot go without."[2] From the official ban to official promotion, the power and moral functions of the same tale but with different revisions are too obvious to be missed here.

Of course, depending upon the values of a society at a time, the reception of a drama is often subject to swings of ideology. But no matter what situations, a drama's function and force are not negligible, as seen previously. The potential influence or the edifying functions of popular dramas on culture and ideology are actually often noticed and sometimes even consciously made use of in history. From this perspective, the constant official bans on certain dramas and promotion of others in history may be regarded as a constant tension between the official ideology and other thoughts that the official ideology tries to suppress. Ming dynasty scholar Tao Shiliang 陶石梁 once remarked that

> Today's drama functions the same as the music of the ancient times. Every time when there was a theatrical performance, even women and children would often be in tears and could not control their emotions when they saw filial sons, respectful brothers, loyal courtiers, righteous persons who went through trials and tribulations, wandering about and encountering various hardships. When one looked around at this moment, everyone else was the same. This is exactly what made [the drama] moving in such a sincere and quick manner. Compared with old scholars sitting on a tiger skin and talking about classic doctrines, or old monks climbing on the dais preaching Buddhist

---

1 The Five Classics refer to *The Classic of Poetry*《诗经》, *The Book of History*《书经》, *The Book of Changes*《易经》, *The Book of Rites*《礼记》, and *The Spring and Autumn Annals*《春秋》; the Four Books refer to *The Great Learning*《大学》, *The Doctrine of the Mean*《中庸》, *The Analects of Confucius*《论语》and *The Mencius*《孟子》.

2 See Xu Wei, *Nanci xulu zhushi* 南词叙录, *Zhongguo gudian xiqu lunzhu jicheng*, 3: 240.

dharma, [this] doubles their effect.[1]

In Chinese history, therefore, scholars and officials have often suggested to have some plays specifically revised so as to make them serve the purpose of moral edification, like Gao Ming's treatment of *Pi pa ji*. But ideology works in complicated ways. While a play extols moral ethics, serving as a tool for official edification, it may at the same time advocate some other popular ideology, an ideology that imperceptibly influences people. One of such ideologies lies in the creation and hence the presentation of images of women. Chinese society has been on the whole under the patriarchal rule for the last two millennia. Men controlled the discursive right, which in turn influenced the way women might be presented in literature and art. The idea of male chauvinism was so deep-rooted in the minds of people that many times they took it for granted that women be portrayed the way they were. That is why even in some writers who openly claimed to be sympathetic for women, one may still find instances of women bashing or at least instances of the distortion of women's image.

We can take as an example the jesting scene at the beginning of Act II in Guan Hanqing's *zaju* play *Jiu feng chen* 救风尘 (Rescued by a Courtesan). This is a monolog by Zhou She 周舍, a playboy, who recounts from his perspective what happened when he accompanied his bride Song Yinzhang 宋引章 home. The description of Song Yinzhang's "stripping herself naked and turning somersaults inside the bridal sedan,"[2] therefore, other than triggering off laughter from the audience, may plausibly be regarded as Zhou She's vilifying attitude towards the moral conduct of a courtesan, which may also be deemed a misogynist version of the popular thought on prostitutes or courtesans at the time. Likewise the comic scene

1 Liu Zongzhou 刘宗周, *Ren pu lei ji* 人谱类记, Vol. 2, in *SKQS.*, 717: 234a.
2 Zang Maoxun, *Yuan qu xuan*, 1: 197.

in which Song Yinzhang is presented to have messed up with her sewing of a quilt is also an exaggerated and mocking comment on a woman's lack of training in her needlework from a male perspective.

Another example comes from the anonymous Yuan dynasty *zaju* play *Yuan yang bei* 鸳鸯被 (Quilt Embroidered with Mandarin Ducks). Here is the plot of the play: Accused by the vice minister in the capital, Li Yanshi 李彦实, prefect of Luoyang, is summoned to the court. Lacking money for his travel to the capital, Li borrows ten silver ingots from Liu Yanming 刘彦明, a local wealthy lord, promising the latter that he will pay back the principal together with interest upon his return. One year has elapsed without any news from Li, and Liu gets angry. So he uses this as an excuse for the hand of Li's beautiful daughter Yuying 玉英, and a nun from the nearby nunnery is asked to serve as a go-between. Hard up for money to pay back the debt, Yuying agrees to go to the nunnery that night to meet with Liu. As a token of her feelings for her would-be husband, she even sends there her quilt embroidered with two mandarin ducks, saying the quilt goes where she is going to wed. As it happens that night, however, Liu Yanshi is taken to the court as a thief by night petrol solders, whereas a young scholar by the name of Zhang Ruiqing 张瑞卿 drops in to the nunnery. After spending a night with Zhang, Yuying agrees to marry him and he goes to the capital for a civil service examination the next day. Later, when Yuying serves in Liu's wine shop as a penalty for her breach of her promise in marriage, it is Zhang and Yuying's father who return and deliver her from her slave labor at the end.

The play professes to portray the marriage between Li Yuying and Zhang Ruiqing, the scholar, but what it actually does is to foreground the tryst scene as a male gaze, representing its voyeuristic tendency, showing Yuying as a sexual commodity sought after by two men. Secondly, by providing her body to whomever comes first to claim her virginity, the image of Yuying reaffirms the feudal doctrine of *funü cong yi er zhong* 妇女

从一而终 (a woman should stick to one husband for her life), hence placing her in a subjected or subjectless position. And lastly, the patriarchal figure of Yuying's father quits at the beginning of the play only to return at the end, which could be taken to imply that trouble and disorder occur with the absence of a patriarch, and, with his return, everything is back in order.[1]

Surveying a number of classical Chinese dramas, Taiwan scholar Zeng Yongyi 曾永义 once remarked: "Chinese drama originated from folk art and aimed at moral edification and entertainment... What it expressed were, therefore, no more than some traditional and religious beliefs and Confucian doctrines."[2] Such beliefs and doctrines not only include praiseworthy morals and conducts, but also contain some old-fashioned feudal ideas and values, which is a fit subject for feminist studies. And to lay bare the ways in which those feudal ideologies were presented or reiterated so as to be internalized by the audience is also to show the functions of drama in this important ideological realm.

II. Performing Characteristics of Chinese Drama

1. Overall Features

Aristotle defined ancient Greek tragedy as "an imitation of an action."[3] This influential theory of mimesis for subsequent Western drama leads to its realistic tendency in everything from characterization to stage performance. Contrary to this mimetic nature of Western drama, Chinese drama has never proposed, nor tried, to imitate as accurately as possible

---

1 For a detailed discussion, see Hongchu Fu, "Historicizing Chinese Drama: The Power and Politics of Yuan *Zaju*," Diss. UCLA, 1995, Ann Arbor: UMI, 1995, pp. 228-238.

2 Zeng Yongyi 曾永义, "Woguo xiju de xingshi he leibie 我国戏剧的形式和类别," *Chung-wai Literary Monthly* 中外文学 2.11 (1974), p. 16.

3 Aristotle, *Poetics*, trans. Malcolm Heath (London: Penguin, 1996), p. 10.

things as they are. Instead, Chinese drama is expressive in nature. As discussed in Chapter One, Chinese drama evolves from songs and dances of the ancient times. Therefore, it never simply takes as its primary goal to narrate a particular story, making an attractive plot out of it. What Chinese drama tries to do is always to combine story telling with songs and dances, making the theatrical performance a comprehensive art capable of various kinds of entertainment to its audience. Because of this, Chinese drama is good at being lyrical rather than at making a theatrically enticing narrative.

We can perhaps take Yuan dynasty *zaju* plays for example, since they form an artistic peak in the development of Chinese drama, and many modern Chinese local dramas such as Beijing operas still retain much of their features. In evaluating Chinese dramas of the Song and Yuan dynasties, Wang Guowei particularly praised Yuan *zaju* drama for its songs, saying "the best of Yuan drama does not lie in its theme and plot structure, but lies in its writing (wénzhāng 文章)."[1] Here by writing is meant the songs composed by Yuan dramatists. To Wang, Yuan dramatists "did not care about the clumsy plot structure, nor did they hide their petty and vulgar ideas or worry about the contradictions in characterizations. All they wanted was to express their feelings and emotions," which came out in the form of songs in the plays.[2]

Dramas of other periods are also like this with their emphasis on songs and dances so much so that audiences come to watch plays not to know the stories to be told, for they may have already known them by heart, but to watch the performances or the interpretations of those stories by particular actors or actresses. Therefore, some scholars call Chinese drama structure a "song-based structure (qǔtǐ jiégòu 曲体结构)," whereas others name it

1 Wang Guowei, *Song Yuan xiqu shi shuzheng* 宋元戏曲史疏证, annot. Ma Meixin 马美信 (Shanghai: Fudan University Press, 2004), p. 177.

2 *Ibid.*

"dramatic poetry (jùshī 剧诗 or xìjùtǐshī 戏剧体诗)."[1] Whatever the terminologies used, they all refer to the fact that Chinese drama emphasizes the beauty of its songs or poetry rather than the soul-stirring plot arrangement and dramatic conflict. It weighs more on musicality than on theatricality. As the modern drama theorist Qi Rushan 齐如山 (1875—1962) put it in very succinct terms, in Chinese drama, "all sounds must be turned into songs, all actions must be made into dances...and there should be absolutely no realism."[2]

Because of these characteristics, there is an interesting phenomenon in Chinese drama: some of its plays' individual acts, especially those famed ones, are often performed alone for the enjoyment of the audience. Those acts or scenes of the plays are usually the ones in which an actor/actress can best show his/her skills at singing or dancing. Such performances are called the performances of *zhe zi xi* 折子戏 (highlights from a play) and they are getting more popular than the performance of entire plays now simply because the audience could appreciate and enjoy some highlights in singing and dancing in those plays in a short span of time.

2. Specific Characteristics

For most traditional Chinese dramas, theatrical performances generally involve songs and dances. The former covers what is called singing (chàng 唱) and speaking (niàn 念), while the latter usually refers to acting (zuò 做) and combating (dǎ 打). These four areas of artistic performance are basic skills for any actor or actress. The specific features of each will be

---

1 See Luo Di 洛地, *Xiqu yu Zhejiang* 戏曲与浙江 (Hangzhou: Zhejiang renmin chubanshe, 1991), p. 55; Zhang Geng 张庚, et al. eds., *Zhongguo xiqu tonglun* 中国戏曲通论 (Shanghai: Shanghai wenyi chubanshe, 1989), p. 140; and Zhu Yinghui 朱颖辉, "Zhang Geng de 'ju shi' shuo 张庚的'剧诗'说," *Wenyi yanjiu* 文艺研究 (1984) 1: 73-84.

2 Qi Rushan 齐如山, "Guoju de yuanze 国剧的原则," in *Qi Rushan quanji* 齐如山全集, 8 vols. (Taipei: no publisher, 1964) , 3: 4.

explained in the following together with other features such as role types, facial makeup, costume as well as stage props.

A. Singing and Speaking

In a broad sense, all utterances in Chinese drama are considered singing. Singing of songs is without doubt singing, but uttering a monolog, or reciting a poem, or even being engaged in a dialog, all needs to follow a specific rhythmic tone, and its pitch and tempo depend on the type of character and the situation in a play. All those "spoken" lines, moreover, are to follow the specific beats of gongs and drums, sometimes drawn-out and sometimes quick-paced, making a chanted and accented "speech." Because of these details involved in chanting those *huabai* 话白 (spoken lines), there is a saying in theatrical circles that "the chanting of spoken lines weighs a thousand pounds whereas singing weighs only four 千斤话白四两唱 (qiānjīn huàbái sìliǎng chàng)", which shows the importance of those "spoken lines" in the performance of Chinese drama.

Likewise, sound generated from being angry, worrisome, regretful, or from crying, laughing, hating, or even from coughing, should all embody some elements of singing. Take the sound of coughing, for instance. Different personalities, different contexts and different musical accompaniments will generate over a hundred kinds of coughing.[1] The only exception is in a clown's speech, which is mostly in plain speech, the purpose of which is just to cause the audience laugh by making this exception to the theatrical norm.

Singing is one of the most important elements in Chinese drama. It is used to express the personality of a character, his or her feelings and emotions, and also to portray some specific theatrical circumstances.

1 See Qi Rushan 齐如山,"Guoju de yuanze 国剧的原则", p. 3.

Because of the priority given to singing in Chinese drama, people sometimes refer to the performance of a play as *changxi* 唱戏 (to sing a drama) whereas to see a play as *tingxi* 听戏 (to listen to a play).

B. Acting and Combating

Generally speaking, all actions in a play have something of dancing. This is because of the principle of non-realism in Chinese drama explained previously. So, to act on stage entails an actor or actress's facial expressions, movements of his hands, eyes, body as well as his walking steps, all of which should follow a strict style. Just take one's walking steps on stage for instance. These are called *taibu* 台步, which is a far cry from the way one normally walks down a street. On stage, one's steps are accompanied either by music or by the beat of gongs and drums to indicate that those are really stylized dancing steps. As a result, a young man has specific walking steps for a young man, so has a young woman or an old woman respectively. What they do is not to show realistically how each one walks, but rather to make those walking steps graceful and pleasing to the eyes of the audience. "The gait assumed by an actor is also meaningful. A noble lady walks with grace and dignity; the flirt sways suggestively in her gaudy costume; fighters stalk; scholars pace thoughtfully; clowns scurry; and officials stride with a grand manner."[1] All the other actions such as horse riding, boat rowing with an oar, or chicken feeding, follow the same principle of being made graceful on stage. Consequently, one sees actors or actresses traveling from one place to another simply by walking a circle on stage. To sleep is always to bend over one's desk or table, because to simply lie down and sleep will be considered too vulgar and awkward for stage presentation. Likewise, to show a man falling sick is always for him

---

1 Josephine Huang Hung, *Classical Chinese Plays* (Taipei: Mei Ya Publications, Inc., 1971), p. 24.

to throw up while to present a woman being sick is almost every time for her to have a stomachache, because those are "presentable" postures on stage.[1]

Another kind of acting that involves series of fighting actions on stage is called *wuda* 武打, which is an acrobatic fighting. This is the stylized representation of ancient warfare and combat in dance form. There are two kinds: one is either unarmed combat or armed combat and the other is somersaults. They are either to showcase the valor of characters or to turn fierce fighting into pleasurable scenes for the audience to enjoy.

C. Role Types

One of the unique aspects of Chinese drama is its use of role types. Rather than having a performer acting a particular character in a play as is the case in Western dramas, Chinese drama has created some role types of character and has a performer assume a specific role type in performance. The origin of and reason for such a dramatic practice is a matter of much controversy. Some have attributed this to the influence of Indian drama,[2] whereas others have come to the conclusion that this is "the inevitable outcome of Oriental culture's emphasis on the generality of people in negligence of their individuality."[3] Although there are some variations for various Chinese dramas in terms of role types, there are generally four basic ones for all of them: the *sheng* 生 (male character), *dan* 旦 (female character), *jing* 净 (painted-face), and *chou* 丑 (clown). Each is subdivided into several groups of more specific types with their own particular

---

1 See Qi Rushan, "Guoju de yuanze," in *Qi Rushan quanji*, vol. 3, pp. 4-5.

2 See Xu Dishan 许地山, "Fanju tili jiqi zai Hanju shang de diandian didi 梵剧体例及其在汉剧上的点点滴滴," Zheng Zhenduo 郑振铎 ed., *Zhongguo wenxue yanjiu* 中国文学研究, 2 vols. (Shanghai: Shangwu yinshuguan, 1927), 2: 26-28; Huang Tianji 黄天骥 & Kang Baocheng 康保成, eds., *Zhongguo gudai xiju xingtai yanjiu* 中国古代戏剧形态研究, pp. 315-330.

3 Fu Jin 傅谨, *Zhongguo xiju yishu lun* 中国戏剧艺术论 (Taiyuan: Shanxi jiaoyu chubanshe, 2003), p. 236.

variations. Everything that helps a performer act the role has been so meticulously stipulated that a performer has to learn assiduously for years before he can perform the role well. Because of the amount of training needed for acting each type of role, a performer will usually stick to the performance of just one type of role during his or her entire career as a professional performer. In what follows, our discussion will give the practice in Beijing opera, which represents the general rule for the majority of other Chinese dramas.

1. The Role Type of *Sheng*

Actors of the *sheng* (male character) category can be divided into three subcategories: warriors are *wusheng* 武生, young men are *xiaosheng* 小生, and old men are *laosheng* 老生, all of which are not mutually exclusive categories. A *wusheng* usually wears heavily embroidered garments, often with four triangular-shaped gaudy pennants, which are called *kaoqi* 靠旗, strapped on to his back. Those pennants are symbols of flags of command in army. Although he is often a warrior or general, the colors of his garments will denote his personality and social rank, and, in general, the elaboration of his headdress is in direct proportion to the importance of the warrior. The role type of *xiaosheng*, on the other hand, did not necessarily indicate a person young in age in classical Chinese drama or in early *Kunqu* drama, but it comes to refer to a young hero in Beijing opera, who may be a young scholar, a prince or simply an ordinary young man in a village. As a refined and handsome gentleman, a *xiaosheng* generally does not wear beards and he wins the heart of a lady by his excellent singing and his exquisite gestures. Since a young scholar often wears a kerchief on his head or flaps a fan with his hand, such a character is also called a *jinsheng* 巾生 (male character wearing a kerchief) or a *shanzi sheng* 扇子生 (male character holding a fan) respectively. A *laosheng* is a typical Chinese:

honest, sincere, learned and yet a bit pedantic. Whether a poor scholar or a valiant warrior, he has to be fastidiously correct with his enunciation and singing. This is because, different from a *xiaosheng* who is more active and energetic, a *laosheng* possesses an air of dignity and grace that makes his action and behavior more sedate and tactful and yet authoritative, which befit his age and character.

2. The Role Type of *Dan*

Although the *dan* category can be divided into six subcategories, the most popular ones are *huadan* 花旦, a "flowery" maiden, *qingyi/zhengdan* 青衣/正旦, a female in dark-colored dress/the main female role, and *laodan* 老旦, an old woman. The *huadan* role usually portrays a beauteous maiden who is vivacious, shrewish or coquettish. It stresses a nimble movement, a quick tongue and a sharp mind. Her flashing eyes, her briskly walking steps and her agile waist movement will specifically keep the audience captivated. To fit her character, a *huadan* often wears brightly-colored costumes and a fancy hair style with sparkling decorations. A *qingyi* is more humble and reserved in character. Her demure behavior, her often downcast eyes and her cautiously mincing steps render her a virtuous lady and a loving mother typical of the Confucian ideal of womanhood. Different from the costumes of a *huadan*, those of a *qingyi* are always simple and subdued in color. In fact, the name of *qingyi* comes from the fact that the actress taking the role often wears dack-colored dress with a white sash. The *qingyi* role stresses singing, so a *qingyi* performer should have a good voice, for she usually has a lot of singing in a play. The role of *laodan*, on the other hand, indicates an elderly woman, whether a poor and rustic servant or a graceful and dignified imperial member. This role requires a performer to have a steady and sedate character and behavior, deep and calm soliloquies and a sonorous singing voice.

3. The Role Type of *Jing*

The role types of *jing* (painted face), also called *hualian* 花脸, are taken by any male character who has some outstanding characteristics such as bravery, honesty, thoughtlessness, or even treachery. The *jing* role types all have painted faces, which distinguish their different personalities: in general, a red face indicates a loyal and righteous figure; a black face denotes an honest, sincere or crude personage; a white face is an indication of a treacherous and cunning person; a yellow face shows a cruel and ruthless character; a purple face represents someone who is both calm, brave and decisive; whereas a blue face signifies a violent, especially an obstinate and unruly person, etc.[1] The role types of *jing* are further divided into *da hualian* 大花脸 (heavily painted face) and *er hualian* 二花脸 (less painted face). The former stresses singing, which should be forceful and resounding, so much so that when the actor sings, the walls actually vibrate along with the powerful force of his voice. The latter mainly dwells on acting, laying emphasis on the actor's movements and postures on stage.

4. The Role Type of *Chou*

Chous are basically clowns on stage. For the fact that they have a little white patch of paint on their eyes and noses, they are also called *xiao hualian* 小花脸 (little painted face). Using everyday language, the role of a *chou* can be taken by various kinds of people on stage, sometimes by a kindhearted, humorously-speaking and comically-behaved character, and sometimes by a fraudulent and crafty, or a miserly and base person. The *chou*s are further divided into *wuchou* 武丑 (military clowns), who are proficient with acrobatics and weapons, and *wenchou* 文丑 (civilian

---

1 See Qi Rushan, *Guoju yishu huikao* 国剧艺术汇考, *Qi Rushan quan ji* 齐如山全集, 6:237-263; Huang Dianqi 黄殿祺, *Zhongguo xiqu lianpu* 中国戏曲脸谱, (Beijing: Beijing gongyi meishu chubanshe, 2001), pp. 160-161.

clowns), who are skillful in cracking jokes, making the audience convulsed with laughter. Whatever characters they are, the role of a *chou* is to provide comic relief amidst some tense plot development.

D. Facial Makeup

Different from ancient Greek drama that used masks, traditional and modern Chinese dramas use facial makeup instead. Early Chinese drama, however, was said to have also used masks. The actor or actress at that time wore a mask by holding in his or her mouth a short bamboo stick attached to the back of that mask. This was possible because the performers then only needed to dance whereas singing was done by different people. As time went by, singing and dancing were gradually combined to be performed by the same performer, and, to be a singer, one could not also hold a mask in one's mouth while singing. Hence people started to paint masks on a performer's face, which has become the practice of facial makeup ever since.[1]

Just as everything else in Chinese drama, facial makeup is also heavily symbolic and it represents a character's personality or temperament rather than to show his real complexion. Generally speaking, a facial makeup implies more negative than positive characteristics. As a result, good and righteous characters all have simple and plain facial painting, whereas the visages of cruel, cunning and treacherous people tend to be covered with heavily glossy lines and colors. Wicked people tend to have their faces painted with a white patch. This is because wicked and treacherous people usually do not show their true faces. What they put out are their false and pretended faces. Therefore, the more wicked a character tends to be, the larger the white patch on his face.[2]

1 See Qi Rushan, "Lianpu脸谱," in *Qi Rushan quanji*, 6:240-241.
2 See Qi Rushan, "Guoju de yuanze国剧的原则," in *Qi Rushan quanji,* 3: 10.

E. Costume

The dazzling display of costume in Chinese drama may often cause people, especially foreign onlookers, to make two false assumptions: one, the performers dressed in period costume reflect the real clothes of the time, and, if not, then, the costume may be randomly designed simply to please the eyes of the audience. In fact, the costume of Chinese drama is not at all the accurate replica of the clothes worn by people at certain periods of time in history, nor does it reflect the regional or seasonal differences. Therefore a performer acting as someone of a certain dynasty in the past may not wear exactly the clothes of the time. Similarly he or she may wear something that may not be the typical clothes by people in that region or during that season. Despite all that, however, one must observe that costume in Chinese drama is rigidly stipulated so much so that there is a saying in theatrical circles that a performer would "rather wear a threadbare costume than to wear a wrong one (*Ning chuan po, bu chuan cuo* 宁穿破,不穿错)."

Like the significations of other elements in Chinese drama, its costume conveys meanings to the audience through its styles, colors, patterns, materials and the ways of wearing.[1] For a headdress, for instance, what a warrior wears will be different from what an official does. Likewise, both an emperor and a minister can wear what is called *mangpao* 蟒袍 (dragon robe), yet different colors differentiate the two.[2] As a general rule, yellow is

---

1 For a detailed explanation, see Zhang Geng and Guo Hancheng, eds., *Zhongguo xiqu tong lun* 中国戏曲通论, pp. 471-475.

2 *Mang* 蟒 in Chinese really means "python." According to Shen Defu 沈德符 (1578—1642) of the Ming dynasty, this robe resembles an imperial robe. In the early years during the reign of Zhengtong 正统 (1436—1449), Emperor Yingzong 英宗 wanted to give a dragon robe as a gift to a foreign chief. His ministers all thought an imperial robe should not be given as a gift to alien people. Therefore, they cut one of the dragon's claws on the robe and called it *mangpao* 蟒袍 (python robe). Hence the theatrical rule that only an emperor can wear a *mangpao* with five claws while all others can only wear a *mangpao* with four claws. See *Wanli yehuo bian* 万历野获编, 3vols. (Beijing: Zhonghua shuju, 1959), 3: 830; or Qi Rushan, *Guoju yishu huikao*, in *Qi Rushan quanji*, 6: 172.

for an emperor or an imperial family; red is for a loyal and honest man; green is for a solemn and awe-inspiring character; brown or gray is for an old man or woman; whereas the color black is reserved for those who are forthright and candid. As a result, a high-ranking and righteous official wears a red dragon robe, a loyal and meritorious one wears a green one, an old minister will wear a white one, whereas those officials who are straightforward, upright and unyielding tend to wear a black dragon robe.

Another fascinating thing for costume in Chinese drama is that civil officials and other non-military characters often wear robes with long and wide sleeves in white color. The white extension of the sleeve is called *shuixiu* 水袖 (water sleeve), for it looks like flowing water when an actor or actress swings and throws it around to express his or her various emotions. The *shuixiu* for men is usually over a foot in length whereas that for women is often between two and three feet. In some specific plays, a *dan* role's sleeve can be as long as two meters to achieve some special effect. The movement of the "water sleeve" is an art in itself. An experienced performer can use it to manifest a wide variety of personal characteristics as well as to provide a rich and colorful display of his or her psychological activities.

F. Stage Props

Stage props are generally called *qimo* 砌末 or *qiemo* 切末 in traditional Chinese drama terms, which are also highly symbolic in use. The principal stage props, a table and two chairs, "sometimes represent themselves but sometimes can also represent anything of certain height such as a mountain, a house, a bridge, a boat, a bed, etc.," when arranged differently.[1] Therefore, a horse whip used by an actor on stage is taken to mean horse-riding, an oar in the hands of a boatman represents the idea of

1 Zhang Geng & Guo Hancheng, eds. *Zhongguo xiqu tonglun*, p. 489.

traveling by boat. Similarly, small flags painted with fish and water waves announce storms, high waves at sea or floods, whereas a plain black or blue cloth painted with white lines resembling a city gate or battlements which is attached to two bamboo poles will indicate a city wall.

Stage props in traditional Chinese drama are mostly not realistic in nature. Candles used on stage, for instance, represent source of light but are not lighted. So is a red lantern, which is generally made of a red cloth to resemble a lantern's outside only. Although the stage props do not need to resemble objects realistically, they do strive to be presented beautifully on stage. As a result, Chinese stage props pay close attention to their decorations. A horse whip, for example, uses silk tassels, the oar of a boat is usually painted colorfully, and the flag resembling a carriage is decorated with embroidery, all of which represent the principle of making things beautiful in decorations. On the other hand, those stage props are also designed so that they can be easily used as a tool for dance. In all, stage props in traditional Chinese drama have three functions: "to arrange space for an action, to indicate and describe the environment for the action, and to express the emotion and significance of the action."[1]

At present time, faced with the challenge by Western drama, many Chinese dramas have also started to use fancy and realistic props. Some even resort to multimedia means to enhance theatrical effects. But these modern innovations are still controversial among some Chinese drama scholars.

III. Evolution of Chinese Theater and Its Influence

Chinese drama has evolved through a long period of time. Similarly,

---

1. Zhang Geng & Guo Hancheng, eds. *Zhongguo xiqu tonglun*, p. 495.

Chinese theater has also experienced a prolonged period of evolution before it becomes what it is today.

1. Earliest Chinese Stage Forms

The idea of a theater in the sense of ancient Greek theater or Elizabethan theater did not really apply to traditional Chinese drama until quite recently. This is because Chinese drama during its early years did not have places specifically allocated for dramatic performances. Since drama was often conducted together with other folk activities such as ritual services, official or private celebrations or bazaar entertainments, it used whatever places available as its location for performance: temples, courts, individual homes or markets. So the earliest Chinese stage was simply an open space for performance, where audiences of various kinds gathered to watch as they pleased. Later on, for better viewing effect, people piled up earth to make raised platforms, which were variously called *pingtai* 平台 (flat stage) or *lutai* 露台 (terrace). This was very much the case before and during the Sui and Tang dynasties (581—907) when Chinese drama was still in its embryonic stage and when *baixi* 百戏 (hundred games) remained a popular form of entertainment then. A flat and open space was what *baixi* performances largely required at that time.

Although the earliest open-space stage for drama performances can be found in the literature of the Han dynasty (206 BC—220AD), it was actually during the Tang period (618—907) when people started to build what was called a *kanpeng* 看棚 (viewing canopy), which could shelter audience from the sun and rain when they were watching a performance, as well as a *yuepeng* 乐棚 (covered performance shelter), which turned performance in the open to that under a roof, thus marking a development in stage design and construction. The covered platform could not only guard the audience against the sun and rain, but also enhance the acoustic effect of the performance by providing echoes there. The covered platforms

for theatrical performances were convenient for drama but they imposed limitations on the performances of some other *baixi* activities that required open space then. So the emergence of those covered stages also marks the independence and maturity that Chinese drama was approaching.

As time went by, those temporary flat stages with viewing canopies were gradually replaced by more permanent structures called *wuting* 舞亭 (dance pavilion), which were often constructed inside a temple. This is because popular entertainments such as hundred games and other songs and dances at the time were still often performed as part of religious services. A *wuting* was a square pavilion with four pillars supporting its roof. Since it had no walls and was open from all sides, audience could watch performances from any side.

2. Chinese Stage at the Mature Age of Chinese Drama

Chinese drama came to its mature age during the Song and Jin period. At the same time, Chinese theater evolved into its stage design—*washe* 瓦舍 and *goulan* 勾栏—which would be typical of later theaters for the next four hundred years until the early Ming dynasty. The *goulan* theater of the Song dynasty was of a closed wooden structure with a covered roof. The audience seats were arranged around three sides of a stage and raised row after row outward. This kind of theater was obviously designed and built for commercial performances and it continued into the Yuan dynasty as theatrical activities became more and more popular during the Jin and Yuan period. Yuan *zaju* play "Lan Caihe 蓝采和" had a good description of such *goulan* theaters, and Tao Zongyi's 陶宗仪 (1316—?) *Nancun chuogeng lu* 南村辍耕录 also recorded an accident about a *goulan* theater that crashed during a performance, resulting in 42 deaths in Songjiang prefecture.[1]

---

1 See Sui Shusen 隋树森 ed. *Yuan qu xuan wai bian* 元曲选外编 , 3 vols. (Beijing: Zhonghua shuju, 1959), 3: 971-980; Tao Zongyi, *Nancun chuogeng lu* 南村辍耕录 (Beijing: Zhonghua shuju, 1959), pp. 289-290.

The *wuting* structure, on the other hand, was also improved during the Yuan period when a wall was added to the back side of a stage, finalizing a transition from a stage that was viewed from all sides to one that only opened to its three front sides. This was largely the result of Chinese drama development. Before the Song dynasty, what were staged were often entertainments such as songs and dances and other hundred games which did not really need specifically to perform toward one certain direction, neither did audience need to choose a certain direction from which to watch the show. As *zaju* drama of the Song dynasty emerged to replace the songs and dances of the hundred games, the shows appeared to orient toward a particular direction and, therefore, audience needed to follow suit. Hence the birth of a theater with three viewing sides. Such a stage actually gained three advantages over the previous ones: first, by arranging the audience towards the front, performers could better suit the audience' s viewing needs rather than heeding audiences both in front and at the back; secondly, such a show that oriented toward the front direction could also enhance acoustic effect in the theater, making the show more appealing; and thirdly, by blocking one side of the stage, a back stage was created where performers could easily make their entrance or exit and where they could also rest, change costumes or do a number of other things.

The *goulan* theater that flourished during the Song and Yuan dynasties marks the formal establishment of Chinese theater for commercial purposes. It reached the pinnacle of its success toward the end of the Northern Song dynasty and continued its popularity into the Southern Song, Yuan and early Ming dynasties. However, the *goulan* theater discontinued during the mid-Ming period, which may be related to the decline of Northern drama such as *zaju* plays then.

3. Theatrical Performances in Restaurants

Theatrical performances continued despite the disappearance of the *goulan* theater during the mid-Ming period. *Jiulou* 酒楼 (restaurant) performances, which actually started during the Song and Yuan period, gradually replaced performances in a *goulan* theater to become popular theatrical activities then. People went to restaurants to eat food and drink wine and, at the same time, they could enjoy various entertainments that included songs, dances as well as theatrical performances. At first, these restaurants did not have regular theatrical performance schedules. What they did was only to provide a location for their patrons to hire theatrical troupes to perform. The restaurants themselves might not necessarily charge the troupes, who were all paid by their patrons. As the *jiulou* performances became more popular, however, the theatrical performances were also gradually becoming more regular in the restaurants. By and by people also started to refer to these restaurants as *xi yuan zi* 戏园子 or *xiguan* 戏馆, which indicates a transition of these restaurants from mainly a place for food and wine to primarily a sort of theater for entertainment. Of course, not all restaurants at that time were like these and since these places still served food and wine, other people could still come in for food while watching performances for free. According to some statistics, towards the early Qing dynasty, there were almost a thousand restaurants in the city of Shengjing 盛京 (present day Shenyang 沈阳) alone, which provided such theatrical performances.[1] There were, of course, much fewer restaurants that were well equipped for and were specialized in theatrical performances. In the capital of Beijing, for example, we now know only a few well-known restaurant names such as *Taiping yuan* 太平园 (Peace Theater), *Bishan tang* 碧山堂 (Green Mountain Pavilion), *Baiyun lou* 白云楼 (White Cloud

1 See *Qing shi lu* 清实录, 60 vols. (Beijing: Zhonghua shuju, 1985—1987), 7: 472a.

Pavilion), *Siyi yuan* 四宜园 (Four Luck Theater), *Yueming lou* 月明楼 (Moonlit Pavilion), etc.

4. Theatrical Performances in Teahouses

Around Emperor Qianlong's 乾隆 reign of the Qing dynasty (1736—1796), teahouses became popular in Beijing. They served tea, melon seeds and other cookies but no food nor wine. Since the teahouses were less noisy than restaurants, they quickly replaced the latter to become a regular place for theatrical performances. These teahouse theaters made a number of improvements in terms of theatrical effect. They enclosed the audience seats and the stage in a closed space so as to be free of any interference by weather. Secondly, such a closed space also enhanced acoustic effect and the overall performing quality, enabling performers to concentrate on their singing and acting, which in turn helped to improve performing art. And thirdly, these teahouse theaters for the first time arranged the audience seats into several areas, and fares vary for different areas. The best seats in a teahouse theater were called *guanzuo* 官座 (official seats), so named perhaps because they were often taken by officials and wealthy lords. They were located on the balcony near the left and right sides of a stage. As for teahouse theater performances, there usually was a playbill posted outside each day to let people know what to expect for each show. In general, a teahouse theater did not sell entrance tickets. What they usually did was to collect money for tea after the audience were all seated. The practice of the teahouse theaters in Beijing quickly influenced other cities in the nation, particularly those in the coastal areas such as Shanghai, Tianjin, Suzhou and Guangzhou, where teahouse theaters mushroomed in late Qing dynasty.

5. Court Theaters

In reviewing the evolution of Chinese theaters, one should be aware that Chinese dramas were often performed at three distinct locations: religious temples, folk and commercial theaters, and court theaters. We have already talked about the first two, so we must also take a brief look at the court theaters, especially the imperial theaters of the Qing dynasty, some of which are still preserved today.

Theatrical activities were a favorite pastime for emperors and court officials of various dynasties. Because of palace resources, they could make the location for theatrical entertainment more elaborate than either the temples or folk theaters. However, until the Qing dynasty, theatrical performances had been held in the palace halls or courtyards since the Han dynasty largely because pre-modern Chinese dramas did not really demand sophisticated facilities for performances. In other words, although Chinese emperors in various dynasties may have established some specialized theatrical entertainment bureaus, there had been no regular or professional theaters created over the years until the Qing dynasty.

Things were changed during the Qing dynasty. Qing emperors and empresses were all theater fans, especially Empress Dowager *Cixi* 慈禧太后 (1835—1908). With the imperial support, the Qing court designed and built very elaborate, three-storied, grand professional stages. Traditional Chinese stages, whether flat or raised, were all one-storied, with the height of about 7-8 meters from the ground to the top of the stage floor. The three-storied grand theatrical stages built during the Qing dynasty were more than 20 meters high. There were specific names for each of the three stories: the top-story stage was named *futai* 福台 (stage of fortune), the middle-story stage was called *lutai* 禄台 (stage of wealth) and the bottom one was labeled *shoutai* 寿台 (stage of longevity). There were altogether four such grand stages built inside the Qing palaces, and they were used to stage shows that simultaneously presented several different realms such as paradise and hell, etc.

6. Changes in Theater Layout

When the teahouse theater was first established for theatrical performances during the mid-Qing period, there were rectangular tables placed in front of theater seats, on which were placed tea cups and cookies. Audience sat around these tables, facing each other with the stage to their sides. They chatted, drank tea and ate some cookies, but to watch a show, they would have to turn their bodies. Also, at that time, there was no electricity yet, so those theaters generally used lanterns instead for lighting. As time went by with the influence from the western theater toward the late Qing period, Chinese theaters, especially those in Shanghai, underwent changes. Seats were arranged so that audience started to face the stage instead of facing each other, and they started to use electric lamps for lighting, and footlights were also developed to create some special effects in lighting for performances. As for the hierarchy of seats, those directly in front of a stage began to be favored, since they were close to the stage and audience could watch more clearly and better there. After all these changes and improvements, then, the modern theater was born in China.

7. Distinctive Features of the Traditional Chinese Theater

In general, there are three distinctive features for traditional Chinese theaters.[1] First, unlike a Western theater where its stage is closed to the audience in the sense that what was on stage was closed off to the audience by what French classical art critic Denis Diderot (1713—1784) referred to as an imaginary "fourth wall" so as to create a realistic illusion, the traditional Chinese theater was open to the audience in the sense that its stage was open to audience interactions from all three sides and what was

1 For details, see Gao Yihua, *Zhongguo xitai* 中国戏台 (Hangzhou: Zhejiang renmin chubanshe, 1996), chapter 3, pp. 97-131.

on stage should not be separated from what was off stage among the audience. Since traditional Chinese dramas never presumed to be realistic, audience came to the theater simply to enjoy or to scrutinize the consummate skills performers displayed. They ate, drank and talked among themselves or even walked inside the theater while the show was going on. Obviously, the theater atmosphere was quite relaxed and audience could loudly cheer or boo at any time during the show. The openness of Chinese theater and Chinese drama was also reflected in the fact that unlike a Western theater where the only lit area is the stage, the traditional Chinese theater was lit both on stage and in the audience area, which facilitated the aforementioned interactions between stage show and the audience.

Secondly, Chinese architecture generally faces south. For a compound with houses around a courtyard such as a typical Beijing *siheyuan* 四合院, the one on the north is always the best house for the host, whereas the ones on both sides are the next best and the one on the south is for the guest. The traditional Chinese theater is just the opposite: its architecture always either faces north or avoids the best direction of facing south by facing either east or west. Its stage, however, always faces the main building. This is because a stage was used to be used for ritual services or to provide entertainment for its patrons. It has to be subjected to a subordinated position. Here, one can already see the low social status of the traditional Chinese drama by merely referring to its architectural design.

Thirdly, in terms of architecture *per se*, a traditional Chinese stage had its unique features. It tended to use two or four pillars in support of its big vaulted roof, whose four corners were always decorated with long and upturned eaves. The vaulted roof not only made the stage a fitting place for ritual services but also caused echoes, rendering a better acoustic effect for theatrical performances. There were usually some couplets written on those pillars, indicating some specific environment for the stage or eulogizing the social climate then. And almost everywhere inside the stage architecture, including its beams, walls or ceilings, was either carved or painted with fine, colorful, and artistic decorations. Together with those upturned eaves, the entire stage architecture really makes a traditional Chinese theater appear in majestic splendor.

Questions for Discussion:

1. What are the various social functions of Chinese drama? Have they always existed or were some more prominent than others at certain times and why?
2. Chinese drama is expressive in nature. How will you explain this in terms of its performing features?
3. What are some of the features in a Chinese drama that strike you as quite different from those in a Western drama?
4. Explain how Chinese theater evolved. Comment on any unique or interesting features in a Chinese theater.

Chapter Five

Introduction and Appreciation of Major Chinese Dramas

I. Introduction to Beijing Opera

Beijing opera was formed and subsequently matured in the then Chinese capital of Beijing during the latter part of the Qing dynasty, hence its name *Jingju* 京剧 in Chinese. Strictly speaking, however, Beijing opera should have been translated as "Chinese national drama," because the character *jing* 京 in *Jingju* does not really mean Beijing 北京 the city *per se*, but rather denote the capital *jing* 京 as in *jingcheng* 京城 (capital city). So Beijing opera is not the drama of Beijing, but rather the drama of the capital, which bears more implications than the city of Beijing alone may have, just as *Kunju* 昆剧 does not really mean the drama of Kunshan 昆山, the city, but rather a form of drama that originated and thrived in the city of Kunshan.

As was discussed in previous chapters, singing and music are the most important aspect of traditional Chinese dramas. Beijing opera has established itself and developed by combining melodies from Huixi 徽戏 (Anhui drama) and Hanxi 汉戏 (Hubei drama) and also by taking elements from some other dramas such as *Kunqu* 昆曲, *Qinqiang* 秦腔 and *Jingqiang* 京腔. Its two main melodies, called *xipi* 西皮 and *erhuang* 二黄, for example, were derived from Hanxi and Huixi respectively. Since its birth at around 1840, the twentieth year of the reign of Emperor Daoguang 道光 of the Qing dynasty, Beijing opera has grown to be a national drama that has integrated the four traditional theatrical skills of singing, speaking, acting and combating in a highly artistic manner, and it has become the most influential and representative drama in China today because of its distinctively nationalistic characteristics, its highly theatrical and artistic attainments as well as its rich heritage of traditional Chinese dramas.

Beijing opera originated and developed in the north. Its two primary sources—Huixi and Hanxi—are also northern dramas. Therefore Beijing opera retains much of the characteristics of the northern music, northern singing and northern manner. For example, its acting and performances of combat are both forceful, dignified and impressive, easily winning audience's applause. As for its theatrical melodies, they belong to what are called *banqiang*-style 板腔体 melodies, which are fairly flexible in melody length and rhythm, because they basically go with rhyming couplets in singing. Such theatrical melodies are very expressive of excited, indignant as well as sorrowful emotions. The accompanying musical instruments used in Beijing operas generally include a small ensemble of percussion instruments and melodic instruments. The former includes a small high-pitched drum (gǔ 鼓) and a clapper (bǎn 板), which are the soul of the entire ensemble. Every performer must strictly follow the beats of the drum and the clapper in singing and in doing almost everything else on stage. As for the latter, the lead instrument is called *jinghu* 京胡, a small, high-pitched, two-string fiddle, and there are also *yueqin* 月琴, a four-string plucked lute, and *sanxian* 三弦, a three-string plucked instrument. Together, those instruments make a Beijing opera aria sound particularly forceful and sonorous, conveying a great momentum.

Because of the social prejudice against women in feudal China, women were generally barred from being actresses performing together with men, and sometimes they were even not allowed to watch plays in a theater during the Qing dynasty. That is why there were no actresses in Beijing

opera before the end of the reign of Emperor Tongzhi 同治(1862—1875) and the beginning of the reign of Emperor Guangxu 光绪(1875—1909). All the roles in a play, male or female, were taken by men.[1] The most fully developed and noteworthy male-acted female role is the *dan* 旦 role type, which is sometimes referred to as *nandan* 男旦 (male-acted female role). And because of this practice, Beijing opera has had some of the best known actors in the nation who were specialized in acting female roles. The Four Great Actors of the *Dan* Role 四大名旦, for example, include Mei Lanfang 梅兰芳 (1894—1961), Cheng Yanqiu 程砚秋 (1904—1958), Shang Xiaoyun 尚小云 (1900—1976) and Xun Huisheng 荀慧生 (1900—1968).

There are many artistic schools in Beijing opera, each bearing the name of its founder, who demonstrates excellent and admiring skills in a certain theatrical role. Take the above Four Great Actors of the *Dan* Role, for example. Mei Lanfang founded the Mei school of Beijing opera art (méipài 梅派), which, after synthesizing features of various *dan* role types such as *qingyi* 青衣 (a female in dark dress), *huadan* 花旦 (a "flowery" maiden) and *dao ma dan* 刀马旦 (a female specializing in martial arts), aims at achieving an artistic perfection in all four areas of Beijing opera art: singing, speaking, performing and combating. Mei Lanfang has also made innovations in Beijing opera music, costume, and even in stage lighting. The Mei school of Beijing opera art has created on stage a series of unforgettable images of tender, kind-hearted, or elegant and stately ancient ladies.

The Cheng school of Beijing opera art (chéngpài 程派), founded by Cheng Yanqiu, through its innovative singing, with its kind of echoing vocal music, is especially good at representing suffering or unfortunate women of middle or lower social statuses, who are tender and submissive

---

1 See Ma Shaobo 马少波,et al., eds. *Zhongguo Jingju shi* 中国京剧史 (Beijing: Zhongguo xiju chubanshe, 1999), pp. 282-293.

in outward appearances and yet of an upright and unyielding character.

The Shang school of Beijing opera art (shàngpài 尚派) established by the actor Shang Xiaoyun, on the other hand, is known for its manly beauty expressed in female characters, which is shown in its characteristically vigorous and straightforward ways of singing together with a clear-cut rhythm, which is well received by many people.

In contrast, the Xun school of Beijing opera art (xúnpài 荀派) initiated by Xun Huisheng is characteristic of its emphasis on the expressions of character psychology and on the beauty and charm of a *dan* role's singing and dancing. Hence it is especially good at creating images of sweet, artless, vivacious and enthusiastic young ladies.

Apparently each of those Beijing opera schools has its own characteristic features that make it different from others and also make it suitable for the performance of a specific character. For actors and actresses in different schools to act the role of the same character in the same play, therefore, they will present the character with various features characteristic of various schools.

Excerpt from *Hegemon-King Bids Farewell to His Concubine*

This play dramatizes a historical anecdote during the famous Battle of Gaixia 垓下之战 in 202 BC between Liu Bang 刘邦 (256—195 BC), the founding emperor of the Han dynasty (206 BC—220 AD), and Xiang Yu 项羽 (232—202 BC), who titled himself Hegemon-King of Western Chu 西楚霸王 (Xī chǔ bàwáng).

Using a strategy by his advisors Zhang Liang and Chen Ping, Liu Bang tore up a peace agreement with Xiang Yu and launched a surprised attack on him. As a brave and yet self-willed general who was not resourceful, Xiang Yu trusted the advice by Li Zuoju 李左车, a strategist originally from the State of Zhao but now sent by Han Xin 韩信 (?—196 BC), commander in charge of Liu Bang's forces, to induce Xiang Yu into Han's trap. Despite the efforts by several of his generals and his loved concubine Yu Ji 虞姬 to try to stop him, Xiang Yu decided to launch his army to meet the challenge by the Han forces and led it all the way into the Jiuli Mountain 九里山 only to find that he was really taken in by Han Xin and his forces were all trapped at Gaixia.

Beijing opera *Hegemon-King Bids Farewell to His Concubine* consists of nine scenes. The following excerpt is taken from Scene Eight, where Han Xin asks his soldiers to learn and sing folk songs of Chu all around Xiang Yu's camps. Hearing this, Xiang Yu's soldiers have become very nostalgic and war-weary and fled in large numbers. Believing Heaven at work against Chu, Xiang Yu starts to feel pessimistic. What follows is the climax of the play when Yu Ji accompanies Xiang Yu in drinking and singing and she also dances with a sword in an effort to enliven Xiang Yu's mood. When they hear that their enemy has launched another assault, Yu Ji, for fear that Xiang Yu may delay his action because of her, quickly slits her throat with Xiang Yu's sword. Shortly afterwards, Xiang Yu is defeated with his remaining soldiers and he also slits his throat by the end of the play. This specific version of the play is one of the representative plays often performed by the noted Beijing opera artist Mei Lanfang 梅兰芳 during the middle of his professional career.

And in the play, the character Xiang Yu is generally taken by an actor of the *jing* 净 role (painted face 花脸) whereas that of Yu Ji is by a performer of the *qingyi* 青衣 role (female in dark dress).

Scene Eight[1]

(Enter eight palace maids with Yu Ji)

1 Zhongguo xijujia xiehui ed. *Mei Lanfang yanchu juben xuanji* 梅兰芳演出剧本选集 (Beijing: Zhongguo xiju chubanshe, 1961), pp. 116-124.

Yu Ji (sings):

(*xi pi yao ban*)
Since I followed the King in his battles to the west and east,
I have endured hardship and suffered from wind and frost year after year.
My only hatred is for the unjust Qin rulers who plunged
So many people into an abyss of misery and hardship.

(Enter four imperial guards and two major eunuchs with Xiang Yu)

Xiang Yu (sings):

(*san ban*)
I killed several Han generals with my spear.
Despite my valor, how could I guard myself
against hidden forces from ten directions?
I have given an order for everyone to stop fighting and go back to his camp.

Two eunuchs: Our King has arrived.

(Exeunt the four imperial guards and the two major eunuchs separately. Yu Ji comes up to look Xiang Yu up and down with concern and welcomes him into the tent)

Yu Ji: Ah, my King!
Xiang Yu (continues to sing):
These battles have involved you and made you often frightened.
Yu Ji: Ah, my King! What is the result of your battle today?
Xiang Yu: Well, I killed several of the Han veteran generals with my spear.

However, I was hopelessly outnumbered and could not win victory. This is really Heaven at work against our state of Chu. Oh, it is not the fault of our fighting!

Yu Ji: Victory and defeat are both common in battle. One should not bother to care about it. I have prepared some wine to share with my King so as to dispel your vexation and worries.

Xiang Yu: Sorry to trouble you then, my lady!

Yu Ji (to court maids): Get wine ready!

Eight court maids: Yes.

Xiang Yu (sings):

(*yuan ban*)
Today I returned defeated, feeling restless.

Yu Ji (continues to sing):
I advise my King not to worry but to feel at ease.

Xiang Yu (continues to sing):
How shall I respond with enemies from ten directions?

Yu Ji (continues to sing):
Patiently guard our position and wait for relief troops.

Xiang Yu: Oh! (continues to sing)
There's no alternative but to drink good wine
to relieve me of all worries and anxieties—

Yu Ji: My King! (continues to sing)

(*yao ban*)
Since ancient times victory and defeat have been common in battle.

Xiang Yu (stretches and yawns) Um!

Yu Ji: My King is tired. How about resting for a while inside the tent?

Xiang Yu: My lady needs to be on the alert then.

Yu Ji: I will do according to your command. You all retire.
Eight palace maids: Yes.

(Xiang Yu enters the tent while the eight palace maids exit separately. It is early summer. Yu Ji comes out of the tent with a lamp in her hand to have an inspection. She then goes into the tent. Enter four night watchmen separately, and, after the night patrol, they exit separately. The second watch is sounded[1])

Yu Ji: Seeing my King is drunk, sleeping inside the tent, I will take a walk outside. (sings)

(*nan bang zi*)
Seeing my King in sound sleep in his clothes inside the tent,
I am walking outside the tent to dispel my sorrow.
Moving my steps forward quietly, I stand still in the wilderness.
Lifting my head, I suddenly see a clear and bright moon in the blue sky.

Clouds are gathering in the clear sky and the moon has just appeared. What a clear autumn scene!
Soldiers: (inside) How much we suffer!
Yu Ji: It is really tragic that despite the bright moonlight, there are voices of sorrow and anxiety heard from everywhere in the fields! Because the King of Qin was unrighteous, fighting occurred everywhere with powerful politicians vying for the throne, plunging people into a state of misery. War also forced those innocent civilians to part with their parents and to abandon their wives and children. How hateful all this

1 In ancient China, night time was divided into five watches (*geng* 更) sounded by a watchman or on a drum tower, so that the first watch is from 7 to 9 pm, the second watch is from 9 to 11 pm, the third watch is from 11 pm to 1 am, the fourth watch is from 1 to 3 am, and the fifth watch is from 3 to 5 am.

is! It is just like

What heroes have for ages been fighting one another for is
To win in a battlefield full of warriors' cold remains.

Han soldiers (sing the songs of Chu inside):

Parents who have been abandoned at home are still there,
Day and night expecting their children to return!

(The third watch is sounded. Enter four night watchmen patrolling)

Watchman A: Folks, have you heard it?
Other watchmen: What have you heard?
Watchman A: The songs sung by our enemies all around here are of the same tune as our home songs. How is this?
Other watchmen: Yes, we don't know why this is.
Watchman A: Oh, I see. This must be that Liu Bang has conquered Chu and the soldiers he has recruited are all our country folks. Therefore what they sing are all of our home tunes. What do you think?
Watchman B: You are right, but what shall we do then?
Watchman C: It doesn't matter. Our King will have his own idea.
Watchman D: Forget about it! What idea does our King have? He only knows about drinking every day, without having any idea at all!
Watchman A: Yes, you are right. Our King does not accept good advice and does not know good people. He trusted Li Zuoju by inviting wolves into our home and was then taken in by our enemy's luring strategy. Now we are all trapped at Gaixia, waiting for our relief troops from Chu every day. Now that Liu Bang has

again taken Chu and has dashed our hope of getting any reinforcements. What shall we do then?

(Yu Ji is eavesdropping)

Watchman B: In my opinion, let us all flee, going back to our separate homes.

Watchman A: Hey, don't talk nonsense! Our King has kept the strictest military order. If anything goes wrong, that would be the end of us all! Let us as well go patrolling now.

Other watchmen: Let us walk, let us walk!

(Exeunt all night watchmen. The fourth watch is sounded)

Yu Ji: Aya! Wait a minute. I just heard many soldiers talking about their minds of leaving because our reinforcements have not yet come. Oh, my King! My King! I am afraid odds are against us now!

(continues to sing)
(*nan bang zi*)
I just heard soldiers chatting and talking.
Everybody revealed a mind of leaving.

Han soldiers (sing the songs of Chu inside):

Why not return, when land is to lie waste?
For whom have we traveled a thousand *li* to fight?[1]

---

1 *li* 里 is a traditional Chinese unit of measurement for length, which has varied considerably over time but now it has the standardized length of half a kilometer or 500 meters.

Yu Ji: Ah! (sings)

(*xi pi yao ban*)
I am thinking alone here,
And have heard again the songs of Chu from the enemy camps.

Aya, wait a minute! How come there are so many voices singing the songs of Chu in the enemy's camps? Why is this? There must be something odd about it. I'd better go in to report to my King. Ah, wake up, my King! Wake up, my King!

(Taken aback, Xiang Yu goes out of the tent with sword in his hand)

Xiang Yu: Well?
Yu Ji: Your lady is here.
Xiang Yu: Why are you in such a panic, my lady?
Yu Ji: I was just taking a walk outside our camp and suddenly heard the songs of Chu coming from the enemy's camps. I don't know why.
Xiang Yu: Really? Was there such a thing?
Yu Ji: Yes, there really was.
Xiang Yu: Let me listen for myself.
Yu Ji: Please, my King.

Han soldiers (sing the songs of Chu inside):

Warriors face death calmly in battlefield.
How many have returned after ten years of fight?

Xiang Yu: Ayaya... My lady! All around are the songs of Chu. Can it be that Liu Bang has already conquered Chu?
Yu Ji: No need to panic. We can send people around to investigate and to

make clear what has happened before we decide what to do.

Xiang Yu: You are right. Where are my guards?

Yu Ji: Where are the guards?

(Enter two eunuchs at the same time)

Two eunuchs: We pay our respects to our King and await your instructions.

Xiang Yu: Now there are the songs of Chu heard all around. Give order to people to take a look and report soon.

Two eunuchs: We take the order. (Exit)

Xiang Yu: Hey, I think there must be something fishy about this.

Yu Ji: Let us wait till our guards report back.

(Enter two eunuchs)

Two eunuchs: We hereby report to our King: they are indeed the songs of Chu from the enemy's camps.

Xiang Yu: Inquire about this more carefully and report back again.

Two eunuchs: We take the order. (Exit)

Xiang Yu: My lady! There are many soldiers from Chu in the enemy's army. It must be that Liu Bang has taken Chu. I think the situation is beyond salvation now!

Yu Ji: People are vying with one another for dominance right now. To lose some occasional battles is quite normal. Let us wait for a few more days for our reinforcements from east of the river. We can then fight again with our enemy. It is hard to tell who will emerge victor at that time!

Xiang Yu: You don't know, my lady! Before, various lords all fought for their own so that I could destroy one and then take on another. Now, all these people have joined forces to attack. Here in Gaixia we have fewer people and have run out of our provisions, so we can never hold out. I am now taking our troops out to fight that enemy and it is hard to predict the result this time. Oh, my lady! Judging by the situation, this is the time when we will be separated from each other!

(sings)
(*san ban*)
We have been in love with and depended on each other for more than ten years.
Now it is evident that I will have to part with you soon.

(Sound of horse neighs)

Xiang Yu: Oh, why was my black steed neighing like this? Groom, bring it here.

(Enter the groom leading the horse)

Xiang Yu: Oh my steed, my steed! You have followed me in fighting east and west with victory in every battle. Today we are besieged in Gaixia... Oh, now there is even no place for your abilities!

(sings)
(*san ban*)
Even the black steed knows the situation is hopeless
So that it neighs and roars repeatedly at the manger!

(Xiang Yu gestures to the groom to take the horse away)

Yu Ji: Oh, my King, it is good that the place at Gaixia has high hills and precipices so that it is hard to attack from the outside. Let us wait for the occasion when we can break out of the encirclement to seek help. That may not be too late!

Xiang Yu: Well, well!

Yu Ji: (with a forced smile) Oh, my King, how about if we drink some more?

Xiang Yu: If so, let us get wine!

Yu Ji: Please, my King!

(Sound of drums and trumpets. Both Xiang Yu and Yu Ji are seated)

Yu Ji: My King, please!

(*Ji san qiang* tune of music. Two drink wine)

Xiang Yu: (throws away his cup) Oh, look at me Xiang Yu!

(sings)

(*qin ge*):

My strength could pluck up a mountain and my might would dwarf the world.

But the times are against me and my steed runs no more.

When my steed runs no more, what can I do?

Ah, Yu, what can I do with you, my lady![1]

Yu Ji: My King sang with such solemn fervor that it made all to cry. Now let your lady sing and dance for a while to relieve you of your worries. How is that?

Xiang Yu: Oh, sorry to bother my lady!

Yu Ji: So excuse me for my immature skills now.

---

1 The English translation of this song is based on Burton Watson's translation in Sima Qian, *Records of the Grand Historian of China,* tr. Burton Watson. 2 vols. (New York: Columbia UP, 1961), 1: 70.

(Xiang Yu stares at Yu Ji, who forces herself to be composed and to avoid Xiang Yu's eyes. She takes up a sword to dance)

Yu Ji (sings):

(*er liu*)
I advice our King to drink and to listen to Yu's songs,
Which will assuage your grief with my graceful dances.
Yingzheng of Qin was unrighteous so the country has crumbled
And valiant heroes everywhere were in war with one another.
Common sayings since ancient times do not deceive me
That it is only a matter of moment whether one wins or loses.
Sit in your imperial tent and drink with a relaxed mind!

(*Ye shen chen* tune of music. Yu Ji dances with her sword)
Xiang Yu: (with a wry smile) Hahaha...

(*Sao tou* tune of music. Enter the chief eunuch)

Chief eunuch: I am hereby reporting to my King: The enemy army is launching a new offensive from four routes.
Xiang Yu: Order all generals to make no mistake in meeting the enemy forces head-on separately.
Chief eunuch: I take your order. (Exit)

(Reenter the chief eunuch)

Chief eunuch: I am hereby to report that the eight thousand of our soldiers have all left.
Xiang Yu: Inquire again about this.
Chief eunuch: I take your order. (Exit)

Xiang Yu: My lady, now that the enemy forces are attacking from four routes, follow me quickly to force our way out of the tight encirclement.

Yu Ji: Oh, my King! How could I want my King to be tied down by me? If you lose your battle this time, just retreat to the east of the river to plan for a comeback. I want to borrow your sword on your waist to kill myself in front of my King so that you will not worry about me!

Xiang Yu: This...my lady, you...you cannot kill yourself!

Yu Ji: Oh, my King!

(sings)
(*ku xiang si*)
The Han army has already seized our land
And all around are the songs of Chu.
When my King's morale comes to an end,
On what shall your humble concubine count to live?!

Xiang Yu: Oh my! Oh my!...

(Shouts inside. Yu Ji is startled and asks Xiang Yu for his sword. Xiang Yu refuses)

Xiang Yu: No, no, you cannot kill yourself!

Yu Ji: (quick-witted) My King, Han soldiers...are coming!

Xiang Yu: Let me take a look.

Yu Ji: (draws out Xiang Yu's sword) It's done! (She slits her throat and dies)

(Enter four imperial guards silently)

Xiang Yu: Oh dear! —Take horse!

(Exeunt the four imperial guards and Xiang Yu)

II. Introduction to *Kunju* Opera

Kunju opera, also called *Kunqu* 昆曲 opera, is one of the earliest forms of Chinese drama, having a history of more than 600 years. The origin of *Kunju* opera has to be traced to the end of the Yuan dynasty (1271—1368), when Gu Jian 顾坚 of Kunshan and other people rearranged and improved the music of the local Southern drama (*nanxi*) and named it *Kunshan qiang* 昆山腔. As was mentioned in Chapter Two, probably after the reign of Emperor Chenghua 成化 (1465—1487), Southern dramas evolved into several diverse theatrical and musical variations, of which the most notable ones were *Haiyan qiang* 海盐腔, *Yuyao qiang* 余姚腔, *Yiyang qiang* 弋阳腔 and *Kunshan qiang* 昆山腔. *Kunshan qiang* developed by incorporating local music and southern folk songs into its melodies, and its performance was restricted within present-day Kunshan 昆山 and Suzhou 苏州 area in southeast Jiangsu province. Initially *Kunshan qiang* was not quite popular and it certainly did not form a competition to other melodies such as *Haiyan qiang* or *Yuyao qiang* until the reign of Emperor Jiajing 嘉靖 (1522—1566) when Wei Liangfu 魏良辅, then a singer and a musician who migrated to Taicang 太仓 from Nanchang 南昌, Jiangxi province, together with a number of other performing singers and musicians, made major changes to the *Kunshan qiang* melody. Keeping the *Kunshan qiang* melody as its core while borrowing some features from *Haiyan qiang* and *Yuyao qiang* respectively, and combining these with the features of Northern melodies, they created a brand new singing genre sometimes dubbed "*shuimo qiang* 水磨腔 (melody as fine and smooth as water)," which was at once soft, exquisite and elegant so that it quickly made *Kunqu* popular.

Additionally Wei Liangfu also made improvement on the accompanying musical instruments to better suit the newly created melody, making the bamboo flute its main musical instrument. The new ensemble of musical instruments rendered *Kunqu* singing a theatrical form with much artistic appeal.

The reform that Wei Liangfu brought to *Kunshan qiang* was indeed revolutionary, but it was only a new melody with no theatrical acting choreographed for it at that time. It was Liang Chenyu 梁辰鱼, a native of Kunshan, who helped to transform *Kunqu* into a new drama with his play *Huan sha ji* 浣纱记. *Huan sha ji* was written specifically for the new *Kunqu* melody and its songs strictly followed the new *Kunqu* prosody. The performance of the play won instant success, which made *Kunju* opera enthusiastically and widely accepted. *Kunju* opera' s popularity then quickly surpassed that of other theatrical melodies at the time and its influence went as far as to the capital of Beijing during the Qing dynasty to become one of the officially endorsed melodies by the imperial court. *Kunju* opera, as a result, dominated the subsequent Chinese theater for almost 200 years.

The performing art of *Kunju* opera is quite intricate. *Kunqu*'s music belongs to what is called *qupai*-style 曲牌体 music, *i.e.,* its arias consist of a suite of songs (qǔ 曲) put together according to certain rules. Its verse follows an irregular pattern but with very strict versification in terms of its tones. In dialogs or in singing *Kunqu* melodies, therefore, clear enunciation is essential to its performance. Compared with other drama forms, the most prominent characteristic of *Kunqu* performance is its lyricism, which is reflected in the combination of its singing and dancing. In terms of its music, *Kunqu* emphasizes a control of sound, the cadence and rhythm of its singing so that its melody sounds especially beautiful and lingering. As for dancing, a *Kunqu* performer has to match each of his or her postures and actions with appropriate dancing movement, which is used either to interpret the verse he or she is singing or to describe a scene, to express the character's situation or his feelings and emotions, etc.

With repeated artistic improvement and revisions over a long period of time, *Kunju* opera has already established a fairly complete system for performance, which has been drawn upon by various other drama forms including Beijing opera. For instance, most of the patterns and techniques of Beijing opera's facial makeup evolved from *Kunju* opera. For its long history and the exemplary role it has assumed for other drama forms, *Kunju* opera has often been regarded as the "ancestor of all dramas 百戏之祖" and "teacher of all dramas 百戏之师." In May 2001, UNESCO awarded *Kunju* opera the title of "Masterpieces of the Oral and Intangible Heritage of Humanity."

There are also various artistic schools in *Kunju* opera. Different from Beijing opera schools, however, each of *Kunju* opera school bears the name of its location to indicate its difference from others. Therefore, *Kunju* operas popular in the south of the Yangtze River, especially in Shanghai, Jiangsu 江苏 and Zhejiang 浙江 Provinces, are generally called *nan kun* 南昆 (Southern *Kunju*), whereas *Kunju* operas active in the northern part of China like Beijing are named *bei kun* 北昆 (Northern *Kunju*). On the other hand, *Kunju* operas popular in Hunan Province 湖南 are called *xiang kun* 湘昆 (Hunan *Kunju*), while *Kunju* operas performed in Sichuan Province 四川 are generally called *chuan kun* 川昆 (Sichuan *Kunju*). The local dialects and local culture that *Kunju* opera has absorbed during the process of its dissemination have generally made various *Kunju* opera schools slightly distinct from one another in terms of their tones and styles of singing.

Excerpt from *The Peony Pavilion*

Written by the dramatist Tang Xianzu 汤显祖(1550—1616), *The Peony Pavilion* is a play that celebrates the power of passion and it affirms and validates one's innermost feelings in a heated philosophical debate between passion/feelings (qíng 情) and reason/rationalism (lǐ理) that was going on during the late Ming. The play dramatizes an extraordinary love story between a sixteen-year-old lady, Du Lining 杜丽娘, daughter of a prefect, and Liu Mengmei 柳梦梅, a young scholar from Guangzhou. As the only daughter in an official family, Du Lining has been brought up strictly according to Confucian ethics, who is not allowed to walk out of her boudoir and to read anything but Confucian canon. It happens that, on a warm spring day, Du Liniang is led by her maid into her backyard garden where, seeing the beautiful spring scenery there, she becomes enraptured with her desire for love, and she returns to her room to dream of her love affair with a young scholar by the name of Liu Mengmei. After that she languishes in lovesickness and dies soon after she paints her own portrait and asks her maid to bury it under a stone in the garden. At this time, her father has received a court promotion and is asked to go to Huai'an 淮安 at once. Before he and his wife hurriedly leave for office, they bury their daughter's body beside a plum tree in the backyard garden and ask her tutor Chen Zuiliang 陈最良 and a nun to build a Plum Convent (Méi Huā'ān guàn 梅花庵观) inside the garden where Liniang's memorial tablet can be set up.

Three year later, Scholar Liu Mengmei goes to the capital for a civil service examination. He gets sick on the way and stays in the Plum Convent. One day, in leisure, he goes into the backyard garden and happens to find the portrait of Du Liniang, which he puts up in his room and prays for every day. Meanwhile King of the Underworld adjudicates that Du Liniang and Liu Mengmei are predestined to marry, so he releases Du Liniang's soul back to visit Liu Mengmei in the Plum Convent. Once recognizing each other at their meeting, they happily enjoy their reunion every night. And Liu further agrees to disinter Du Liniang's body at her request to bring her back to life. When all this is done, they go to the capital together and Liu tops the list in his civil service examination. Liu then goes to see Du Bao, Liniang's father, only to get arrested and tortured for being a grave robber and an impostor. All is well that ends well when the emperor comes in and pardons all. At the end of the play, the emperor gives the verdict that Du Liniang and Liu Mengmei be officially wedded.

The Peony Pavilion consists of fifty-five scenes in all, the longest of all the plays by Tang Xianzu, and, although nowadays the play is seldom performed in its entirety, it usually takes about 20 hours to perform the whole play. The following excerpt is its tenth scene describing vividly Du Liniang's excited as well as sentimental emotions at seeing the beautiful spring scenes at her own backyard garden. Her thoughts generated during her stroll at the garden sets off everything that is to follow in the play. It is one of the most celebrated scenes of the play and also one of the most often performed scenes on stage.

In this play, the character of Du Liniang is generally taken by an actress of the *gui men dan* 闺门旦 (a female in her boudoir) role, that of Liu Mengmei is done by an actor of the *jin sheng* 巾生 (a male wearing a kerchief) role, whereas that of Chun Xiang, Liniang's maid, is performed by an actress of the *tie dan* 贴旦 (an extra female) role.

Scene Ten: Waking from a Dream[1]

（Enter Du Liniang）

Du Liniang (sings):

(*Rao di you*)
Awakened from my dream by orioles' singing,
I stand inside the small secluded courtyard,

---

1 English translation of this scene is largely based on two previous translations: Tang Xianzu, The Peony Pavilion, Mudan ting, 2nd ed., trans. Cyril Birch (Bloomington: Indiana University Press, 2002), pp. 42-52; Tang Xianzu, Mudan ting 牡丹亭, Chinese-English bilingual ed. ed, Xu Shuofang 徐朔方 & Yang Xiaomei 杨笑梅, trans. Wang Rongpei 汪榕培, 2 vols. (Changsha: Hunan renmin chubanshe, 2000), 1: 118-143.

Amidst the springtime beauty all around.

(Enter Chunxiang the maid)

Chunxiang (sings):

With the aloes wood burnt to ashes
And the remaining embroidery thread cast aside,
Do you care more about spring this year than last?

Du Liniang (recites):

(*Wu ye ti*)
I gaze at the distant Plum Blossom Pass at dawn,
Forlorn with last night's rouge undone.

Chunxiang (recites):
From a side view,
You are leaning against the balustrade,
The coils of your hair being dressed with silken swallows.

Du Liniang (recites):
Where are the scissors that can cut off
Or the comb that can untangle my grief?
I feel depressed for no reason.

Chunxiang (recites):
I have told the orioles and swallows
That urge flowers to bloom

To lend the spring for you to see.

Du Liniang: Chunxiang, have you given an order for the paths to be swept?
Chunxiang: Yes, I have.
Du Liniang: Bring my mirror and my gown.

(Exit and reenter Chunxiang with the mirror and the gown)

Chunxiang (recites):

She'll face the mirror when she's done her hair
And add more scent before she changes her robe.

Here's the mirror and the gown.

Du Liniang (sings):

(*Bu bu jiao*)
Gossamer swings
to and fro
In the air,
Gleaming idly across the yard
And making the spring as graceful as a rippling thread.[1]
I pause
Awhile
To straighten my hair ornaments,
When all of a sudden,
The mirror stole a half-glance at my face,

---

1 To show the inserted words (*chen zi* 衬字) in the original, I have rendered them here indented and in a smaller font.

Throwing my lovely hairstyle out of place.

(walks in the room)

As I

walk

In my chamber,
How could I show myself in full view?

Chunxiang: You are beautifully dressed and adorned today.
Du Liniang (sings):

(*Zui fu gui*)

You say

My dress is beautifully red
And my flowery hairpins gleam with gems.

But don't you know

It has always been in my nature to love beauty?

And yet,

This bloom of springtime no eye has seen.

It doesn't matter

If my beauty should amaze the birds
And, out of shame for the comparison,
Cause fish to sink and wild geese to fall to earth.

But it matters

If petals are to close and the moon is to hide her face,
While all the flowers tremble.

Chunxiang: It's time for breakfast. Please come.

(Both walk)

Look,
(recites)
While the golden paint along the corridor glitters sporadically,
Mosses make a green mass near the pool and the building.
To walk on grass I fear to soil my newly embroidered socks;
To love flowers I keep tugging my little gold bells.[1]

Du Liniang: Without coming to the garden, how could I ever come to see the splendor of spring like this?

(sings):
(*Zao luo pao*)
I see
How deepest purple and brightest scarlet
Open their beauty
Only to
Crumbling wells and walls.
Lovely scene on a bright day is of no avail.
Who enjoys real contentment and delight?

My mother and father have never mentioned such lovely scenes.

---

1 This refers to a prince of the Tang dynasty who strung tiny gold bells on red thread to hang on the stems of flowers and instructed his gardener to tug the thread when necessary to scare off birds that may harm those flowers. See Wang Renyu 王仁裕, et al. *Kaiyuan tianbao yishi shizhong* 开元天宝遗事十种, ed. Ding Ruming (Shanghai: Shanghai guji chubanshe, 1985), p. 73. Another interpretation is young women in ancient China wore tiny bells on their feet, similar to present-day jewelry chain by the foot. This is both for the beauty of the lady and for training her walking steps without causing the bells to jingle—true lotus steps for ladies. Therefore, the phrase in question here could refer to the fact that the young ladies, for fear of stepping on flowers and also of causing the bells to jingle, had to strain their feet and hence hurt their feet. The "*xiao jin ling* 小金铃," therefore, is used here as a metonymy for the lady's feet. See http://www.yuleshow.com/?p=437 (12 Aug. 2011).

Du Liniang:
Chunxiang:
(sing)
The flying clouds at dawn and the drizzling rain at dusk,
The emerald pavilion shrouded in rosy clouds;
Fine threads of rain amidst slices of gentle breeze,
Gilded pleasure boat in waves of mist:
All the glories of spring are little treasured by screen-secluded maid!

Chunxiang: All the flowers are in bloom now, but it is still too early for the peony.
Du Liniang (sings):

(*Hao jie jie*)
The green hillside bleeds with red azaleas
While willow twigs lie soft upon roseleaf raspberries.

Oh, Chunxiang,

However fair the peony,
It
Comes late in spring!

Chunxiang: Look at orioles and swallows in pairs!
Du Liniang:
Chunxiang:
(sing)
Gaze out at leisure:
Swallows chatter and swiftly fly
While orioles sing their way across the sky.

Du Liniang: Let us leave.
Chunxiang: One can indeed never weary of enjoying this garden.
Du Liniang: Say no more!

(They begin to leave)

Du Liniang (sings):

(*Ge wei*)
Let him feel attached who enjoys unwearyingly.
It is all in vain
Even though
One's visited all the gardens and pavilions.
Far better it will be,
As first elation passes,
If we find back in our chamber
Some pastime for our idle hours.

(They arrive at the chamber)

Chunxiang (recites):

I open the door to the west chamber
And make the bed in the east chamber.
I fill the vase with purple azalea,
And add aloes in the incense burner.

Please take a rest now, young mistress, and I'll go and report to Madam.
(Exit)

Du Liniang (sighs and then recites):

Back from a spring stroll to a silent room,
I try on the spring's new adornments.

Oh, spring, now that you and I have forged a mutual attachment, what shall I do when you leave? Oh, such weather makes me feel so drowsy. Where's Chunxiang? (looks around and then lowers her head again, murmuring) Oh Heaven! Now I do believe how annoying the spring's splendor can be. I often read about ancient girls in various poems and ballads who felt passionate in spring and became grieved in autumn. They were all telling the truth! Here I am sixteen now and yet no successful scholar has come my way. Stirred by my spring passion, where can I find one? In the past, Lady Han found a way to a meeting with a scholar named Yu, and Scholar Zhang met Miss Cui quite by chance. Their love stories are told in the books *Poems on the Red Leaves* and *The Life of Cui Hui*.[1] These lovely ladies and talented scholars started with clandestine meetings but all ended in happy marriage. (heaves a long sigh) Born and brought up in a renowned official family, I've already come of age and yet have not made a marriage union. Truly I am wasting my youth here with time flying by! (weeps) What a pity that my beauty is as bright as a flower but my life is as hopeless as a leaf!

(sings)
(*Shan po yang*)
I am so distraught that
I cannot dispel my springtime thoughts of love,
And hidden bitterness comes all of a sudden
for my cherished man.

---

1 According to the context, *The Life of Cui Hui* (*Cui Hui zhuan* 崔徽传) seems to be the playwright's mistake in confusing it with *The Life of Cui Yingying* (*Cui Yingying zhuan* 崔莺莺传) by Tang dynasty writer and poet Yuan Zhen元稹 (779—831).

For my beauty since I was little,
Those selected have been one after another of eminent families,
All
To promise a happy marriage.
But for what happy match
is
This springtime of my youth so cast away?
My
Thoughts and dreams who could perceive?
I have but
To remain shy and reserved as before.
Think of it,
By whose side will I be in my dream
That silently
Passes away
Along with
The passing of springtime?
To defer the thought?
But where to reveal my true desires!
Tormented,
Where but to Heaven shall my lament be made!

I feel rather tired, so I'll lean on the table and take a nap.

(She falls asleep and begins to dream of Liu Mengmei, who enters with a willow-twig in his hand)

Liu Mengmei (recites):

Orioles' songs get sweet in warm days
While people wear smiling faces in romance.
Tracing my path by fallen petals in the stream,

I am Ruan Zhao coming to Mount Tiantai today.[1]

I've followed the footsteps of Miss Du along the path, but how is it that I've lost sight of her now? (looks back) Oh, Miss Du! (Du Liniang rises, startled from her sleep, and greets Liu Mengmei. Liu continues) I was looking for you everywhere, so this is where you were! (Du Liniang looks aside without uttering a word) I just happened to snap half a twig off a weeping willow in the garden. Miss Du, since you are so deeply versed in classics, couldn't you compose a poem to honor the twig? (Surprised and yet pleased, Du Liniang is about to speak but holds back her tongue)

Du Liniang (asides): I have never seen this young man before. Why does he come here?

Liu Mengmei (with a smile): Miss Du, I am dying of love for you!

(sings)
(*Shan tao hong*)
For you,
A fair lady as beautiful as a flower
Whose beauty will fade just as water flows and time flies,
I am in search everywhere.
But you are pining secluded
in
Your chamber.

Lady, come with me just over there where we can talk.

---

1 A reference to the legendary story about two men named Liu Chen 刘晨 and Ruan Zhao 阮肇, who went astray to Mount Tiantai 天台山 and found romance with two fairy ladies there by chance. See Liu Yiqing 刘义庆, *You ming lu* 幽明录, ed. Zheng Wanqing (Beijing: Wenhua yishu chubanshe, 1988), pp. 1-3.

(Du Liniang gives Liu Mengmei a shy smile, but refuses to move. Liu tries to pull her by the sleeve)

Du Liniang (in a low voice): Where to?
Liu Mengmei (sings):

Turn beyond
This railing for peony,
Closely beside
The mound of Taihu Lake rocks.

Du Liniang (in a low voice): But what to do, sir?
Liu Mengmei (also in a low voice, sings):

I shall
Unbutton your collar,
And loosen your gown.
You cover your face with your sleeve
And
Bear with me patiently for a while,
Then drift into gentle slumber.

(Du Liniang turns away, blushing. Liu advances to take her in his arms, but she resists)

Liu Mengmei:
Du Liniang:

(sing)
Where
Was it
That we have met before

So we now behold each other in all seriousness?

Do we not

Want to speak a word for our meeting in this lovely place?

(Exit Liu carrying Du off by force)
(Enter Flower Goddess with bundled hair, dressed in red and strewn with flowers)

Flower Goddess (recites):

The flower goddess cherishes the world of flowers,
So she examines the springtime's work for one more year.
Drenched in the rain of red petals,
The heartbroken beholder anchors his yearnings amid the colorful clouds.

I am Flower Goddess in charge of the prefect's back garden in Nan'an. Because Liniang, daughter of Prefect Du, and the scholar Liu Mengmei are predestined to be married later, Miss Du is now so sentimental about her spring stroll that she has enticed Scholar Liu into her dream. To cherish in compassion the fair sex is a special concern of a flower goddess's, and that is why I am here to watch over her and to ensure that she enjoys the pleasure of "cloud and rain."[1]

(sings)
(*Bao lao cui*)

It is all

The surge of earth and sky.

He looks like

1 A phrase for love-making common in classical Chinese literature.

A wanton bee swirling to stir
The gale of her desire,
Both with
Loving stares,
Opening parts,
And trembling souls.
This is
A mating of shadows,
Consummation within the mind,
And a karmic appearance.

Oh,

My flower palace is now sullied by foul lust.

I'll drop a flower petal to wake her up. (She scatters some petals in the entrance to the stage)

How could
She
Tear herself away from
Her fond dream and her consummated spring passion?
But petals gleam and flutter down
Like
Crimson pieces.

The scholar's dream is but half-complete. When it is over, he'll see Miss Du back to her chamber. I am leaving now.

(Exit)

(Enter Liu Mengmei and Du Liniang, hand in hand)

Liu Mengmei (sings):

(*Shan tao hong*)

For this brief moment

We give in to nature

And make grasses for our pillow, flowers as our bed.

Are you all right, Miss Du?

(Du Liniang lowers her head)

Rearrange the clouds of your hair,

Where red petals get loosened

While emerald hairpins are aslant.

O, Miss Du, please do not forget

How closely I clasped you

And with what tenderness we consummated,

Longing only

To make of our two bodies one single flesh,

But quiveringly bringing forth

A glistening of rouge raindrops in the sun.

Du Liniang: Are you leaving now, sir?

Du Liniang:

Liu Mengmei:

(sing)
Where

Was it

That we have met before
So we now behold each other in all seriousness?

Do we not

Want to speak a word for our meeting in this lovely place?

Liu Mengmei: Lady, you must be tired. Please take a rest. (He sees Du Liniang back to where she was sleeping, and gently pats her on the back) Lady, I am leaving. (looks back) Lady, please have a good rest and I shall come and see you again.

(recites):
She came with spring time's gentle passion;
She went to sleep after a brief "clouds and rain."

(Exit)

Du Liniang (wakes with a start and calls in a low voice) Young sir, young sir! Oh, have you left me? (falls asleep again)

(Enter Madam Du)

Madam Du (recites):

My husband sits in his prefect's office
And my daughter stays in her boudoir
Yet she has embroidered her skirts
With flowers and birds all in pairs.

Child, my child, why are you asleep here?

(Du Liniang wakes and calls the scholar)

Du Liniang: I was coughing.
Madam Du: What's wrong with you, my child?

(Du Liniang is startled, rises to her feet)

Du Liniang: Mother, it's you!
Madam Du: My child, why don't you do some needlework or a little reading to enjoy yourself? Why were you sleeping here during the day?
Du Liniang: Just now I took a stroll in the back garden. Annoyed by the sudden noise of the birds in spring, I came back to my chamber. As I could find no way to while away the time, I dozed off for a moment. Please forgive me for my failure to greet you at the door.
Madam Du: The back garden is too lonely and deserted, my child. You must not go strolling there again.
Du Liniang: I'll follow your advice, Mother.
Madam Du: Go and read in your study.
Du Liniang: Since the tutor is not here, we are having a break.
Madam Du (sighs): A girl has her own feelings and emotions when she has come of age. I'd better leave her alone. Just as the saying goes,

(recites):
Moiling and toiling in the children's wake,
Many a pain must a mother need to take.

(Exit)

Du Liniang (watches her leave and heaves a sigh) Oh, Heaven! You are really lucky today, Du Liniang! Chancing to come to the back garden, I found flowers in bloom everywhere and, therefore, felt sentimental about the beautiful scenes. After I came back in low spirits, I fell into a midday slumber in my chamber. Suddenly I saw a handsome and elegant youth by the age of twenty, who broke off a twig from a willow in the garden. He said to me with a smile, "Lady, as you are so versed in classics, why don't you compose a poem in honor of this willow twig?" I was just about to make a reply when I thought to myself that since we had not known each other before and neither did I know his name, how should I so lightly enter into conversation with him? As I was thinking like this, he came forward and said a few fond words; and then taking me in his arms, he carried me to a spot beside the peony pavilion and beyond the railings lined with tree peonies, where we had the "joys of cloud and rain" together. Passion was matched by passion, and indeed a thousand fond caresses and a million tenderness passed between us. After our bliss was accomplished, he took me back to where I had been sleeping and said repeatedly, "Take a rest." Then I was just about to see him off at the door, when my mother came and woke me up. Startled, I was in a cold sweat, realizing it was all a daydream. I hastened to greet my mother and was duly given a lecture. Although I made no reply, how can I now free my memories of all that happened in my dream? Now I feel uneasy whether sitting or walking, and suffer from a sense of loss. Ah, mother, you asked me to go and read in my study, but what kind of books can bring me relief? (covers her face with her sleeve and weeps)

(sings):
(*Mian da xu*)
Enjoyment of fragrant "cloud and rain"
Only
Brought me to the edge of my dream,
When Mother called me, alas! and broke
This slumber by window's gauze.

A cold sweat soaked my dress,

Making

My mind blank, my footsteps falter,
My thought hesitate, and my hair slant awry.

Almost

I am exhausted with my mind and emotion,
Not able to tell which is comfortable, to sit or to stand?

Then

Let me go to sleep.

(Enter Chunxiang)

Chunxiang (recites):

Rid cheeks of powder's traces for evening makeup,
Add more incense to the burner for the damp of spring.

Young mistress, your quilts have been scented. It's time to go to bed.

Du Liniang (sings):

(*Coda*)
As my springtime's thought and the stroll tired me out,
I need no incense to scent my embroidered quilts in order to sleep.

Ah, Heaven!

Since I still miss the dream,
It should not be too far away.

Leisurely spring excursion begins from painted halls, (Zhang Shuo)

The scattered plums and willows cannot stop the fragrance of flowers. (Luo Yin)
You ask where Liu and Ruan met their fairy loves? [1] (Xu Hun)
Looking back against the east wind, one finds his heart broken. (Wei Zhuang)

III. Introduction to *Yueju* Opera

Also called Shaoxing opera 绍兴戏 because it originated in Chengxian County 嵊县 near Shaoxing in the northeast of Zhejiang province, *Yueju* opera is currently the second largest form of drama in China, having a history of about a hundred years. It is a major drama form in Shanghai and in Zhejiang, Jiangsu, Anhui, Fujian and other provinces, with its influence mainly in the south of China, although it is performed in some major cities and in some provinces in the north, too. At its peak during the early 1960s, professional *Yueju* opera troupes were found in almost all of China except a few provinces and autonomous regions such as Tibet, Guangdong and Guangxi provinces. According to some rough statistics, there were about 280 professional *Yueju* troupes with many more amateur troupes then.[2]

During the spring festival in 1906, six *chantefable* amateur artists from Chengxian' s rural area in Zhejiang province first put on a show based mainly on a local melody called *luodi changshu diao* 落地唱书调. Artists sang to the accompaniment of a rhythmic "didu," "didu" sound made by a drum and sandalwood clappers. Hence the drama form was originally called *didu ban* 的笃班 (didu troupes) or *xiaoge ban* 小歌班 (small singing troupes). The earliest *xiaoge ban* was comprised mostly of local peasants who were amateur performers and who put up performances during slack

1 See Note # 1 in page 229.
2 http://baike.baidu.com/view/16781.htm (29 July, 2011)

seasons in farming. Later, as their popularity grew, there gradually emerged professional *xiaoge ban* troupes that regularly staged shows in places like Tonglu 桐庐, Fuyang 富阳, Haining 海宁 and Hangzhou 杭州 in Zhejiang province.

But it was in Shanghai that the *xiaoge ban* eventually thrived. In spring of 1917 it first came to perform in Shanghai. Since the *xiaoge ban* was good at learning from other dramas such as Beijing opera or Shaoxing drama 绍剧, it made a series of important improvements on and innovations in its melodies and performing art, which helped to enhance its reputation, and it started to perform under the name *Shaoxing wenxi* 绍兴文戏 (Shaoxing opera in singing and acting[1]) in some teahouses in Shanghai.

The earliest performers in *Shaoxing wenxi* were all male. In 1923, the first batch of female performers were recruited and trained in Chengxian and they gave their first performance in Shanghai the following year. The all-female cast captured the essence of *Shaoxing wenxi* and helped push the beauty and gracefulness of its melody to a new artistic height. Therefore the all-female troupes won almost instant success and their popularity grew by leaps and bounds in Shanghai. In comparison, those troupes with only male performers, because of their lack of good young performers to succeed them, gradually declined and were eventually replaced by the all-female troupes. Since then, *Shaoxing wenxi* (name changed to *Yueju* opera in 1938) was dominated by female performers until the 1950s when some *Yueju* opera troupes started to recruit male performers to experiment male and female performers acting on the same stage. But until now there are still far more female performers than their male counterparts in *Yueju* opera.

Like the melodies of Beijing opera, those of *Yueju* opera also belong to what is called *banqiang*-style 板腔体 music. However, singing in *Yueju* opera is very refined, leisurely, sweet and moving so that it is especially

1 *Wenxi* 文戏 is characterized by singing and acting without acrobatic shows as in Beijing opera.

good at lyricism; as for its acting, refined by generations of master artists, it has become quite vivid and exquisite, which is particularly suitable for the expression of one's feelings and emotions. It is no coincidence that the first Chinese violin concerto under the name *Liang Shanbo and Zhu Yingtai* (sometimes with the English title as *The Butterfly Lovers*) was precisely based on the *Yueju* opera music.

Like other dramas, *Yueju* opera also has numerous artistic schools, each bearing the name of its founder who has usually excelled in singing. Those *Yueju* opera schools vary according to their variations and emphases placed on melody, rhythm as well as the accented and unaccented beats (*ban yan* 板眼) used in music, hence presenting different artistic images on stage. Some of the major schools in *Yueju* operas include Yuan school 袁派 of *Yueju* opera art founded by actress Yuan Xuefen 袁雪芬 (1922—2011) who specialized in the role of *qingyi* (female in dark dress), Yin school 尹派 of *Yueju* opera art established by actress Yin Guifang 尹桂芳 (1919—2000), who excelled in the role of *xiaosheng* 小生 (young man), Fan school 范派 of *Yueju* opera art founded by actress Fan Ruijuan 范瑞娟 (1924—), who also specializes in the role of *xiaosheng*, and Fu school 傅派 of *Yueju* opera art initiated by Fu Quanxiang 傅全香 (1923—), who is known for her role of *huadan* 花旦 ("flowery" maid).

Excerpt from *Liang Shanbo and Zhu Yingtai*

The romance between Liang Shanbo and Zhu Yingtai is one of the four great Chinese folk legends known by almost every Chinese. There have been numerous adaptations of this tale in dramas, TV series, movies and even music and ballet dance.

Sometimes abbreviated as *Liang Zhu*, the *Yueju* opera version narrates a tragic love story between Liang Shanbo, a scholar from Kuaiji 会稽 (present-day Shaoxing), and Zhu Yingtai, daughter of a wealthy family in

Shangyu 上虞, Zhejiang province.

Although in traditional China, girls were discouraged from going to school, Zhu Yingtai nevertheless persuaded her father to let her be disguised as a man in going to school. It happened that on her way to the academy in Hangzhou 杭州, Yingtai chanced to meet Liang Shanbo, who also went to study there. They chatted and felt so close to each other that they decided to become "sworn brothers."

During the three years in the academy, they were classmates and also roommates. As days went by, Yingtai gradually fell in love with Shanbo, who, however, was too ignorant to notice any of her feminine advances. One day, Yingtai received a letter from her father asking her to return home at once. Before she left, Yingtai revealed her mind to her teacher's wife and asked her to be a matchmaker. Reluctant to part with Yingtai, on the other hand, Shanbo went with her for eighteen *li* in seeing her off at the Changting Pavilion.[1] Failing to make Shanbo see her love for him on the way, Yingtai had to volunteer as a matchmaker herself for her "ninth sister" at home to Shanbo and hence asked the latter to come to her home before they parted with each other. Meanwhile, Liang Shanbo was duly elated when he was told about Yingtai by his teacher's wife, and he came hurriedly to Zhu Yingtai's home later only to find Yingtai already betrothed by her father to Mr. Ma Wencai 马文才, son of a local prefect. Heartbroken, Liang Shanbo returned home gloomy and depressed and fell sick thereafter. He soon died of lovesickness.

On her wedding day, Zhu Yingtai insisted that she visit Liang's grave before going on to the Ma residence. In mourning white dress, she cried and knelt before Liang's tomb. All of a sudden, there came a huge thunderstorm with whirlwinds blowing. The grave opened up instantly with a clap of thunder, and Yingtai threw herself in to join Shanbo. After the

---

1 See Note # 1 in page 209 for the definition of *li* 里 in Chinese.

storm, Liang Shanbo and Zhu Yingtai turned into a pair of butterflies that emerged from the grave. They flew freely in the air and would never to be separated again.

The play consists of thirteen scenes. What follows is Scene Four, one of the most memorable scenes in the play that enjoys great popularity, where Zhu Yingtai tries several ways, using one metaphor after another, in an effort to let Liang Shanbo see her affection for him before their parting. The melodies in this scene are especially sweet and soft, expressing vividly Yingtai's unvoiced love for Liang Shanbo.

In the play, the character of Liang Shanbo is taken by a performer of the *xiaosheng* 小生 (young man) role whereas that of Zhu Yingtai is acted by a performer of the *qingyi* 青衣 (female in dark dress) role.

Scene Four: Seeing Each Other Off for Eighteen *Li*[1]

(Scenery: Half way on the journey where Liang Shanbo sees Zhu Yingtai off)

Chorus behind: With affection as deep as sea for being three years of classmates,
Liang Shanbo finds it hard to part with Zhu Yingtai.
Hand in hand, he takes her to descend the hill
Before they come onto the road to Qiantang.

(Enter Liang Shanbo, Zhu Yingtai, Sijiu—Liang Shanbo's servant, and Yinxin—Zhu Yingtai's maid)

Zhu Yingtai (sings): On the branch of a plum tree outside the door of our

---

1 The play script is from Zhongguo xijujia xiehui ed. *Zhongguo defang xiqu jicheng: Shanghai shi juan* 中国地方戏曲集成上海市卷, 2 vols. (Beijing: Zhongguo xiju chubanshe, 1959), 2: 577-582.

study
Hundreds of birds perch in pairs.
The chatter of all the magpies on the tree
Must have brought good news to you, Brother Liang.

Liang Shanbo (sings): Descending the hill came two brothers;
Magpies are in pairs in front of doors.
They have always brought good news,
To congratulate my younger brother on your safe journey home.

Zhu Yingtai: Please, Brother Liang.

Liang Shanbo: Please, my younger brother.

Zhu Yingtai (sings): Going out of the city and through the pass,
We see but a woodcutter gathering firewood on the hill.

Liang Shanbo (sings): How hard it must be to work from morn till eve
And what hardship it is to gather firewood for a living!

Zhu Yingtai (sings): For whom does he cut his firewood
And whom do you see off down the hill?

Liang Shanbo (sings): He cuts firewood for his wife
And I see my younger brother off down the hill.

Zhu Yingtai (sings): We have passed one hill after another,

Liang Shanbo (sings): And come to the Phoenix Hill in front.

Zhu Yingtai (sings): Hundreds of flowers are in bloom on Phoenix Hill,

Liang Shanbo (sings): But there lacks the Chinese herbaceous peony to match the true peony.

Zhu Yingtai (sings): If you, Brother Liang, loves peony,
You can come with me to my house.
There is a fine peony in my home
And it is not hard for my brother to pick up its flowers.

Liang Shanbo (sings): Although the peony is fine in your home,
It is a pity I cannot come so far to pick up its flowers.

Zhu Yingtai (sings): On the clear water pond with green lotus leaves,
Mandarin ducks swim and play all in pairs.[1]
O Brother Liang, if Yingtai is a woman in her makeup,
Would you like to match her as a pair of mandarin ducks?

Liang Shanbo (sings): To match, and to match as a pair of mandarin ducks—
What a pity that Yingtai is not a woman in her makeup!

Yinxin (sings): We've come to a big river in front,

Sijiu (sings): There come a pair of big white geese,

Zhu Yingtai (sings): The male goose is going ahead
And the female one is calling it brother from behind.

Liang Shanbo (sings): I have not seen any goose opening its mouth,
So where is there a female goose calling a male one?!

Zhu Yingtai (sings): Haven't you seen a female goose smiling at you,
Laughing at you, Brother Liang, for being as dumb as a rock?

Liang Shanbo (sings): Now that I'm as dumb as a rock,
Don't call me Brother Liang from now on.
(gets upset)

Zhu Yingtai (apologizes) Brother Liang...

Yinxin (sings): There is a single-log bridge in front.

Liang Shanbo (goes on to the bridge first): My younger brother, please come over!

---

1 Mandarin ducks always stay in pairs: one male with one female. Hence Chinese people like to use the image of mandarin ducks to refer to the everlasting love between a man and a woman.

Zhu Yingtai (sings): I am both nervous and timid.
Liang Shanbo (sings): Your brother will help you cross the bridge.

(Liang Shanbo helps Zhu Yingtai cross the bridge. They come to the center of the bridge)

Zhu Yingtai (sings): You and I are like Cowherd and Weaving Maiden
crossing the bridge of magpies to meet.[1]

(Liang Shanbo helps Zhu Yingtai descend the bridge. Sijiu and Yinxin follow them and cross the bridge)

Liang Shanbo:
Zhu Yingtai:

(sing)
Crossing the river, we have come to another village.
Inside the village, a yellow dog is barking.

Zhu Yingtai (sings): It is not barking at the man ahead,
But only barking at the lady behind.

Liang Shanbo (sings): My younger brother is being absurd with your words,
For where is there a lady here?
Be bold and not be frightened,
For I will beat the dog while you pass through the village.

Zhu Yingtai (sings): There is also a well in front;

---

1 This is a reference to a Chinese folk legend that a poor cowherd met and fell in love with a fairy who came down to the earth to take a bath. Both lived happily with the fairy working as a weaving girl and the cowherd going out to herd cows every day until one day when the Queen Mother of the West 西王母 in heaven heard of this and ordered the fairy to return to the celestial world and allowed the couple to meet only on the seventh day of the seventh month in the lunar calendar. According to the legend, therefore, on that day all the magpies will fly to the place where they will form a bridge for the loving couple to cross and meet once every year.

I don't know how deep the water therein.
(throws a pebble into the well)

Liang Shanbo (sings): It doesn't matter if water is deep or not,
But it matters that we make haste with our journey.

(Zhu Yingtai asks Liang Shanbo to see each other's faces in the well, so they help each other to the well and look beneath)

Zhu Yingtai (sings): Look at the two mirrored faces at the bottom of the well.
With a man and a woman smiling at each other.

Liang Shanbo (sings): I am unmistakably a man,
So you shouldn't take me as a woman!

Liang Shanbo:
Zhu Yingtai:
(sing)
Walking past the well, we have come to a temple.
It is a temple for Bodhisattva Guanyin in front.[1]

Liang Shanbo (sings): The Temple for Guanyin, the Temple for Guanyin,
The Guanyin who grants people sons sits high on the dais.

Zhu Yingtai (sings): Bodhisattva Guanyin will be our matchmaker.
Please come, let you and I bow to each other as bride and groom.

(She pulls Liang Shanbo so they are both on their knees together)

---

1 Bodhisattva Guanyin (观音菩萨) is Bodhisattva Avalokitesvara, commonly known in English as Goddess of Mercy and Compassion for the Chinese, who believe that Guanyin will grant children to people who pray before her.

Liang Shanbo (sings): My younger brother is getting more and more absurd.
How can two men bow to each other as bride and groom?
Let us go.

Liang Shanbo:
Zhu Yingtai:
(sing)
Leaving the ancient temple, we walk straight.
Yinxin (sings): And we see a cow coming this way.
Sijiu (sings): The cowherd is riding on its back,
Yinxin (sings): Singing folk songs to relieve him of his worries.
Zhu Yingtai (sings): What a pity it is playing guitar to an ox
that doesn't understand!
How regrettable it is that Brother Liang is as dumb as a rock!
Liang Shanbo (sings): It is not that I have gotten angry,
But why did you compare me to this and that without an end!
Zhu Yingtai (sings): Brother Liang, please do not get upset.
I am apologizing and admitting my fault.
Liang Shanbo: It's alright. Let us hurry up.
Zhu Yingtai (sings): I am much indebted to you for your deep affection, Brother Liang.
You have climbed the hills and crossed the rivers
in seeing me off.
It is a common saying that there will be an eventual parting even though one sees the other off for a thousand *li*.
Please stop here, Brother Liang, and return to the academy.

Liang Shanbo (sings): Our affection runs deep as sworn brothers
vowed at the Thatched Bridge,
Please allow your brother see you off
at the Changting Pavilion.

Liang Shanbo:
Zhu Yingtai:
(sing)

We traveled eighteen *li* to see each other off at the Changting Pavilion;
We traveled eighteen *li* to see each other off at the Changting Pavilion.

(Liang Shanbo and Zhu Yingtai enter the pavilion and are seated. Sijiu and Yinxin rest outside)

Zhu Yingtai (sings): You and I will be parted as far away as two swan geese.
Liang Shanbo (sings): Do you have anything for me to take care of, my brother?
Zhu Yingtai (sings): I want to ask you one thing before parting.
Does Brother Liang already have a wife at home?
Liang Shanbo (sings): Since you knew long ago that your brother is not married,
Why do you ask this again today?
Zhu Yingtai (sings): If Brother Liang has not decided with your marriage,
Your little brother wants to be your matchmaker.
Liang Shanbo (sings): If my younger brother wants to be my matchmaker,
Could I ask who is the one you want to introduce?
Zhu Yingtai (sings) It is the little Ninth Sister in my family.
I wonder if Brother Liang likes.
Liang Shanbo (sings): How old is your Ninth Sister this year?

Zhu Yingtai (sings): The same age as mine—twins as we are.
Liang Shanbo (sings): Does your Ninth Sister look like you?
Zhu Yingtai (sings): Her character and looks are the same as those of Yingtai.
Liang Shanbo (sings): I wonder if your father is willing or not?
Zhu Yingtai (sings): My father asks me to choose a talented young man.
Liang Shanbo (sings): If so, many thanks to my younger brother's kindness.
Zhu Yingtai (sings): Come early, Brother Liang, with your bridal sedan chair.
I'll make an appointment with you that on the seventh of the seventh month—
Liang Shanbo: On the seventh of the seventh month,
Zhu Yingtai (sings): —You'll come to my home.
Chorus behind (sing): Reluctant to part at the time of parting,
I have endless words that I want to express from my heart,
Only wanting you, my Brother Liang, to come at an early date.

— Curtain —

Questions for Discussion:

1. What are the performing characteristics of Beijing opera? Why is it commonly regarded as the representative of Chinese drama?
2. Xiang Yu is defeated and he commits suicide along with his favorite concubine Yu Ji at the end of the Beijing opera *Hegemon-King Bids Farewell to His Concubine*. In what respect could he be viewed as a tragic hero?
3. What are the performing characteristics of *Kunju* opera? Why is it considered "the ancestor of all dramas" in China?

4. What do you make of Du Liniang's dream in the *Kunju* opera *Waking from a Dream*? Is it simply a revelation of a young lady's long-suppressed sexual desire? What cultural significance may the scene convey?
5. How much do you know about the art of *Yueju* opera? What are some of its performing features? Why are there more female performers in *Yueju* opera?
6. What, you think, has caused the tragedy in the play *Liang Shanbo and Zhu Yingtai*?
7. The Chinese play *Liang Shanbo and Zhu Yingtai* is often compared with Shakespeare's *Romeo and Juliet*. To what extent are they comparable?